ARTICULATION DISORDERS

REMEDIATION OF COMMUNICATION DISORDERS SERIES
Frederick N. Martin, Series Editor

RONALD K. SOMMERS

Kent State University

ARTICULATION DISORDERS

Prentice-Hall, Inc., Englewood Cliffs, New Jersey 07632

Library of Congress Cataloging in Publication Data

SOMMERS, RONALD K.
  Articulation disorders.

  (Remediation of communication disorders)
  Bibliography: p.
  Includes index.
  1. Articulation disorders.   2. Articulation
disorders in children.   I. Title.   II. Series.
RC424.7.S65 1983   616.85′5   82-12381
ISBN 0-13-049080-6

© 1983 by Prentice-Hall, Inc., Englewood Cliffs, N.J. 07632

Printed in the United States of America

10 9 8 7 6 5 4 3 2 1

Editorial production/supervision by Virginia Cavanagh Neri
Interior design by Maureen Olsen
Cover design by Maureen Olsen
Manufacturing buyer: Edmund W. Leone

ISBN 0-13-049080-6

Prentice-Hall International, Inc., *London*
Prentice-Hall of Australia Pty. Limited, *Sydney*
Prentice-Hall of Canada, Ltd., *Toronto*
Prentice-Hall of India Private Limited, *New Delhi*
Prentice-Hall of Japan, Inc., *Tokyo*
Prentice-Hall of Southeast Asia Pte. Ltd., *Singapore*
Whitehall Books Limited, *Wellington, New Zealand*

This book is dedicated to Virginia,
my forgiving and sacrificing wife

Contents

Articulation as the basic integrator of speech 1

The basis for therapeutic intervention 22

Traditional and historical approaches
to articulation remediation 63

Linguistic concepts and articulatory
remediation 75

The operant paradigm applied to articulation remediation 143

Articulation-therapy aspects of orofacial abnormalities and neurological disorders 165

FOREWORD

With the information explosion of recent years there has been a prolif-eration of knowledge in the areas of scientific and social inquiry. The speciality of communicative disorders has been no exception. While two decades ago a single textbook or "handbook" might have sufficed to provide the aspiring or practicing clinician with enlightenment on an array of communication handicaps, this is no longer possible—hence the decision to prepare a series of single-author texts.

As the title implies, the emphasis of this series, *Remediation of Commu-nication Disorders,* is on therapy and treatment. The authors of each book were asked to provide information relative to anatomical and physiological aspects of each disorder, as well as pathology, etiology, and diagnosis to the extent that an understanding of these factors bears on management procedures. In such relatively short books this was quite a challenge: to offer guidance without writing a "cookbook"; to be selective without being parochial; to offer theory without losing sight of practice. To this challenge the series' authors have risen magnificently.

Ronald Sommers is the ideal author of a book dealing with clinical remediation of articulation disorders. Dr. Sommers' background is unique because he has both clinical and university experience. His clinical expe-rience includes fifteen years devoted to providing services to speech-language- and hearing-impaired children in a public school setting. From this rich experience, Dr. Sommers embarked on a full-time commitment to university teaching and research, a career that has spanned fourteen years. Many of the doctoral and masters studies he has directed have dealt in large measure with aspects of defective articulation and phonological disorders.

FREDERICK N. MARTIN
Series Editor

The present effort seeks to provide speech/language pathologists and students in training to be speech/language pathologists with some guidelines which may be useful in making choices about therapy for the articulatory-defective person. It is not my intention to promote a particular philosophical basis for articulation diagnosis and treatment except in one regard: The decision about whether articulation therapy will be provided or not and the specific type of therapy which will be used should be based upon the recognition that not all children and adults with such disorders are alike. Modern research evidence is very supportive of the position that the makeup and capabilities of many articulatory defective persons are not alike. Since, ideally, treatment decisions should stem from diagnostic studies, it is my opinion that adequate studies of the person with the problem should be completed before decisions concerning therapy are made and therapy begun. The disappointing thing is that too many persons receive articulation therapy in the absence of adequate study of their problems. In fact, one can find speech pathologists who fail almost completely to prescribe the type of therapy based upon the outcome of diagnostic findings except for some simplistic articulation testing results. The assumption in all this is the belief that articulation therapy methods must be highly suited to the makeup and capabilities of the defective person, demanding that a number of different methods of approach be in the speech pathologist's armamentarium.

Many of the approaches to articulation therapy presented in this document have similarities and differences. Contrasting them is troublesome for two reasons: First, they overlap both in their theoretical bases and procedures, and secondly, since their originators or proponents have, for the most part, not written extensively about their use, detailed case studies are not available for comparison purposes.

Perhaps something should be said about the "newer" or more modern articulation therapy approaches in contrast to the older, more traditional ones. We can frequently see the therapy blueprints of the past in the "newer" approaches. The axiomatic statement "There is nothing new under the sun" may be shopworn, but it stubbornly refuses to die. Many of the important ideas related to articulation disorders were born in the past. We owe a great deal to Martha K. Scripture, Sara Stinchfield-Hawk,

Robert West, Ollie Backus, Jane Beasley, Lee Travis, Charles Van Riper, Martha Hall Powers, Robert Milisen, Eugene McDonald, and many others. Although small in number, our ancestors were intelligent, dynamic, and dedicated professionals; and much of what they pioneered is alive and useful today. One can see exciting modifications of their basic therapeutic ideas and approaches in the modern orientations frequently advocated.

The advent of two major theoretical and applied bodies of knowledge within the past decade has allowed for the development of many of the "newer" articulation therapy orientations. Both of these, the operant movement in speech pathology and the application of distinctive-feature concepts and assessment, have been sharply influential in changing the orientation to articulation therapy. I discuss these in separate chapters knowing full well that the operant paradigm is largely the backdrop for many distinctive-feature applications to articulation therapy. A third related movement, perhaps of lesser impact, is the attempt to improve articulation in defective children by strengthening their linguistic performances, particularly the improvement of defective syntax. This type of programming is lightly touched upon in Chapter Four, as is a description of some aspects of using phonological-process information to guide therapy.

It is also apparent that any effort to present information about the corrective process in defective articulation is not going to escape the reality that articulation is a very complex basic aspect of speech and linguistic processing. Much of the new information about coarticulation, linguistic aspects of speech production, and acoustic phonetics has not been effectively tied into therapy strategies for the articulatory defective. We eagerly await the use of the body of current information, which must be exhaustively related to implications for therapy; and we long for the new vital information that is sure to come from our future generations of speech scientists, speech pathologists, and psycholinguists.

My examination of the strengths and weaknesses of older and newer articulation approaches will not, however, address the question of the general efficacy of articulation therapy, particularly as applied to children. The two almost unstudied questions are for whom articulation therapy is most effective and what type of therapy is best under the circumstances surrounding the individual with the problem. But I do not feel adequate to answer these questions and only hope that this effort illuminates some of the elements in these decisions.

Finally, I will assume responsibility for presenting some of my personal beliefs about both the state-of-the-art and preferences for therapy approaches under certain conditions. I trust that these opinions and preferences will not be too deceptively hidden in my writings.

○ACKNOWLEDGMENT

I would like to express my heartfelt thanks to Mary Ann Reiser and Patty Glass for their assistance in the preparation of sections of this manuscript.

RONALD K. SOMMERS

ARTICULATION DISORDERS

Articulation as the basic integrator of speech

○BASIC ELEMENTS OF SPEECH PRODUCTION

The Traditional View of Speech Production For many years the elements that allow human speech to be produced have been conveniently separated into four major types: respiration, phonation, resonance, and articulation. Implicit in this early classification is the belief that each of these types is independently and uniquely involved in speech production. Some recent publications (perhaps because the authors stressed structures and morphological aspects of speech rather than physiology) also divide the speaking process into these four types of activities (Eisenson and Ogilvie, 1971; Van Riper, 1978). This approach seems largely characteristic of that used early in a science when the best that one can hope for is simple classification of events or behaviors. Fortunately, our understanding of the speech-production process has advanced beyond the simplistic classification represented by these four divisions. Modern evidence confirms the holistic and dynamic nature of speech production, and these traditional classifications, while convenient, are no longer very meaningful. Both phonetic (acoustic processing basically devoid of meaning) and phonemic (syntactic, semantic, and morphologic meaningful signals) developments in linguistics and speech science have altered these traditional notions of speech production most irrevocably. Thus, modern philosophies and evidence confirm that speech production is an inextricably intertwined, masterful linguistic process that man is uniquely specialized to adopt with relative ease. It is one process, not four, and the integration of respiration, phonation, resonance, and articulation functions in human speech is accomplished using a highly perfected, complex, linguistic code. We will briefly evaluate the four traditional classifications of speech production using more modern evidence and opinion concerning this marvelous process's nature and functions.

In the traditional view of speech production respiration appears to assume a fundamental position; it is the first necessary step, if you will. It has been recognized for many years that man has a central control mechanism for the regulation of respiration, which is located in the limbic system. As seems characteristic of most sciences, the gross musculature that controls and regulates the respiratory act has been studied first and discussed as prominent in its completion. Thus, the diaphragmatic actions, particularly elevation and retraction of the rib cage, have historically been thought most vital for normal human respiration. This process, however, deals with the required inspiration and expiration required for life and has perhaps less relevance to that required for normal speech production. Recent revelations have been reasonably successful in identifying the less apparent but very necessary components of respiration needed for normal speech production under various speaking conditions.

Among the prominent researchers of the effects of speech production on air pressure in the lungs is Ladefoged. Results from a number of his experiments show that the previously considered sluggishness of the systems subserving respiration is erroneous when air pressure for speech is studied (Ladefoged & McKinney, 1963; Ladefoged, 1963). In the latter experiments, Ladefoged successfully determined that subglottal air pressure is regulated in normal adult speakers by the act of voicing. Voiceless sounds were determined to have lower subglottal air pressure requirements than voiced sounds, presumably because there is a higher rate of air flow on voiceless sounds. He further reported that regardless of the intonation patterns used by his speakers, nouns of the form *insult* always were accompanied by a physiological correlate of stress with an extra increase in subglottal pressure. This increase always came earlier than it did in corresponding verb forms. Differences in peak mouth pressure for various classes of speech sounds were also identified. Slow buildup for mouth pressure in the production of both voiced /d/ and /v/ were contrasted to the more rapid ones for voiceless /p/ and /f/. Peak mouth pressure for voiceless fricatives was found to occur during the first part of the sound. Thus, Ladefoged's findings support different requirements for subglottal air pressure to maintain accurate articulation, and these determiners include whether the sounds are voiced or voiceless, grammatical class (nouns/verbs), stress, and the specific intraoral breath pressure requirements for classes of speech sounds.

The sensitivity of the intercostal muscles to regulate certain of the air-pressure and air-flow requirements for normal speech can be seen in results of electromyographic studies reported by Ladefoged, Draper, & Whitteridge (1958). These investigators found that a burst of intercostal muscle activity occurs before stressed sections of connected speech and that these bursts vary in intensity as a function of how much stress the speaker is required to produce. Perhaps more exciting was their finding that these bursts of intercostal muscle activity were related to specific classes of speech sounds with some words beginning with fricative-plosive sequences showing two bursts of activity. Bursts were frequently detected before long vowels and production of /h/. These findings suggest that articulatory requirements may be accommodated, to some degree, by very rapid and frequently changing fine-muscle activity in the chest. As in most studies in speech physiology, the small number of subjects studied poses a serious problem in the ability to generalize about the findings. However, at least for the speakers studied, results tend to show that the articulatory demands of connected speech can be detected at the beginning stage of speech, that is, the fundamental requirements of air flow and air pressure.

These complex relationships suggest that the respiratory mechanisms that regulate speaking must alter their performances rapidly and accurately if normal speech is to occur. In effect, the respiratory, speech regulatory system has characteristics of an articulatory system.

Phonatory aspects of speech production, studied over many centuries (Muller, 1848; Russell, 1928), have also been undergoing study related to the multifaceted demands of human speech. The general notions of physiology mechanisms, the overlaid, life-sustaining purpose of the ana-tomical structures, have been largely displaced by a combination of the relevant and dynamic physiological functions as viewed by the fundamental mechanisms of linguistic control of laryngeal function.

Historically, authoritative phoneticians and linguists have disagreed concerning aspects of laryngeal functioning, particularly voice-onset timing required for different types of stop-consonant productions (Lisker & Abramson, 1971). Distinctive features have been designated by some (Chomsky & Halle, 1968) to explain the underlying events that produce varying voice-onset times for stops. Their original four distinctive features, used to explain the phonetic aspects of voice timing are: (1) voice, (2) tensity, (3) glottal constriction, and (4) heightened subglottal pressure. Regardless of whether distinctive features operationally control these elements of voicing or whether the hypothesized timing system of Lisker and Abramson (1971) is a more scientifically viable explanation, it is clear that laryngeal structures are modified by information received in the encoded linguistic material that makes speech possible. Thus, under varying conditions, the presence or absence of information concerning which phonemes must be produced is provided also to laryngeal structures in order that all the requirements for production are properly met. The exact nature of these complex processes, while somewhat better understood today, comprises a formidable challenge for future investigators.

An example of how the laryngeal structures work to facilitate the articulatory aspects of speech production can be seen in results of electromyographic studies of normal speech. Clear evidence has been reported that speakers increase muscular activity to open and close the glottal opening for different speech sounds to meet changing air-flow requirements (Sawashima & Miyazaki, 1973). Voiced sounds require significantly greater air flow than voiceless ones (Lieberman, 1977, p. 93). Sounds requiring the greatest amount of air flow, /s/ and /p/, show significantly more opening for the /s/ than for /p/. Lieberman (1977, p. 93) contends that the speaker's greater glottal opening for /s/ is necessary to produce the noise that results when a constriction is made near the

speaker's teeth. These findings provide further evidence of the interde-
pendence of speech structures and processes in the production of the final
product. It seems likely that future investigations will uncover additional
evidence that laryngeal activity is even more specifically tied into the more
traditional view of the articulatory process.

In the older concepts of speech-production mechanisms the velum was
considered to be an articulator, since it serves to increase or decrease the
amount of nasality in speech, thus contributing to speech intelligibility.
This structure's role in the articulatory process has been expanded and
revised as a result of newer information concerning its functions. In effect,
the nasal, nonnasal segments of speech have been found by newer research
techniques to be more continuous than dichotomous, influenced by
coarticulation, and related to the order of various consonants and vowels
in connected speech (Moll & Daniloff, 1971). The velum is also, therefore,
a recipient of encoded linguistic information, which specifies in advance
what position the velum must assume to allow a specific syllable to be
produced by signifying both what preceded the syllable and what followed
it. This complex coarticulatory activity has been found to occur in the
velum, showing the activity of this organ to be sensitive, precise, and
complex. Many of the "markers" (linguistic signals programmed to denote
changes) related to velar-movement patterns which may be associated with
suprasegmental factors, such as stress and duration, await further investigation; and it seems likely that these important elements of speech
production can also be linked to the task.

The articulatory component of the speech signal has been seen to
regulate the activity of a number of elements of the speech-production
system. While certain classes of speech sounds may commonly control
some aspect of speech production, for example, laryngeal closure patterns,
the uniqueness of each sound of the language may be detectable in specific
requirements needed in its production; and these unique requirements
may manifest themselves in one or more of the elements of the production
system. My concept of the "upper" and "lower" articulators is depicted in
Figure 1–1.

flexibility of the articulatory process

When speech is studied using acoustical or auditory techniques
such as spectrographic analysis, it appears easier to detect characteristic
acoustic patterns, or "targets," among speakers who say the same message
than to detect precise articulatory patterns, or "targets," using high speed
photography or similar methods. Findings from the work of Ladefoged,
DeClerk, Lindau, and Papcun (1972) support the belief that different
patterns of articulatory movement can be used by speakers to obtain
comparable acoustic patterns, or "targets." The correlation between the

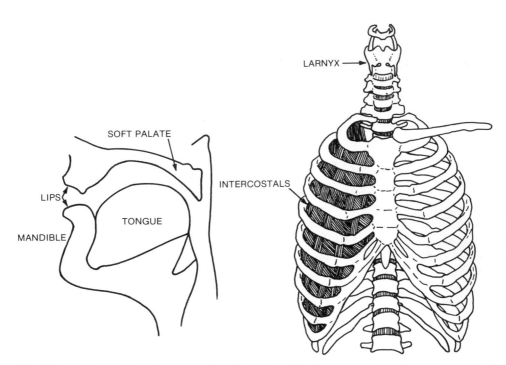

FIGURE 1–1 The traditional concept of the "articulators" (left), now termed the "upper articulators," and the author's concept of the additional ones (right), now termed the "lower articulators."

acoustic events in connected speech and the articulatory one is thus not impressive across speakers. While difficult and troublesome for researchers to observe, the functioning of the upper articulators does yield information that a wide variety of articulatory target positions and patterns of movement can be used to produce the same message. This characteristic of speech probably allows individuals to modify their speech production to conform to their particular anatomical, perceptual, and linguistic restraints. The concept of articulatory posturing as a variable, individual process attests, once again, to the alleged dynamic nature of speech; and the phenomenon may have some implications for the remedial process in articulatory disorders.

concepts of place and manner of phoneme production

Using examples from recent speech-physiology literature, the author has attempted to show that the articulatory process is a specific regulator of many of the major structures and systems that contribute to speech production. The ancient concepts of place and manner of articulation, while perhaps too simplistic, may yet be viable, since both upper and lower articulatory systems appear to show preliminary signs of having specific place duties and responsibilities for certain phonemes and classes of phonemes. There appears to be sufficient variation in muscular activity and physiology to suggest manner influences as well. For example, the specific manner requirements for /s/ production demand more opening of the glottis for /s/ than for other voiceless consonants.

○ THE EMERGENCE AND IMPACT OF DISTINCTIVE-FEATURE CONCEPTS

Since distinctive-feature approaches to articulation therapy have become topics of interest recently, a brief historical account of their development, nature, and some of their limitations may be profitable at this juncture. Although distinctive features have only relatively recently been adopted by some portion of the speech pathology profession and applied to the remedial process in young children severely impaired in their phonological development, their basic principles have been known and conjectured about by linguists for many years. Some linguists have been seriously attempting to discern "universal truths" that explain languages, and this quest has probably stimulated their interest in applying distinctive-feature concepts to linguistic theory.

Among the applications of distinctive-feature concepts is that which hopes to explain the intricacies of the phonetic elements of human speech by specifying universal features that allow for the fine differentiation of human speech sounds. Thus, the phonological rules of the language would "speak" to the neuromusculature systems responsible for the speech process and regulate their activities in a most tidy and efficient manner. Man, after all, is a highly systems-oriented animal who operates far above chance levels to perform his daily linguistic functions.

Distinctive features have also been applied to an understanding of speech perception, for example, theories of speech perception such as the Analysis-by-Synthesis Theory of Halle and Stevens (1959). Perhaps a concise view of the development of distinctive-feature systems and their application to theory and practice may be profitable at this point due to the high impact that they currently have on the interest and thinking of many speech pathologists, clinical researchers, linguists, psycholinguists, neurolinguists, and speech scientists.

Although no lengthy comparison of distinctive-features systems will be tendered at this time, some of them are more applicable and understandable to the speech pathologist than others. All systems appear to endeavor to categorize speech sounds differently, yet all systems form new classifications of sounds not conceived earlier in phonetics and linguistics.

Furthermore, some systems appear very abstract and nontraditional when viewed in light of the older concepts of place, manner, and voicing of speech sounds. Finally, many systems lack clinical verification, while portions of others appear to be better supported by research evidence.

Presumably, the major goal of distinctive-feature systems is to describe the unique, characteristic elements of phonemes in a language. Thus, each phoneme in a language should be able to be represented by a unique collection (or bundle) of features, and it is recognized in all the major distinctive-feature systems that each feature is present or absent from the 'bundle.' (As we shall see later, this assumption has come under heavy fire by some critics.)

The distinctive-feature systems that have emerged have differed in their basic purpose, orientation, and complexity. A wide variety of terms has been manufactured to describe the features of a number of them, and this situation has fostered some degree of confusion among readers and consumers. Most of the feature systems appear to be basically dissimilar for two reasons: First, the correlates of features have been acoustic, articulatory, perceptual, or some combination of the three. Secondly, while some originators have been intrigued with the universal applicability of features, others have been more interested in a more specific application to the consonants and phonology of spoken American English. This tendency appears to have resulted in six related, but theoretically different feature systems.

Using acoustic correlates, Jakobson, Fant, and Halle (1951) presented an early feature system with the claim of 'universality,' that is, a set of features applicable to all languages, and 'economy'—a set of features that describe linguistic competence. They postulated an acoustical classification of features according to function for each of eight binary oppositions. This conceptualization included the classification of consonantal/nonconsonantal and vocalic/nonvocalic features into a category of 'fundamental source features.' Other categories included nasal/oral distinctions as comprising a 'supplemental resonator feature,' compact/diffuse as a 'resonance feature', grave/acute and tense/lax as 'tonality features,' and the continuant/interrupted and strident/mellow features as 'secondary consonantal source features.'

Perhaps the simplest feature system was an early one proposed by Miller and Nicely (1955). This system consisted of only five features: place, duration, affrication, voicing, and nasality. All features represented articulatory correlates except duration which was based upon an acoustic correlate. Only sixteen English consonants were described by the system. Feature evaluation used 0 to indicate feature absence and 1 for feature presence. The exception to this scoring was that for the feature 'place,' 0 denoted front, 1 mid, and 2 back consonants. The features appeared to account for the basic elements in the old traditional concept of articulation of place, manner, and voicing as elements in sound production. Later, Singh and Black (1966) added three features to the Miller and Nicely (1955) system. These three features consisted of retroflexion, liquid, and a fourth value for place. Place in their modified Miller and Nicely system was scaled as 1 front, 2 mid-front, 3 mid-back, and 4 back. This modification appeared to show further evidence that the use of distinctive features to describe physiological aspects of articulatory function were of greater interest than more theoretical linguistic ones to some persons associated with research in speech science.

In a somewhat related conceptualization, Halle (1964) located his correlates of features acoustically and derived an eight-feature system that applied to eighteen English consonants. He used the same + and − binary procedures for distinctive-feature presence or absence for the following: vocalic, consonantal, grave, diffuse, strident, continuant, voiced, and nasal features.

Wickelgren (1966) criticized Halle's (1964) feature system, describing it as unnatural in its ability to describe the articulatory process. He maintained that no simple acoustic or articulatory description could account for speech. He then provided a parsimonious description of the admissable sound sequences in different languages and went on to present a feature system of his own that was more conventional in its ability to describe the phonetic analysis of consonants. To accomplish this, Wickelgren (1966) specified that place and manner of production characteristics for consonants could be divided into: (a) openness of the vocal tract, (b) manner (three values), and (c) place (five values). Voicing and nasality were conceived of as exactly the same as in the Halle (1964) and Miller–Nicely (1955) systems. In contrast to the Miller–Nicely (1955) systems, Wickelgren's accounted for manner of articulation with the single dimension of openness, while the former system used two dimensions for this purpose (affrication and duration). Halle's (1964) system employed four dimensions for the same purpose (vocalic, consonantal, continuant, and strident). It should be observed that the Wickelgren system was basically interested in the prediction that a consonant is coded in short-term memory as a set of distinctive features rather than a discrete unit of speech. Thus, Wickelgren did not intend to develop a feature system which would provide a comprehensive description of the articulation of each consonant in English.

Subsequently, Chomsky and Halle (1968) elaborated upon earlier feature concepts and proposed a feature system to be used in an analysis of generative grammar in which syntactic, lexical, and phoneme sequencing rules were also studied. Their system was considered to have universal applicability to the languages of the world. In it were groups of features that were designated 'major class features,' and these included the vocalic/ nonvocalic, consonantal/nonconsonantal, and sonorant/nonsonorant features. Their second major classification consisted of 'cavity features' and was composed of nine subclassifications consisting of coronal/noncoronal, anterior/nonanterior, distributed/nondistributed, covered/noncovered, and further subclassification of 'tongue body features' that included high/ nonhigh, low/nonlow, back/nonback and of 'secondary apperture features' including nasal/nonnasal and lateral/nonlateral. While most of the features of the elaborate feature system of Chomsky and Halle were related to the place concept of articulation of speech sounds, a few were related to the manner of articulatory production of such events. Among these, in their third major classification, were those of continuant/non-continuant and release and tense/nontense features. In their four classifications they described 'source features.' These consisted of voiced/ voiceless and strident/nonstrident features. Their fifth classification contained 'prosodic features.' Conforming to earlier views of the reality of distinctive features, Chomsky and Halle asserted their binary existence and scored them 0 if absent from speech and 1 if present. This comprehensive system was subsequently used in articulation-therapy experiments by investigators who maintained the view that features were binary and scored children's responses as + for feature presence and − for feature absence (McReynolds and Huston, 1971; McReynolds and Bennett, 1972; and McReynolds and Engmann, 1975). Table 1–1 contains the distinctive-features combinations of English phonemes as conceived by Chomsky and Halle (1968).

Singh and Polen (1972) devised a more recent feature system that appeared to emphasize the physiological aspects of the articulatory process. Their system distinghished between twenty-two English consonants using a binary coding system of 0 and 1 to specify the perceptual dimensions of a feature. A total of fourteen different articulatory components were included in seven different features. In order to locate features that may be more important than others and a developmental sequence for them, Singh and Polen (1972) conceived of a perceptual rather than acoustic or articulatory model to describe the consonants of English. This system eliminated six pairs of consonants, since they were indistinguishable in their feature system. For the remainder of consonants seven features were described: (1) place (front/back), (2) labial, (3) voicing, (4) sonorant, (5) nasal, (6) stop, and (7) sibilant. Perceptual referents of the articulatory aspects of features included: (1) advancement, (2) height, and (3) retroflexion. Although the perceptual aspect of the Singh and Polen (1972) system was unique, portions of the earlier acoustic and articulatory models, used, for example, by Chomsky and Halle (1968) and others, were maintained.

The validation of distinctive features has been troublesome from the beginning. Problems have arisen when distinctive features have attempted to be identified in spectrograms due to imprecision of measurement and limitations in reliable assessment of some of the acoustic parameters. The

TABLE 1-1
The Chomsky–Halle (1968) Distinctive-Feature System.

	r	l	p	b	f	v	m	t	d	θ	ð	n	s	z	tʃ	dʒ	ʃ	ʒ	k	g	ŋ	h	i	u	eɪ	oʊ	aɪ	ɔɪ	ɪ	ʊ	ɛ	ʌ	o	x	ɔ	w	j
Vocalic	+	+	−	−	−	−	−	−	−	−	−	−	−	−	−	−	−	−	−	−	−	−	+	+	+	+	+	+	+	+	+	+	+	−	+	−	−
Consonantal	+	+	+	+	+	+	+	+	+	+	+	+	+	+	+	+	+	+	+	+	+	−	−	−	−	−	−	−	−	−	−	−	−	+	−	−	−
High	−	−	−	−	−	−	−	−	−	−	−	−	−	−	+	+	+	+	+	+	+	−	+	+	−	−	−	−	+	+	−	−	−	+	−	+	+
Back	−	−	−	−	−	−	−	−	−	−	−	−	−	−	−	−	−	−	+	+	+	−	−	+	−	+	+	+	−	+	−	+	+	+	+	+	−
Low	−	−	−	−	−	−	−	−	−	−	−	−	−	−	−	−	−	−	−	−	−	+	−	−	−	−	+	−	−	−	−	−	−	−	+	−	−
Anterior	−	+	+	+	+	+	+	+	+	+	+	+	+	+	−	−	−	−	−	−	−	−												−		−	−
Coronal	+	+	−	−	−	−	−	+	+	+	+	+	+	+	+	+	+	+	−	−	−	−												−		−	−
Round	−	−	−	−	−	−	−	−	−	−	−	−	−	−	−	−	−	−	−	−	−	−	−	+	−	+	−	+	−	+	−	−	+	−	+	+	−
Tense																							+	+	+	+	+	+	−	−	−	−	+		−		
Voice	+	+	−	+	−	+	+	−	+	−	+	+	−	+	−	+	−	+	−	+	+	−												−		+	+
Continuant	+	+	−	−	+	+	−	−	−	+	+	−	+	+	−	−	+	+	−	−	−	+												+		+	+
Nasal	−	−	−	−	−	−	+	−	−	−	−	+	−	−	−	−	−	−	−	−	+	−												−		−	−
Strident	−	−	−	−	+	+	−	−	−	−	−	−	+	+	+	+	+	+	−	−	−	−												−		−	−

Table 1 (pp. 176–177) in *The Sound Pattern of English* by Noam Chomsky and Morris Halle. Copyright © 1968 by Noam Chomsky and Morris Halle. Reprinted by permission of Harper & Row, Publishers, Inc.

lack of precision of some measurements made using spectrographic analysis was compounded by the inabilities of some investigators to arrive at precise and reliable judgments of what was being measured. The articulatory components of distinctive features have been much more difficult to identify due to the imprecision and very delicate problems involved in FMG and cinefluoragraphic studies. While investigators have made valiant efforts to validate the presence or absence of features from specific phonemes, many issues are in doubt and are largely not well confirmed by the evidence gathered to date. Thus, the 'distinctiveness' of distinctive features has been controversial, perhaps due to the various techniques used to identify them and the measurement problems.

A number of different procedures have been used to identify distinctive features. The definition of the acoustic correlates of features was attempted in the early work of Jakobson, Fant, and Halle (1951). Spectrographic representations of the parameters of their distinctive features was the principal approach that they used, and they reported the successful identification of the acoustic correlates of each of their features. Miller and Nicely (1955) and Singh and Black (1966) also studied the acoustic correlates of speech using spectrographic information, but, in addition, they studied the articulatory correlates of their features. Articulatory correlates alone were studied and described by Halle (1964) and Chomsky and Halle (1968) while Wickelgren (1966) described both the articulatory and perceptual realities of his distinctive-feature system. The extent to which any of these investigators adequately and precisely defined the acoustic, articulatory, or perceptual correlates of the distinctive features that were of interest to them is perhaps debatable, in spite of the fact that the best technologies available at the time were assigned to the task.

○CRITICAL VIEWS OF DISTINCTIVE FEATURES

As time has elapsed and more persons in the speech and language remediation professions have considered the implications of distinctive-feature theory and systems to the corrective process in phonological disorders, the anticipated numbers of critical views have increased. While proponents of distinctive-feature use in the remediation of phonological disorders have rather vigorously promulgated and published accounts of their beliefs and experiences, certain adversarial points of view have gradually emerged. Most of these challenge the pragmatic use of a theoretical system to a direct clinical intervention process.

One of the first to express discomfort with distinctive-feature use in phonological disorders was Walsh (1974), followed by Winitz (1975), and Parker (1976). The misuse of a theoretical, explanatory system in clinical remediation was stressed by Walsh who maintained that distinctive-feature systems of the Chomsky and Halle (1968) type were designed originally to describe and clarify the nature of "autonomous phonemics and transformation grammar." Thus, such features were abstract and not clearly related to the physical aspects of speech.

Use of a distinctive-feature system in articulation therapy was questionable according to Walsh, since he felt that the binary notion of distinctive features was only applicable to an abstract classificatory system and remediation techniques for articulation therapy are largely phonetic. He further contended that the abstract nature of distinctive features (particularly the Chomsky and Halle system, 1968) makes the + or − feature concept inadequate for use in articulation therapy since clinicians frequently rely upon phonetic approaches. This binary view, if applied at the phonetic level, would restrict clinicians doing therapy to from one to eight distinct front-back positions or articulations. Walsh found this inadequate for most therapy, stating that the number of distinct consonant positions for English is actually from fourteen to sixteen (Walsh, 1974).

Walsh refuted the economy of the Jakobson features which had been earlier claimed by Winitz (1969) as an advantage over the more traditional ways of classifying articulatory behaviors (bilabial versus labiodental, for example). He believed that using Jakobson features such as grave/acute and continuant/interrupted in lieu of the more traditional descriptors would be uneconomical in the corrective process since such features would not allow for any differences between bilabial and labiodental fricatives or an interdental in contrast to an alveolar stop. Walsh also observed that use of Jakobson features would not discriminate among the place of articulation of liquids despite the many motor differences required for their production.

Walsh was of the opinion that speech clinicians need phonetic feature systems based on "language-specific articulation features." He proposed two advantages of such systems over the types of abstract, universal features of the type presented by Jakobson and his colleagues. The first he described as "contextual or facultative variation in speech," which could be accomplished using a phonetic feature system; and, secondly, he suggested that for children having serious misarticulations that "do not result in the split, shift, or merger of autonomous phonemes may be described in terms of subphonemic features." He then went on to provide the reader with his "tentative" phonetic feature system to be used by speech clinicians. Since this system may be more specifically relevant for use by speech clinicians than other more abstract ones, the features and their definitions are as follows:[1]

---

[1] H. Walsh, "On Certain Practical inadequacies of distinctive feature systems," *Journal of Speech Hearing Disorders* 39(1):32–44 (1974). Reprinted by permission.

SEGMENTAL FEATURE

Segment. The segmental feature specifies that a phoneme is present or absent in a given environment. Thus, "segment" indicates that a phoneme has been omitted.

VOCAL TRACT CONFIGURATION FEATURES

Open. A relatively unobstructed oral tract is characteristic of true vowels.

Stopped. Full occluded stop consonants and affricates, but not fricatives and sonorant sounds, are positively marked by this feature.

Constricted. Constricted sounds include fricatives, glides, nasals, and liquids, in the production of which the degree of openness in the vocal tract exceeds that of the stop consonants and is less than that of vowels.

CONSONANT PLACEMENT FEATURES: LOWER

Lower lip. This feature normally pertains to bilabial and labiodental phonemes /p/, /b/, /m/, /w/, /f/, /v/.

Tongue tip. The tip of the tongue is the lower articulator, either contextually or habitually, of certain varieties of /t/, /d/, /s/, /z/, /θ/, /ð/, /l/, /r/, /n/, /tʃ/, and /dʒ/.

Tongue blade. This feature is the normal lower articulator for /ʃ/ and /ʒ/, also for certain retracted varieties of consonants normally produced with the tongue tip.

Tongue dorsum. The dorsum serves as the lower articulator for /k/, /g/, and extremely retracted varieties of /r/.

CONSONANT PLACEMENT FEATURES: UPPER

Upper lip. The upper lip is the normal articulator for /p/, /b/, /m/, and /w/. It is sometimes substituted for the upper teeth in misarticulated labiodental fricatives.

Upper teeth. This feature applies in normal speech only to /θ/ and /ð/, but serves as the upper articulator for certain consonants usually articulated at the tooth ridge.

Tooth ridge. The tooth ridge is the characteristic upper articulator for /t/, /d/, /s/, /z/, /l/, /n/, and the extended varieties of /j/, /r/, /ʃ/, /ʒ/, /tʃ/, and /dʒ/.

Prepalate. The forward edge of the hard palate is the place of articulation for the retracted varieties of /r/, /ʃ/, /ʒ/, /tʃ/, and /d/ dʒ/, and for extremely forward articulations of velar stops.

Velum. The normal locus of articulation for /k/ and /g/.

Tongue Positions for Vowels

The monophthongs of American English are best described by reference to the positions of the tongue body in relation to its "neutral" position just before speaking. The tongue features along the vertical axis are high, mid, and low and along the horizontal axis front, central, and back. For the description of normative vowels one need not use all of these oppositions. The monophthongal vowels, for instance, may be specified as follows:

	/ɪ/	/ɛ/	/æ/	/ə/	/a/	/ʊ/	/ɔ/
Front	+	+	+	−	−	−	−
Back	−	−	−	−	−	+	+
High	+	−	−	−	−	+	−
Low	−	−	+	−	+	−	+

Diphthongs should logically be described bisegmentally according to the terminals of the transition.

Release Features

In most distinctive-feature systems, release features are neglected in favor of major class features and placement features. However, for several English phonemes the manner of release constitutes the actual distinctive marker. Among the distinctive release features for English are retroflex, lateral, nasal, frication, and abrupt. No distinctive-release feature is provided for glides, since misarticulations resulting in glides usually are the consequence of the nonapplication of a typical release feature, often accompanied by, or resulting from a shift in articulation.

Supplementary Features

Features that supplement oral configuration, placement, and release features may be distinctive or redundant. Typical supplementary articulation features are voice, aspiration, length, fortis, and lip rounding.

By using features of this type, the speech pathologist is in a better position to see precisely what sort of articulation problems are involved in a given case. For instance, the common contextual or habitual substitution of /j/ for /l/ would be described in Jakobsonian features as a change in such features as vocalic, consonantal, and coronal, which are used to differentiate large classes of sounds. However, regarding what occurs in the context of actual speech, the substitution may be described as follows:

	/l/	/j/
Lower Articulator:	+ tongue tip →	− tongue tip
	− tongue blade →	+ tongue blade
Upper Articulator:	+ tooth ridge →	− tooth ridge
	− prepalate →	+ prepalate
Release Feature:	+ lateral →	− lateral

When the substitution is described in these terms, the misarticulation can be seen either as a retracted articulation rendering a lateral release impossible or as a motor failure requiring compensatory articulation in a retracted position.

Similarly, the common substitution of /θ/ for /s/ would be indicated according to the common models as + strident → − strident, which describes not a change in articulation, but rather the consequence of a change in articulation. The substitution is better explained in articulatory terms:

		/s/		/θ/
Lower Articulator:	either	+ tongue tip →		+ tongue tip
	or	+ tongue tip →		+ tongue blade
Upper Articulator:		+ tooth ridge →		− tooth ridge
		− upper teeth →		+ upper teeth

The substitution is thus easily explained as a forward shift in articulation, which impedes the production of sibilance.

In precisely the same way, the common substitution of /w/ for /r/ can best be explained as compensatory articulation at the lips and the velum when the motor gesture for retroflexion is insufficient.

○ OTHER CRITICISMS OF DISTINCTIVE-FEATURE APPLICATIONS

Some of the difficulties of applying an abstract distinctive-feature system on the order of that by Chomsky and Halle (1968) were discussed by Winitz (1975) in light of some distinctive feature applications to articulation therapy reported by McReynolds and Huston (1971). These latter investigators studied the articulation disorders of some young severely defective children. Using the Chomsky and Halle (1968) system, they evaluated the feature usage of one young child who was consistently defective in his productions of /t/, /d/, /f/, /v/, /s/, /z/, /θ/, /ʃ/, and /ʒ/. They concluded that stridency was the single feature misused by this individual, with all other features present at one time or another as segments of other correctly produced sounds. It appeared that the acquisition of + coronol as seen in this feature requirement of /t/, /d/, /s/, /θ/ and /z/ was expected by McReynolds and Huston because this subject could consistently artic-ulate /n/ correctly, and this phoneme has + coronal as one of its features. This type of assumption was seriously questioned by Walsh (1974) who contended that features can be converted into phonetic segments; but as they are defined and used in phonology, they are not phonetic units in the usual sense. Thus, they lack the concreteness and specificity required to approximate the physiological gestures required for transfer to other phonemes.

While Winitz (1975) was very protective of the McReynolds and Huston (1971) opinion that features not produced in target sounds will appear in the production of other sounds, he supported Walsh's view that "the Chomsky–Halle feature system may pose problems in interpretation for some features if statements about physiological capabilities are made" (p. 25). Perhaps, then, both Walsh and Winitz might agree that in the example given by McReynolds and Huston the ability of the one child to generalize the + coronal feature from his correct use of it in /n/ might pose problems since /t/, /d/, /s/, /z/, and /θ/ are sounds whose physiological gestures are remarkably different from /n/. The extent, therefore, to which features can generalize when partially acquired is complex, obviously poorly understood, and seriously challenged under some conditions.

A basic assumption of a system advocated by McReynolds and Engmann (1975) for the determination of the percentage of distinctive-feature acquisition that children have mastered based upon the Chomsky and Halle (1968) system was attacked by Winitz (1975). He stated, "It is therefore incorrect, in the strictest sense, to speak of "the percentage of correct distinctive features" because articulatory productions, not phonological abstractions, are of concern. A distinctive feature can be assigned only to a phonological grammar; it cannot be partially correct. The easiest way out of this definitional straight jacket is not to discard important data, but to recognize that the special vocabulary of a discipline has been violated" (pp. 26–27). Winitz's last statement is capable of being interpreted as indicating some discomfort on his part with the use of an abstract system based on generative phonology in the articulation-therapy process.

Winitz (1975) posed an additional concern regarding the use of distinctive features in articulation therapy. He cautioned that an important limitation in their use relates to their basic original purpose, namely, to identify elements to explain or accommodate the phonological grammars of adult languages. He felt it improper to use such feature systems to describe the phonemic errors of young children. He concluded that distinctive features should be devised specifically for young children and applied to an understanding of their phonological rule systems.

In an informative and comprehensive article Parker (1976) clarified the nature of generative phonology and phonemic theory and put under attack a number of persons from the speech pathology/language areas for their misinterpretation and misuse of distinctive features in the correction of children's misarticulations. His frequent contrasts and examples of the differences implied in each approach were directed at demonstrating that a phonemic view of distinctive features would assume a direct one-to-one correspondence between distinctive features and the speech signal itself.

But, he pointed out, in generative phonology no assumptions of this part are necessary or implied, and a speaker–hearer's linguistic competency is what is most relevant.

Parker (1976) suggested that the important distinctive-feature system originally developed by Jakobson, Fant, and Halle (1952) was phonemic in nature and that the well known subsequent system presented in *Sound Pattern of English* (1968) was much more generative–phonological in nature. This change, he maintained, was related to a discrepancy between the physical speech signal and the abstract linguistic system, and it represented a significant departure from phonemic theory.

Since generative phonology and phonemic theory are confusing for most practitioners, some of the clarifying elements quoted directly from Parker may be helpful as these pertain to distinctive features and their application to the correction of children's misarticulations. Parker maintained that their terminologies were part of the confusion and went on to define important terms and contrast them within each of the two theoretical frameworks.

> The problem is that they use the same or similar terms to mean different things: underlying form is not equivalent to phoneme; phonological rule does not mean the same thing as phonemic rule (allophonic statement); and the two theories use the term phonetics to mean two different things.

He further illustrated his point by saying that

> . . . underlying forms are more abstract than phonemes. Underlying forms describe morphemes (the smallest units of meaning) and phonemes describe allomorphs (the different phonemic manifestations of morphemes). For example, (photo) is one morpheme, but it has three allomorphs: /foto/ in *photo*, /fotə/ in *photograph*, and /fətə/ in *photography*. Generative phonology represents morphemes rather than allomorphs in the classificatory matrix, because it is a fundamental aim of generative theory to capture what the speaker–hearer knows about his language. And it seems to be part of the speaker's knowledge that more than one word may be formed from a single morpheme. Consider *Canada* and its derivative *Canadian*. In a generative grammar the phonetic representation of these two words would be derived from one form (morpheme) listed in the lexicon (a list of all the morphemes of the language), whose second vowel is /æ/. That is, the second *a* in Canada and Canadian would be represented in the classificatory matrix by /æ/, even though /æ/ does not appear on the surface in either word. By the application of a series of phonological rules, the /æ/ would become /æ/ in *Canada* and /e/ in *Canadian*. Conversely, phonemic theory makes no attempt to show the relationship among different occurrences of one morpheme, that is, among its allomorphs. In phonemic theory both words would have different phonemic representations, /kæ n d/ and /k nedI n/, respectively. Each phoneme is associated with an invariant set of phones and thus no phonological rules in the generative sense are motivated.[2]

[2] F. Parker, "Distinctive Features in Speech Pathology: Phonology or Phonetics." *Journal of Speech Hearing Disorders*, 41(1) 23–39 (1976).

Although some speech and language pathologists have claimed that a distinctive-feature approach to articulation therapy for preschool children has as much or greater efficacy than nondistinctive (traditional) approaches (Pollack and Rees, 1972; Costello and Onstine, 1976), experimental evidence to support this assertion is extremely limited both in the number of reports and the scope of the experiments reported. A detailed description of such approaches and their possible strengths and weaknesses is contained in Chapter IV.

⊙DISTINCTIVE FEATURES AND THE SPEECH SIGNAL: SOME RECENT EVIDENCE

Under the direction of the author, Gowman (1979) completed a comprehensive study of the degree of distinctive-feature acquisition achieved by ninety articulatory-defective children—thirty four-year olds, thirty five-year olds, and thirty six-year olds. Within each age level there were ten mildly, ten moderately, and ten severely articulatory-impaired children. Gowman determined the percentage of acquisition of the thirteen distinctive features in the Chomsky and Halle (1968) system using a method for determining percentages of acquisition developed and tested by the author (This system is described in Chapter II.).

Although the Chomsky and Halle (1968) system has been the most popular in use by speech–language pathologists, it has been criticized by some authorities (Walsh, 1974; Parker, 1976) as too abstract and more theoretical than applicable to remediation of children's articulation disorders. Gowman and the author attacked this problem by relating feature acquisition to basic elements of the speech signal.

Three aspects of the speech signal used to make choices for children to receive remediation and help select primary and secondary targets for therapy are the consistency of misarticulation, severity and stimulability performances for individual phonemes and across all defective ones. To test the former, Gowman used the McDonald Deep Test (1964). A version of the Carter and Buck Prognostic Speech Test (Carter and Buck, 1958) developed by the author assessed both individual phoneme stimulability and an overall stimulability percentage for all defective phonemes. Thus, on both measures percentages of individual phoneme consistency and stimulability were gathered, along with overall percentages of each of these factors. Total severity was judged using the total number of defective phonetic contexts. These factors appeared to us to be prime elements of the "speech signal" of young children and major factors in the clinical-management program for such children.

The major thrust of this effort was prediction. Is it possible that combinations of distinctive features from the "abstract" Chomsky and Halle 1968 system would be predictive variables in the individual and overall consistency of these ninety children, and would such variables be equally predictive of subjects' individual phoneme and overall stimulability performances, as well as severity? The analysis took the form of stepwise regression using distinctive-feature combinations to first predict individual defective-phoneme consistency measures followed by a prediction of average phoneme consistency across each child's total number of defective phonemes. Regression was completed using all ninety subjects combined and then three times additionally so that prediction could be studied in the thirty four-year olds, thirty five-year olds, and thirty six-year olds separately. An identical set of procedures was used to test subjects' individual and overall stimulability performances, first with all ninety subjects combined and then again for each of the three age groups. Finally, using the total number of phonetic contexts in error from the deep tests as a measure of severity, one separate regression analysis was completed for all subjects again followed by one done at each of the three age levels. Results from a total of seventeen separate regression analyses showed that various combinations of nine poorly acquired features ($+$ strident, $+$ continuant, $+$ coronal, $+$ vocalic, $-$ strident, $-$ voice, $-$ anterior, $-$ back, and $-$ high) in various combinations could predict the speech-signal performances of the children to an amazing degree. Some multiple correlations were almost perfect. Among the many surprising findings were the following:

> The feature $+$ coronal alone had a single correlation with all subjects' overall percentage of consistency at .786, and, in concert with the eight other features used as predictors, resulted in a multiple correlation of .910.
>
> Prediction of individual phoneme consistency and overall consistency was very high at all three age levels and near one hundred percent at the four-year level.
>
> The feature $-$ high alone had a single correlation with all subjects' overall severity of .920, and the other eight features elevated the correlation to .980.
>
> Overall stimulability performances for defective phonemes for all subjects combined could not be predicted nearly as well as the consistency and severity factors. The overall multiple R was .550 and statistically significant.
>
> Prediction of individual phoneme stimulability was not possible for some phonemes but occurred for others at specific age levels.

The belief stated by some writers that the features from the Chomsky and Halle 1968 system were not related to the speech signal seems totally challenged by these many findings. Indeed, if measures of individual phoneme and overall phonemic performances of young children used in the Gowman investigation are legitimate measures of the "speech signal," then the Chomsky and Halle 1968 feature system is almost perfectly related to many of them. Use of such feature systems by clinicians, therefore, in planning and conducting articulation therapy may be very meaningful in view of the importance attached to them in modern applied approaches to articulatory remediation.

SUMMARY

Attempts to relate aspects of speech production with complex and seemingly abstract linguistic control systems have been extremely limited. However, the interest of a rather small group of investigators who are applying newer strategies and much more sensitive measurement systems appears to be contributing to a beginning understanding of how speech physiology is influenced by linguistic encoding of the message. Older ideas of the articulatory system seem now to have been destroyed or severely challenged in terms of their validity. If anything, the dynamic nature of the process and its complex sets of interactions of the basic elements of respiration for speech, phonation, velarcoupling, resonance, and articulatory patterns have begun to show their common denominators. We see increasing evidence that the old concept of phonetics or motor phonetics, while not discarded as fraudulent beliefs, have yielded to the influences of the linguistic impact and the precise nature of control these variables have on the coordination of this totally fantastic system.

Although termed too abstract to be useful to the speech-language pathologist by some and perhaps in violation of some basic linguistic precepts, distinctive features have been adopted by some speech-language pathologists and presumably manipulated in the corrective process with young children having phonological disorders. The older concepts to describe aspects of the articulatory process that described aspects of place, manner, and voicing do not seem defeated by distinctive feature systems. Rather, such systems appear to have contributed to much finer distinctions of these three basic parameters of the articulatory process, and many features of different systems seem to show more distinctiveness in the identification or specification of these three elements.

Attacks on the abstractness issue, raised particularly against the Chomsky and Halle (1968) feature system widely used by speech-language pathologists, seem unfounded based upon some recent evidence showing strong predictive relationships to a number of aspects of young children's phonological skills including total degrees of defectiveness, consistency of phonemic error production, and some relationships to stimulability performances. Such measures are clinically relevant, evaluated, and used to guide the intervention process by large numbers of speech-language pathologists. Inclusion of distinctive feature concepts, coarticulation studies, linguistic ties to the specific aspects of the physiology of speech, and related investigations of the mechanisms of speech have stimulated a great deal of new thinking, and it appears all this is just a bare beginning.

The basis for therapeutic intervention

○ THE ARTICULATORY-DEFECTIVE PRESCHOOL CHILD

One of the salient aspects of early child development is speech and language acquisition. This process has been the focus of some investigators for many years, yet little of substance is known about many of its basic elements. Clearly, more attention is being directed at understanding this complex yet perfectly normal process at this time than at any other time in history.

Not only are researchers from a number of related disciplines, for example, speech–language pathology, speech science, psycholinguistics, and psychology, interested in speech–language acquisition but, very significantly, so are many parents of young children. If a child's speech and language capacity is badly underdeveloped, parental concerns are frequently centered on these aspects of development. Children who cannot talk or who have speech that is so impoverished in its structural aspects that it is unintelligible are very disturbing to parents. It is not unusual in clinical practice to find the chief complaints of parents to be either "He's not talking" or "He doesn't speak clearly." This concern may be telegraphed to parents because little or no speech or very unintelligible speech and poor comprehension of language are advertised very well by children exposed to other persons.

The old unwritten rule that one should ignore a lack of speech and language until the child is three years of age or older seems to be waning, and more and more concerned parents want professional judgments by trained professionals concerning such conditions. Thus, the impetus for providing more and better quality clinical services for preschool children has been characteristic of the 1970s. The availability of such services will emerge as a major emphasis in the 1980s, spurred by national legislation that affects all states, school districts, and protectorates of the United States, that is, PL-94–142, The Right to Education Act. This massive piece of legislation, which supports principles such as providing total services in the "least restrictive environment," continues to make huge changes in state, regional, and individual school district programs for handicapped children. This law mandates special-education services for children from age zero to twenty one. Thus, many specialists, including, of course, speech-language pathologists and audiologists, have rather suddenly been confronted with the need to adequately assess many of the skills of preschool children.

The incidence of communication disorders in preschool children has not been reported. A conservative estimate of the percentage of young school-age children who are considered under the guidelines of PL 94–142 as handicapped is ten percent. It is likely that the percentage of preschool children with handicaps would be of the same magnitude or perhaps somewhat higher, since some small portion of very young children showing, for example, delayed development in speech and language might fall into a normal range of performance as they grow older. The incidence of those in the estimated ten percent of preschool handicapped who have a component of articulatory defectiveness is probably substantial, since this is a common area of related defectiveness in many types of handicapping conditions. Some visually impaired and certain types of physically impaired children may enjoy normal speech and language development. But children with many other types of severe handicapping conditions do not, and one expects to find disordered or delayed articulatory development as one element in their constellation of problems.

speech- and language-impaired preschool children

Again, the number of such children is unknown, but clearly many thousands of preschool children have serious speech and/or language impairments. Children in this category may have related problems in fine-motor skills, inadequate perceptual functioning, and social development; however, their primary area of difficulty is their poor ability to communicate using speech and aural language. The etiology of their problems is frequently unknown, although many will show signs of slow maturation of their central nervous systems. Such children are often found by careful psychometric assessment to have intelligence within or approaching the normal range using tests such as the *Wechsler Preschool Intelligence Scale* (Wechsler, 1955) or the *Leiter Scale* (Leiter, 1951). They do not have sensory defects, are not seriously emotionally disturbed, and have no gross physical impairments. Researchers have rather consistently found, however, that compared with normal speech- and language-functioning children of the same ages, they frequently fail to show the normal left-hemispheric processing of various types of dichotic stimuli (Sommers and Taylor, 1972; Starkey, 1974; Pettit and Helms, 1974; Davis, 1978; Kucera, 1980).

Since researchers have found that normal speech- and language-functioning children as young as three (Nagafuchi, Kimura, 1963; Lowe-Belle, Berlin, Berlin, 1972; Bryden, 1965) and four (Starkey, 1974) do show significant left-hemispheric processing for different types of dichotic stimuli, the finding that some young speech and language impaired do not may be interpretable as showing a slower rate of CNS maturation. An alternative hypothesis is that these findings denote a disarray in speech and language processing that may not necessarily disappear even though the speech and language disorder may ameliorate over time and with remedial effort. Such a hypothesis is somewhat supportable by results from a number of independent studies of adults who stutter, almost all of whom developed this disorder in early childhood. Investigations by Curry & Gregory, 1969; Perrin & Eisenson, 1970; Sommers, Brady, & Moore, 1975; Davenport, 1979; and Barrett et al., 1979 have contained evidence that more stutterers have significantly less left-hemispheric processing and more tendency to be right-hemispheric processors of dichotic stimuli of various types than normal adult speakers. We have also found evidence that children who have retained their stuttering behaviors after age ten frequently have less left-hemispheric processing of dichotic words and digits than normal children of the same ages (Sommers, Brady, & Moore, 1975).

handicapped children having concomitant speech and language impairments

Very young children suffering with various types of handicapping conditions are also impaired in their abilities to communicate verbally. The range of defectiveness in the major handicapping condition is from mild to profound, and, of course, this is true for the communication impairment as well. The impact of the major handicap appears to be significantly related to the degree of speech and language impairment. This is most obvious in the case of mild versus severe mental retardation and mild versus severe hearing impairment. In both of these handicapping conditions the degree of impairment of speech and language is closely related to the degree of intelligence in the first instance and hearing loss in the second, since the range is great in both dimensions. The intelligibility of speech of the young deaf child in contrast to one having mild hearing loss is grossly deficient in many aspects, namely, accurate use of appropriate phonemes; proper use of supersegmental factors; adequacy of syntactical, morphological, and semantic elements; and vocal abnormalities. This same situation appears to characterize the speech and language of the mentally retarded; that is, at the high end (IQs 50–75), children may be very slow in learning speech and language and use it poorly in contrast to normal speaking ones; at the low end (IQs 25–50), many such children develop some degree of verbal communication much later with all elements of speech and language poorer than the mildly retarded. Some of these children never really develop meaningful use of verbal communication. The articulatory component of the problem is obviously much more affected in the severely retarded with occasional, rare exceptions.

Many types of physical disabilities in young children have components

of defective speech and language. Those affecting the functioning of the
neuro-musculature system underlying speech and language appear to be
most devastating to these processes. Certainly, cerebral palsy, in its wide
range of forms, can impair many vital elements of these functions. Again,
it is generally the case that the more pervasive the physical involvement
the greater the chances for impaired speech and language. Other factors
are also influential in influencing the degree of speech and language
impairment, of course, such as the specific type of cerebral palsy (spastic,
athetoid, etc.); the speech and language resiliency of the individual;
environmental variables; intelligence; presence of hearing loss; and specific
paralysis of the respiratory, laryngeal, palate, tongue, mandible, lips, and
other oral–facial structures.

Owing to the severe dysarthria that characterizes many of the more
involved cerebral palsied children, their articulation is grossly affected and
their speech intelligibility often is poor. The great effort required by some
of the more severe cases to speak probably inhibits efforts to do so; and
this situation is in turn detrimental to the development of expressive
language in its syntactical, morphological, and semantic forms.

The young child with cleft palate is most often noticeably deficient in
being able to communicate. Although modern surgical and prosthetic
approaches have improved the speech plight of such children, many do
not develop articulatory and other speech skills in the normal way. As in
the case of some other developmental anamolies, cleft palate has the
occasional unfortunate tendency of occurring along with other defects.
Some preschool children with multiple handicaps have cleft palate and
other disorders such as mental retardation, hearing loss, visual defects,
and emotional disturbance. The majority of victims, however, escape with
only the cleft palate or cleft palate and cleft lip.

Children labeled as "autistic" frequently have communication disorders.
Many have echolalia or "parrot speech" in which they repeat whole
sentences, phrases, or words apparently without comprehending the
message. Their auditory comprehension of language appears to be more
of the communication problem than their expressive language, and it has
been observed by Fay and Butler (1968) that their articulatory abilities
may often be found to be within normal limits for their ages. While many
young children showing autistic-type behaviors may have impaired communication abilities related to comprehension, and thus need this type of
language training and other services, articulation therapy *per se* is frequently not required.

developmental apraxia

The term "developmental apraxia," or "developmental verbal
apraxia," has been used by some American and British clinical and

research personnel to describe a certain variety of symptoms, the most obvious of which is a unique pattern of severe articulatory defectiveness in the absence of other serious linguistic difficulties. The sequelae of this disorder are not definitively established, although a surprisingly large number of important investigations have been completed within the past five years and interest in identifying them seems great at this time. (We shall also see, in a later chapter, that some authorities have established specific articulation therapy methodologies for children described as having developmental apraxia). Clinical experience tends to show that some portion of severely articulatory-defective young children are troublesome for many clinicians and slow to remit their articulation errors under therapy. It is commonly observed that traditional approaches to remediation for them may be inefficient and ineffective (Macaluso–Haynes, 1978).

Head injuries, certain diseases of childhood, toxic conditions, tumors, and other traumatic conditions may result in apraxic symptoms in children's speech. We term this "acquired apraxia," but fortunately, the condition is uncommon, and many children of young age show recovery from it to an impressive degree. The condition termed "developmental" or "congenital apraxia" is probably more common than the acquired form, and its etiology remains unknown.

In the distant past the term "developmental aphasia" was popular with some speech/language pathologists to describe children who manifested serious central language-processing problems including poor speech output and reduced or impaired auditory comprehension of speech. Rosenbek (1972) makes a distinction between the condition referred to by some as developmental aphasia and that of developmental apraxia contending that the latter condition is characterized by normal or near normal comprehension of speech but severely impaired articulation. A fundamental delineating concept that characterizes writings concerning apraxia in adults has also been applied to developmental apraxia. This suggests that one form of developmental apraxia may be present when the speed and accuracy of muscles involved in speech appear to be within normal limits for involuntary movements of a spontaneous nature and successful imitation of the articulators can be accomplished. However, in spontaneous speaking articulatory patterns of movement may break down (Morley, 1965). This condition appears to reflect a type of difficulty in inserting the phonological elements successfully into the linguistic stream, and, as such, may be a motor-encoding disorder which impairs the development of a reliable coarticulatory function.

Not unlike the confusing nomenclature that has been applied to aphasia and related disorders in adults, apraxia in children has been given various labels. The identification of a second form, a nonverbal or oral apraxia, (again borrowed from a concept and assessment procedure applied to adult apraxia) refers to the inability of the child to be able to produce voluntary, nonspeech motor movements, such as yawning, tongue-clicking, and lip-puckering. Rosenbek (1972) and others have maintained that if the child cannot imitate or can only partially imitate movements of his articulators, "oral apraxia" is present. Thus, it appears that we have two distinct possibilities; and we have various combinations, such as: (a) developmental apraxia in the absence of any problems with imitation of articulatory movements and production of nonverbal patterns of movement, (b) nonverbal or oral apraxia alone, (c) combinations of the two phenomena. It appears to this writer that the combination of events would most likely be found to occur. It also should be acknowledged that the existence of any of these conditions as representing meaningful, clinical, and etiological categories may be severely questioned by some at this time. The resolution of the existence of these conditions as entities will, of course, require a substantial amount of research effort. These efforts appear to be increasing in a promising manner.

developmental history of apraxic children

Based on his clinical experiences and records, Eisenson (1972) reported some tentative impressions concerning the developmental histories of young children thought to be "articulatory apraxic." Certain aspects of their development were normal while others were not. Differences were reported in speech and language development, feeding habits, and motorical skills. The child's early auditory responses to various speech/nonspeech sounds is normal, perhaps reflecting good sound localization, discrimination, and recognition abilities. In infancy babbling may be present, but lalling (self-sound imitation) and later echolalic responses may be very limited to absent. Expressive abilities are weak, and the child may imitate speech poorly and not interact verbally to the degree that normal children do. Apraxic children, according to Eisenson, may be "lazy chewers" and prefer easily digested foods and liquids. Such children may be clumsy, late walkers, and poorly coordinated; and some portion of them may reflect evidence of neurological dysfunction.

symptomotology of developmental apraxic children

Some of the characteristics of young developmental apraxic children to be presented are based largely upon case studies and observations by experienced professionals; other information is available from group studies, some rather comprehensive in nature. None of the characteristics is well enough researched to be a conclusive sign of this disorder, and it is likely that all are not required to support a diagnosis. Furthermore, assuming that developmental apraxia in children is a viable diagnostic entity, future studies may show that other symptomologies are related to many of these and are perhaps better indices of the condition.

Among the historical observers of children having poor speech intelligibility was Orton (1937). He laid the framework for the now reactivated hypothesis of incomplete or confused cerebral dominance as basic to speech, reading, and writing problems in some children in this classic work, *Reading, Writing, and Speech Problems in Children.* He observed that children having developmental apraxia developed hand preferences later than others and were much slower in learning in talk. Using measures of "external dominance," for example handedness, eyedness, and footedness, Orton appears to have been considerably ahead of his time since he postulated that a lack of unilateral cerebral control for speech, reading, and writing was focal in such disturbances and reflected a better natural endowment in the cortex of one hemisphere. Recently, some impressive scientific evidence that seems supportive of Orton's contention was reported by four physician/researchers who studied the cerebral asymmetry of twenty four developmental dyslexic persons between the ages of eleven and forty-seven. They reported that ten of the subjects evidenced a reversal of the pattern of asymmetry usually found in right-handed persons, with computerized brain tomograms showing their right parietoccipital region wider than their left. The verbal IQs of the ten subjects with reversed asymmetry were twelve points lower than the fourteen with normal left areas, that is, wider than the right; and four of the ten had histories of delayed speech development in childhood (Hier and others, 1978). They concluded that reversal of cerebral asymmetry alone is not adequate cause for dyslexia or verbal disabilities, but that its existence may be a risk factor, especially for boys in whom the incidence of dyslexia is four times as great as girls. They estimated this risk for those having the reversed cerebral asymmetry to be five times greater than for individuals having the normal larger area in their left parietoccipital regions.

An ever-increasing literature leads us to the conclusion that the severely articulatory-defective child tends to be an inferior performer on a variety of perceptual, motor, and linguistic tasks. There is some related research evidence to show also that children having less severe articulatory defects may be poorer performers than normal speaking ones, but the evidence to show that the severely defective is inferior is gathering.

This population of severely defective children has prompted investigations by a number of researchers, who support the assertion that developmental articulatory apraxia is an entity. A strong suggestion from a number of investigations is that the developmental apraxic child may be one subtype of the more general group of children having severe articulatory problems.

Performances of some severe articulatory-defective children on certain perceptual/lingustic tasks may reflect the existence of subpopulations. Severe articulatory-defective, young, school-age children studied by the author and his colleagues (Sommers, Moore, Brady, and Jackson, 1976) were found to process dichotic words significantly less in their left hemispheres than comparable children having mild/moderate articulation problems or normal articulation. Not all of the severe defectives failed to show significant right-ear effects, however, but ten of fifteen failed to show any ear effect or had reversed ear effects. Thus, average left-hemispheric processing in one group of severe defectives was normal and one group's performance was aberrant. This suggests a possible division and the likelihood of the existence of a subgroup whose etiology and other characteristics might be different.

A similar finding was made by Davis (1978) who studied the dichotic word processing of forty-four preschool children enrolled in special training programs for learning disabilities. Their problems almost always included deviant or delayed articulatory development and general linguistic deficiencies. Subjects had normal hearing, intelligence tested and found to be within or close to normal limits, frequently poor physical coordination, and no major emotional disturbances. While their average right-ear scores were significantly lower than comparable normal subjects, seventeen of forty-four children had normal right-ear effects, sixteen had no significant ear effect, and eleven had reversed or left-ear effects. These findings again point to the existence of subgroups within a sample of young speech- and language-impaired children most of whom had significant numbers of articulation errors along with other linguistic deficits.

Probably many investigations of the performances of severe articulatory-defective young children where significant inferiority on some task was identified might contain information to show that some portion of the severe group performed normally. For example, findings from the Jenkins and Lohr (1964) investigation revealed that it was the group of severe articulatory-defective children that manifested the poorest fine-motor abilities. Most likely some portion of the severe group's members performed somewhat like the normal and mildly defective subjects in this study. Because of our cursory knowledge about these populations, we expect that global classifications such as "severe articulatory defective" may subsume many relevant differences in subjects. The author is reminded that he once saw the oralform discrimination and two-point difference limen scores on a spastic, quadraplegic young man whose articulation and other elements of speech were almost perfect, yet the scores on each test were extremely poor.[1] If both of these measures have

---

[1] This author is grateful to Eugene T. McDonald for this enlightening experience, State College, Pennsylvania, 1967.

been found almost consitently to relate to speech proficiency in children and adults, how can this be? One obvious explanation is that this person had the requisite skill in his auditory system to compensate for the poor feedback information that was transmitted by the defective tactile and kinesthetic mechanisms in his oral structure. Does he therefore represent a subtype of this disorder, an extremely rare one? Identification of the subtypes of severe-articulatory defectives seems to have begun, and this activity is long overdue.

An ambitious investigation was completed by Arndt, Shelton, Johnson, and Furr (1977) to determine if subgroups of misarticulating school children could be identified and discriminated accurately based upon the uniqueness of their patterns of reponses on a large number of school achievement, oral structure, and auditory processing tasks. Subjects were considered to have predominate (but not exclusive) misarticulations of either /r/ or /s/ phonemes. Although the authors evidenced disappointment to the extent in which they succeeded in locating subgroups, their data do tend to show that those having largely /r/ defects had patterns of perform- ance on certain tasks different from those having largely errors of /s/.

In perhaps a more definitive test of the subgroup-existence hypothesis, McNutt and Hamayan (1982) studied the performances of 60 children averaging nine years eleven months of age who were defective in articu- lation with a group of comparably aged normal-speaking control subjects (39 in number) on measures of auditory processing and memory, language and cognition, oral sensory and motor skills, and other factors such as sex, handedness, and parental occupation. Using a form of factor analysis followed by discriminant analyses, these investigators reported the exis- tence of 12 subgroups of articulatory defectives. On many measures that earlier studies in which homogeneous groups of articulation defective children have been found to be inferior to normal-speaking children, McNutt and Hamayan's findings seem to suggest that such overall poorer average performances may have been heavily influenced from subgroup members deficient in certain skills. As such, this investigation seems particularly illuminating and appears to provide good evidence to support the existence of subgroups in the large population of children having defective articulation.

the concept of developmental apraxia

Yoss and Darley (1974) found that one group of thirty moderately severe to severe articulatory-defective children, averaging four to six years of age, were significantly poorer in their abilities to perform isolated, volitional oral movements based upon a modification and elaboration of the test by De Renze and others (1966) for oral apraxia. This subgroup's articulation performances were significantly different from the better performing group on the types of articulatory errors produced, and their neurological ratings were significantly poorer. This study has the additional value of the specification of the types of phonological errors that separated the two groups using a spontaneous-speech sample and a repeated-speech task. Stepwise, discriminant function analysis was used to determine if these factors could provide significant discrimination of the members of each group. Using this statistical procedure, their findings indicated that ninety percent of correct classification of subjects was possible using six variables: neurologic ratings, sum of two-feature errors, sum of distortion errors, sum of three-feature errors, sum of prolongation and repetition errors, and sum of addition errors. In a similar analysis using the spontaneous-speech analysis, the resulting correct classification of subjects was again highly accurate (ninety percent). The five variables used were: neurologic ratings, sum of distortion errors, sum of one-place errors, sum of addition errors, and sum of omission errors. Three of the five predictors were the same as in the repeated-speech analysis, and, interestingly, sum of omission errors was a significant predictor of their spontaneous speech. (Probably errors of omission are less likely to occur when subjects repeat the examiner's words.)

Of further interest was their report that the group having inferior isolated volitional oral movements, considered to be the developmental apraxics, had twice as many errors of voicing as the other severe group. On tasks such as tieing shoelaces, buttoning, etc., the developmental apraxics were inferior to the other severe articulatory defectives, suggesting poorer development of some fine and gross motor skills. Motor defectiveness in this group was also seen in some of the articulators, since their diadochokinetic performances rates were significantly slower than the other subjects. Many of these findings seem related to suggestions of earlier investigators concerning the constellation of symptoms labeled developmental apraxia.

In a follow-up investigation highly similar to that reported by Yoss and Darley (1974), Williams, Ingham, and Rosenthal (1981) found some evidence for certain types of speech characteristics to differentiate the performances of fifteen children having inferior abilities to perform volitational oral movements and fifteen having better abilities all of whom had a wide range of articulatory defectiveness. Some of the findings from the Yoss and Darley study were not confirmed, particularly important being the lack of neurological ratings to differentiate to two groups. Williams, Ingham, and Rosenthal cited possible differences in the populations of the two investigations, such as severity of articulatory defectiveness, and possible methodological differences as reasons for some lack of agreement in findings. Their investigation also provided evidence for significantly inferior performances of their thirty articulatory defective children compared with a matched group of thirty normal speaking children on tasks involving imitation of volitional oral movements, auditory sequencing, and diadochokinetic rates.

Aspects of the symptomotology of developmental apraxia have also been described in detail by Rosenbek and Wertz (1972) as a result of a review that they completed of fifty developmental apraxia-of-speech cases. It was their opinion that a number of generalizations about the existence of unique speech and language characteristics could be arrived at. These include the following:

> Their receptive language abilities are superior to their expressive expressive ones.
>
> Oral, nonverbal apraxia frequently, but not always, is associated with apraxia of speech.
>
> Frequent transposition of sounds within words can be identified in some children.
>
> The condition frequently occurs in conjunction with childhood aphasia and dysarthria, but it may be found without significant degrees of these conditions.
>
> Articulatory errors occur most frequently on fricatives, affricatives, and consonant clusters and, therefore, vary with the complexity of the required articulatory adjustments and demands of speech sounds categorically.
>
> Articulatory accuracy in spontaneous, connected speech is worse than one might expect based upon responses from single words obtained from standard articulation tests.
>
> Repetition of sounds in isolation may be adequate.
>
> More vowel errors may tend to characterize their types of phonemic errors than in others having misarticulation.
>
> Phonemic errors may tend to be inconsistent.
>
> When misarticulating phonemas, groping and trial-and-error behaviors may be present.

Although Rosenbek and Wertz's case review did not locate large numbers of developmental apraxics who had signs of neurological dysfunction, thirty-eight percent of their sample evaluated neurologically were reported as having neurological deficits, including muscle weakness, spasticity, hyperkinesia, and hyper- and hypoflexia.

Many readers will note that the symptomotology reported by Rosenbek and Wertz is very reminiscent of that found in the recent literature dealing with apraxia of speech in adults. Those developmental apraxic children whom the author has seen were most often highly consistently defective in their articulation, showed very poor stimulability, deviant and badly underdeveloped distinctive-feature systems, poor fine-motor skills, some expressive-language inferiority (although marginal receptive linguistic abilities), poor volitional control over their articulators, correct production of syntactical units to denote the presence of syllables and words without, however, very intelligible speech. (A detailed case study of a remarkable young child who exhibits many of the symptoms of developmental apraxia will be presented later in this chapter.)

In a research report Snyder, Marquardt, and Peterson (1976) provided additional evidence concerning the abilities of developmental apraxic children to complete volitional and sequenced motor productions of their articulators and other valuable information concerning their expressive and receptive linguistic abilities. These investigators studied the performances of one group of young normal-speaking children, one group having "functional articulation disorders," and one group they considered as apraxic based upon the application of the Yoss and Darley (1974) study's test battery. Using the *Northwestern Syntax Screening Test* (Lee, 1969), they concluded that the functional articulatory-defective subjects and the developmental apraxic ones tended to be inferior to the normal-speaking children on the receptive syntax subscale, but the differences failed to reach statistical significance. On the expressive subscale of the NSST, however, the performances of both the functional misarticulating children and the apraxics were inferior to the normal subjects, and the apraxics' scores were lower than the functional misarticulators' scores. In an earlier report Benton (1964/65) had observed that children having apraxia of speech also had expressive-language errors taking the form of "telegraphic" speech in which certain parts of speech such as conjunctions, prepositions, and articles were omitted. These findings may question the general assumptions that the expressive and receptive linguistic abilities of developmental apraxic children are completely normal and that the only deficiency is their uniquely motor-impaired articulation.

Perhaps the low-keyed, national controversy surrounding the use of the term "apraxia of speech" to describe adult apraxia will eventually settle around a related problem in children. Opponents of the speech-only concept of this disorder in adults point out that this disorder almost always has linguistic deficits other than phonology, thus the correct descriptor should be "apraxia of speech and language" (Martin, 1974). Efforts to locate "pure" apraxic adults (having normal linguistic abilities) have been very difficult, although after exhaustive searching a few such persons have been located (Square, 1980). Most apraxia in adults, indeed, exists on a continuum of defectiveness and coexists with aphasia. Does this mean that developmental apraxia in children is also likely to imply the existence of other linguistic problems, especially in other expressive-language components? Information from the Rosenbek and Wertz report (1972 would support a positive response to this question.

syntax and articulation

The linguistic component that appears to be most related to children's articulatory abilities is syntax (Panagos and Klich, 1979). One of the most revealing investigations that ties severe articulatory defectiveness in children to syntactical skills was completed by Shriner, Holloway, and Daniloff (1969). Thirty children having large numbers of phonemic errors were matched with thirty normal-speaking ones. Children were six to nine years of age. Subjects' spoken language samples were evaluated, and the results indicated that the severe articulatory defectives were poorer in grammatical usage. They also used shorter sentences as measured by the mean length of response (MLR). The investigators hypothesized that children with severe articulation problems may tend to use shorter sentences, thus reducing the probability of their making an articulation error. This tendency, then, reduces the opportunity for them to experiment with new syntactical forms; therefore, they do not develop this aspect of their language adequately.

Other investigators have provided earlier evidence of the tie between articulation and syntax in children. Menyuk (1964) studied ten normal-speaking children and ten having "infantile" speech (as well as, apparently, many misarticulations). Subjects were three to five years of age. Spoken-language samples and a sentence repetition constituted her data. She concluded that the rule systems that the speech-impaired children used were very general and primitive in contrast to the normal speakers. Some support for her findings came from a subsequent study by Van Denmark and Mann (1965) who studied fifty articulatory defectives and fifty older normal-speaking children's spoken-language performances. They reported a significant between-group difference in favor of the normal subjects when aspects of structural complexity were analyzed, and they concluded that the articulatory defectives tended to be deficient in areas of grammatical completeness and in their complexity of verbal response.

Collaborative evidence for a strong relationship between aspects of syntactical functioning and articulation followed, with Whitacre, Luper, and Pollio (1970) reporting a more general linguistic deficiency in children having a wide range of articulation errors in contrast to normal speakers. Subjects, aged six to seven years, were studied using a word-association test, an implicit-phonology test, and a sentence-repetition test. The articulatory defectives were found significantly inferior to the normals on all tests, and the authors concluded that such children are also impaired in language abilities that require knowledge of phonological rules, form class, and sentence structure. It appears that this conclusion fits the model of a close tie between the phonological deficits and the syntactical ones.

After using different language tests on a wider range of young school-age children Jackson and the author (Jackson and Sommers, 1971) presented related evidence. We studied twenty-five public school children's articulation and receptive and expressive linguistic abilities using the *McDonald Deep Test* (McDonald, 1968), the *Menyuk Sentence Repetition Test* (Menyuk, 1968), the *Northwestern Syntax Screening Test* (Lee, 1969), and the *Illinois Test of Psycholinguistic Abilities* (Kirk, 1968). Subjects ranged in age from six to ten years with a mean of seven. Five of the children were normal in speech and language, five were mildly defective in articulation, five were moderately defective in articulation, five were severely defective in articulation, and five were enrolled in special classes because of minimal brain dysfunction. All had either mild or moderate articulatory defectiveness. On all tasks the five subjects having a serious number of misarticulations were the poorest performers. The moderately defective five subjects were approximately one year delayed in their linguistic skills compared to the normal and mildly defectives. Finally, the McDonald articulation test error scores were found to be excellent predictors of some of the linguistic measures, particularly the Sentence Repetition Task error scores (r = .930, Significant = .001, N = 25). The results demonstrated rather clearly the strong relationships that exist between the extent of articulatory impairment and other linguistic abilities in children of these ages.

The sentence-repetition abilities of nine children, aged four years, six months to six years, six months, were evaluated by Dukes and Panagos (1973). All were found to have multiple misarticulations and were considered to have unintelligible speech but normal receptive-language skills. The investigators stated that they hoped to relate the grammatical data to symptoms of verbal apraxia, to elucidate the nature of the underlying encoding disorder, and to analyze grammatically sentences that the children indicated they understood. Since their conclusions were pointedly related to the phonological/syntactical relationship and may be helpful in gaining insights into it, they are detailed below.

> The type of syntactic rule used by the children was a better predictor of the distribution of their errors than their use of lexico-semantic features.
>
> Since all errors were omissions, the transformational component is probably not fully developed, thus making it difficult for these children to establish base sentences during repetitions.
>
> As syllable complexity increased, the percentage of phonemic errors increased indicating the presence of nonexpansion trends in the phonological system.
>
> A substantial percentage of nonexpansion errors were found across distinctive features.
>
> Fewer distortions, as opposed to segmental errors involving systematic changes in place and mode of articulation, suggest that adequate control of articulation took place once a segment had been chosen.

Dukes and Panagos concluded that these nine young children, whom they referred to as "deviant" in speech, lacked an adequate transformational basis to encode speech. They functioned syntactically and phonologically at bare minimum levels. Their transformational skill weakness is a negative influence on their motor–speech performances. Believing that their subjects suffered from verbal apraxia, they went on to explain that this disorder is a symptom of cerebral dysfunction which disturbs the normal acquisition of coordinated and voluntary movements of the articulators. The inadequate cerebral control is thus the common element between their poor articulatory skills and poor syntactical ones.

Evidence of increased articulatory severity in children as a function of the existence of errors of omission has been reasonably well accepted. For example, we have strong evidence from a number of investigations that an error of omission generally detracts primarily from speech intelligibility (Jordon, 1960). Errors of omission are probably the most primitive type of articulation error, since they represent the most immature aspects of the phonological system in the infant, with errors of substitution, addition, and distortion usually occurring later in infancy and early childhood.

When many omission errors are seen in children's speech, the general impression is for severity to be increased along a number of related dimensions. For example, Prins (1962) and Frisch and Handler (1974) have demonstrated that children having omissions perform distinctly differently on tasks from those having normal speech or articulatory errors of the substitution type and not the errors of omission. Prins (1962) reported that children who had omission errors were inferior performers in both auditory and motor skills, and Frisch and Handler (1974) found them frequently to receive poorer overall neurological ratings. In the investigation performed by this author and his colleagues (Sommers, Moore, Brady, and Jackson, 1976), many subjects who were severely defective in articulation and frequently found to have either no ear effect or a left-ear one on dichotic tasks had errors of omissions; whereas subjects with mild or moderate errors whose dichotic processing was essentially normal had errors of substitutions and distortions. Interestingly Rosenbek and Wertz (1972) said that the prominent errors in developmental apraxia are omissions, and they provided some support for Handler and Frisch's finding of poorer neurological development in young children who have errors of omission.

When many consonant sounds are omitted from speech, we obviously have very limited distinctive-feature acquisition taking place. This implies that many phonological rules are not operational and probably also suggests that the transformational rules (discussed by Dukes and Panagos and others) are very limited also. The failure of young children to arrest syllables with consonants ("open-syllable syndrome"), first brought to our attention by Renfrew (1966), has been related to the severely articulatory-defective young child in both the Yoss and Darley (1974) and Jackson and Sommers (1971) studies. In the former it denoted developmental apraxia; in the latter it was linked to increased general-language impairment and increased severity of the articulatory component. One might, therefore, reason that children having severe articulation defects characterized by errors of omission (and other predictors from the Yoss and Darley data) will be generally linguistically impaired.

The above information has been an attempt to focus attention on the existence of developmental apraxia in young children. Based upon this author's clinical experience with numbers of young children that have evidenced some or many of the symptoms described in the literature and upon the strength of the data and observations of others, some of the issues involved are problematical. Although this condition probably does exist, it rarely occurs in "pure" form. Most likely it reflects a continuum of difficulty, and most often expressive language is affected by weaknesses found in language comprehension not very obvious without careful assessment. Following is a description of a child who has been known by the author for two and half years. Almost all of the major symptoms of developmental apraxia could be seen in his behaviors. When younger, he was the "purest" form of this disorder personally encountered.

At the age of two, J.K. was not talking. Both parents were professional persons relatively young in their careers. An older brother had normal speech and language development. J.K. was born after a ten-month pregnancy period and labor of seven hours. His mother reported that she knew something was wrong with him right at birth. His early development was characterized by late walking, general clumsiness, frequent childhood illnesses, resistance to toilet training, and frequent crying; and when he attempted to speak words, he could produce only monosyllables beginning with bilabial stops followed by low front vowels. Parental concerns about his lack of speech and language resulted in a referral to a private speech/ language pathologist who diagnosed his problem at the age of three as developmental apraxia.

More extensive evaluations of his development began when he reached four years of age. His speech was now characterized by unintelligible utterances that appeared to be syntactical units correctly organized and used. Echolalia was noted to occur for words, phrases, and sentences some portion of the time. He cried in the presence of many of his examiners and sought to terminate the sessions by trying to leave. His mother reported that J.K. had occasional word-finding problems. A closer look at his expressive language indicated that he was making reasonably long sentences and using them meaningfully; they contained verb forms, articles, prepositions, and some pronouns. All words were monosyllables using bilabial stops or velar stops, and he basically voiced all utterances. Telegraphic speech was present with slow rate, equal timing of utterances, reduced inflection, but adequate control over loudness. Oral apraxia was severe, with little or no voluntary control over his tongue and zero ability to perform sequenced, voluntary movements of his articulators.

Other evaluations by specialists revealed that his hearing was normal.

Medical specialists described him as having an awkward gait, gross- and fine-motor impairment, balance problems, depressed muscle tone, no obvious pathological weaknesses, no evidence of a major component of emotional disturbance, a visual problem of acuity plus occular apraxia. The clinical psychologists found his IQ on the *Slossen IQ Test* to be 88, his M.A. 4-0, with a C.A. of 4-2. On later verbal-intelligence tests his IQ was depressed coming out 62 on the *Wechsler Intelligence Scale for Children* and 60 on the *Stanford–Binet*. On the *Columbia Mental-Maturity Scale* his deviation score was 89, and he was later tested on the *Wide-Range Achievement Test* and found to have average word-recognition skills and low-average math skills. It appeared that highly verbal intelligence tests may have underestimated a number of his intellectual skills, and later (ages five, six, and seven) both teachers and psychologists generally agreed that his learning rate for many activities suggested that his intelligence was normal to dull–normal.

Over a span of three years in which J.K. received intensive speech and language training and special schooling, repeated language and speech testing studied his expressive and receptive linguistic abilities. These scores reflect the fact that although his unintelligible speech was the primary concern, other aspects of his language were weak. Thus, a diagnosis of developmental apraxia for speech *and language* might be justified.[2]

C.A.	TEST*	SCORE	AGE EQUIVALENCY
5-3	TACL	50 correct	3-1
5-3	G.F. Artic.	69 errors	
5-5	Dichotic Word Pointing	Right 17 Left 19	No ear preference
5-11	TACL	66 correct	4-0
6-3	G.F. Artic.	60 errors	
6-3	TACL	70 correct	408
6-3	Menyuk S.R.T.	4 errors	
6-4	D.S.S.	209/46	4-5
6-11	TACL	78 correct	5-7
6-11	Menyuk S.R.T.	6 errors	
6-11	G.F. Artic.	43 errors	

* These tests are: TACL (Test of Auditory Comprehension of Language, Carrow, 1973); G.F. Artic. (Goldman–Fristoe Test of Articulation, Goldman & Fristoe, 1969); Dichotic Word Pointing Test (Starkey, 1974); Menyuk S.R.T. (Menyuk Sentence Repetition Test, Menyuk, 1964); and D.S.S. (Developmental Sentence Scoring Test, Lee and Canter, 1971).

[2] Certain approaches to the correction of his severely defective articulation will be described in Chapter Four.

The author would like to present a description of another child who may be legitimately considered to reflect symptoms of developmental apraxia. Like J.K., this child, R.O., was enrolled in a special private school for young children having developmental problems. Intelligence testing had repeatedly confirmed the presence of normal to near-normal ability, and audiological assessment suggested normal hearing. He had a history of delayed speech and language development, but information in his case history suggested that his language was most impaired in its defective phonology. He became of increasing concern to his parents, teachers, and speech/language specialists because he appeared to be developing into a stutterer.

When seen by the author, R.O. was precisely seven years of age. His articulation was improved but reflected many misarticulations including a few omissions of consonants as they arrested syllables, some distortions of stressed /ɝ/ and unstressed /ɚ/ in some contexts, and numerous substitutions in which earlier developing consonants were substituted for later developing ones, for example, t/tʃ/.

Items involving R.O.'s ability to perform volitional, sequential movements of his articulators were poorly performed. For example, when asked to "first smile and then stick our your tongue," he reversed the order of the instructions. He also reversed "first whistle and then smile," and when three volitional, sequenced commands were given, he could only do two of them correctly. At one point, he was instructed to "move your tongue from side to side and then smile." He moved his tongue in and out and then gave a clumsy smile. He could not voluntarily move his tongue to his alveolar ridge either through verbal instruction or by imitating the examiner.

His performances on a sentence repetition test revealed expressive deficits in language. He frequently omitted articles, verb forms, and prepositions.

His concepts of left and right directionality seemed impaired. His overall visual/motor performances were more like those of a child four years of age. Testing showed him to be rather consistently left-eyed and left-footed, but to prefer his right hand for coloring, writing, cutting, and other fine-motor activities. His ear-preference score on the *Dichotic Word Pointing Test* was not established, the right-ear score being 17 and the left-ear score 19.

His nonfluencies resembled real stuttering behaviors. He was much more likely to produce these symptoms when imitating the examiner's sentences, but they occurred in his spontaneous speech as well. He seemed aware of his moments of stuttering and appeared to "grope" for production and release. These took the form of phoneme, syllable, and phrase repetitions and prolongation of some consonants and vowels accompanied by tremor and distortions of his articulators. Stuttering was more likely to occur on some initial consonants in words than others.

diagnostic studies of speech and language

The phonological disabilities of young children (less than five years old) will be emphasized in this section, albeit it is appreciated that many young children will have delayed or deviant linguistic performances of other types.

Case-History Information With rare exception, one or more parents of the preschool child can be interviewed and serve as an informant. If foster parents have reared the child, they or others, such as grandparents, other relatives, ward mothers, and personnel who may have interracted consistently with the child during his or her development, can also serve. Even with the real or foster parents, however, one encounters a wide spectrum of abilities to recount salient aspects of infant and child development. Nevertheless, clinicians take advantage of all the information that they can entice from informants in order to gain a better understanding of the child and his disorder.

A wide variety of information appears to characterize the early lifespans of children having speech and language disorders. The developmental landmarks, for example, age of crawling, walking, eating with a spoon, first words, and so forth, of some children who ultimately show articulatory deficiencies in their development may not be remarkable. It is clear that some portion of young school-age children having misarticulations are notoriously slower in some aspects of their development, and this slowness may not be solely restricted to their speech (Eisenson, 1972). Their perceptual, cognitive, and motor development may also be poorer than children of comparable basic mental ability who have the good fortune to develop speech at normal rates. Probably global linguistic problems, that is, serious delays in all aspects of language, have the most pronounced effect on many aspects of early child development. In those rare instances in which the problem is associated with singular or near-singular influences, such as defective articulation development, in the absence of other linguistic impairment of any significance, the likelihood for some other developmental landmarks being within normal limits seems increased. (However, we do not know enough of the specifics of these instances to make wide-scale generalizations). Clinical experience suggests, also, that more failures to attain developmental landmarks within a normal time frame can be found in the case histories of severe articulatory defectives than in the mildly defectives. Thus, the suggestion is that clinicians make the good effort at gathering case-history information, particularly if the young child has a severe problem in articulation and the related linguistic impairments that most often accompany this disorder.

Child Assessment An assessment of the degree and quality of phonological acquisition in a young child will usually be made as part of a larger diagnostic process in view of the possibilities of related impairments. Language and perceptual assessment techniques and tools will probably be involved in this larger process; however, the author will focus largely on those pertinent to studies of phonology.

In contrast to older school-age children, these very young children are most often referred by parents who are very concerned about speech. Again, in contrast to many older ones, young children are likely to be severely impaired in their communication skills. Low levels of general functioning often preclude the use of regular articulation tests such as the Goldman-Fristoe one (Goldman–Fristoe, 1969). When very young children can recognize pictures of common objects, some traditional articulation assessment can be accomplished. However, since testing many of them in this fashion may be difficult if not impossible, assessment may be made using a method of having the child repeat the test stimuli words from the articulation test.

Spontaneous speech samples constitute the most thorough way of evaluating children's articulatory skills (Faircloth & Faircloth, 1970; Sommers & Sitler, 1980; DuBois and Bernthal, 1978; Panagos, Quine, & Klich, 1979). The first three investigations found a lack of correspondence between children's traditional or imitated articulation of single words and accuracy of articulation of the same phonemes in spontaneous, connected speech. The third found that the accuracy of articulation in connected speech was affected by grammatical complexity and characteristics of the utterances. The extent to which good correspondence might occur in very young, severely impaired children (two-, three-, and four-year olds) is unknown; but judging from the studies of somewhat older articulatory defectives (five years and older), probably the most accurate way to assess their articulation is to get a substantial sample of it from their spontaneous speech.

Obtaining an adequate sample of a young child's speech is often not a simple task. Although Diedrich (1980) has demonstrated that a three-minute-talk task provides sufficient data to complete a reasonable assessment of school-age children's articulation of certain phonemes (principally /s/ and /r/), some speech sounds occur so seldom in American English, namely, /v/, /dʒ/, /tʃ/, /θ/, that the examiner cannot get adequate representation of the performances of young children on these sounds. The alternative is either having the child respond to pictures or objects to get the basic information or using the method of imitation of words, syllables, or the sound in isolation to supplement the evidence from the spontaneous-speech sample.

In order to get cooperation for any involvement the examiner of the young speech-defective child needs a variety of tactics, toys, tools, etc. Frequently, a disturbed and frightened child will respond best and become spontaneous in speech if the examiner provides the parent (usually mother) with the toys, pictures, games, etc., leaves the testing space, and allows the parent to get the speech sample (this may be tape-recorded or the examiner can record it live either via an amplification system or by standing outside a partially open door). Observation of the child/parent interaction *per se* may also prove insightful, since the parent (mother again most often) may reveal some portion of her management strategies with the child and show the verbal and nonverbal interaction systems that operate between parent and child. These observed behaviors, then, may comprise a preliminary network of information, which will decide on the need for and content of any parental counseling that will provide a comprehensive program of management.

○ THE ARTICULATORY-DEFECTIVE YOUNG, SCHOOL-AGE CHILD

Most speech and language therapy provided anywhere in the world is available to school children in the United States. Therapy is given to children in grades one to three (Bingham et al., 1961; Sommers and Hatton, 1979), and approximately sixty-five percent of the children receive direct training for the correction of their defective articulation. Thus, an historical commitment to serve articulatory-defective children has been maintained over the last two decades, although the percentage of children in school-therapy caseloads with other, related problems has increased (notably language disorders) while the percentage of articulatory defectives has decreased (Bingham et al., 1961; Sommers and Hatton, 1979).

Most articulation therapy provided in public schools in our country is delivered using a small group; however, some more severe or difficult-to-manage children are seen individually. Parents of these articulatory defectives are not involved in the therapy process to any appreciable degree, although the required Individual Education Programs mandated by PL 94–142 have brought some parents' attention to the service that their children will receive. The extent of parent involvement is highly variable with some school clinicians entering parents into special training to assist their children and some making frequent contacts via practice workbooks, telephone calls, and scheduled conferences and meetings of various types. While probably improved over the past two decades, a meaningful involvement by parents of articulatory-defective children in the corrective process remains disappointing.

familial and environmental factors

This section focuses upon some of the older information that concerns the identification and possible effects of familial and environmental variables on the acquisition of articulation skill. Much of this work was accomplished using young, school-aged articulatory defectives, but in a few instances very young children and their families were studied. Research in this area is diminishing, but many questions of importance need resolving if we are to get adequate, clear pictures of the nature of these disorders.

Socioeconomic Levels of Articulatory-Defective Children Based largely upon two factors, namely, parental occupations and parental educational levels, a number of early studies were completed that sought to determine a relationship between the macrovariable of socioeconomic level and articulation proficiency in children. In a very early study of infants, Irwin (1948) sampled the frequency of production and types of phonemes produced by very young infants by gathering speech samples from them monthly for thirty-nine months. He reported that the types of phonemes used during the first year and a half were very similar in all children, and the frequency of their occurrence was also comparable. After eighteen months, however, children from upper socioeconomic classes forged ahead in both dimensions. The suggestion was that the amount of parental stimulation of the young child's speech and language is greater in upper socioeconomic families. An alternative thesis, of course, is based upon Lennenberg's hypothesis that some highly verbal and linguistically superior children are innately endowed for the development of such abilities.

In an early (1942), exhaustive investigation of fifty preschool children, Beckey (later to be a prominent authority in articulation disorders as Ruth Beckey Irwin) reported that a larger percentage of her fifty preschool, delayed-speech children came from lower socioeconomic status. Children having the most severe articulatory defectiveness tended to be from families from the lowest socioeconomic stratum. She additionally reported that children without articulation errors and those who "outgrew" them tended to come from higher socioeconomic classes.

Birth Order, Family Size, and Specific Errors In a convention report Shriberg (1975) summarized his investigation of certain socialization factors and error-specific phonological defectiveness. He was particularly interested in studying children who misarticulated /s/ only, /r/ only, those having both /s/ and /r/ defects, and normal speakers. He reported information relating to family structure, including family size and birth order. Among his significant findings was information that differences in some of these variables did exist as a function of the specific phonemes misarticulated. He found that two out of three /r/ and /s/ children and four out of five /r/ children were other than first born. A different pattern was found for the /s-;-;/ children and normals with one out of two, other than first born. Children defective only in /r/ were significantly more often born later.

Shriberg also provided information on ordinal position in both two-child and three-child families. Within two-child families /s/ children were significantly more often first born. In three-child families children with errors on both /s/ and /r/ were often second children. No /r/ and /s/ child was born first, and /r/ children were more frequently the third child. These findings appeared very intriguing, and an effort was mounted to replicate portions of Shriberg's investigation.

Those portions of Shriberg's study that related to singular phoneme defectiveness of /s/ or /r/ were investigated by Galathris (1977) using 145 children from grades one to six in the Youngstown, Ohio public schools. Subjects were screened from a larger population of 984 and found by articulation testing and measures of spontaneous speech to misarticulate either /s/ or /r/ but not both. Of the total of 145, seventy-seven were /s/ only and sixty-eight /r/ only defectives. All subjects came from lower to upper-lower socioeconomic neighborhoods, and the sample was almost equally divided into black and white children.

Some of the evidence to show links between specific singular-phoneme defectiveness and family size and birth order reported by Shriberg was also found in Galathris' data. Some of his findings were not confirmed in her data.

Birth order was investigated for /s/ and /r/ children. Significantly more first born children were found in the /s/ group (twenty-two percent) than in the /r/ group (twelve percent). In Shriberg's study similar findings were reported in the first born with /s/ group (forty-seven percent) versus /r/ group (twenty-one percent).

Within two-child families, Shriberg found a significantly larger percentage of first born /s/ defectives (eighty-three percent) than /r/ defectives (thirty percent). For second born, he reported twelve percent were in the /s/ group and seventy percent in the /r/ group. Galathris' findings were similar except that her percentage differences were not as great. The /s/ group in first-born children was thirty-two to forty percent in the /r/ group. In second-born children, the /s/ group had fifty-eight to sixty percent in the /r/ group.

Birth order in families having four or more children was analyzed by Galathris. Results indicated a significantly higher percentage of /r/ children (forty-six percent) compared to /s/ (thirty-one percent) within this category.

These results confirm Shriberg's finding that /r/ children are more likely to come from larger families.

Results from tests of proportions looking at /r/ defectives and /s/ defectives separately, did show a birth-order affect with both /r/ and /s/ defectives having considerably more last-born than first-born children in their samples.

In three-child families, Shriberg reported that children with /r/ errors were one-hundred percent other (first or third) child and not a middle child. In the /s/ group he found ten percent were middle children compared to eighty-one percent other (first or third). In the Galathris study, forty-seven percent of the /r/ group was found to be middle children compared to forty-four percent for the /s/ group subjects. Also, fifty-three percent for the /r/ group were other (first or third) versus fifty-six percent in the /s/ group. Shriberg reported that the /r/ children were more often the third child and this was found also in this investigation.

Results from both of these investigations leave many unanswered questions. A tendency for some relationship to be similar suggests the possibility that for these types of articulatory defectives, macrovariables such as family structure and socioeconomic variables may be related to likelihood for specific phonological defects. If confirmed by future investigators this will imply that aspects in the socialization process (child rearing, that is discipline, affection, acceptance) might be operational variables to restrict or modify early sound learning. If /r/ defectives do often come from large families and tend to be later born, then aren't the /r/ defective's parents older than /s/ defective ones? If so, perhaps they suffer a higher risk factor at having some type of minimal CNS damage at birth. The speculation can easily be continued, but these data are very preliminary, puzzling, and provocative.

Maternal Adjustment In a classic effort Wood (1946) studied the maternal and paternal adjustment and personality of fifty pairs of parents of articulatory-defective children and reported that many of the mothers showed unhealthy signs of adjustment including tendencies to be neurotic. The fathers' ratings were not basically different from the control sample used by the test makers, thus reflecting normal attitudes and adjustment. This study attracted a great deal of attention, and other researchers over a period of two decades entered into this difficult research area.

Some portion of the research evidence to support and elaborate upon Wood's findings was reviewed by Bloch and Goodstein (1971) who were unhappy with the quality of most of it and concluded that the evidence was not strong enough to draw any generalizations concerning the existence of certain defective personality types or a general maladjustment hypothesis in mothers of articulatory-defective children. Although the area is difficult to research and problems have arisen concerning the validity of some of the assessment procedures, lack of control groups, and designs that may not have been precise in other ways, there is appreciably more consistency than inconsistency in the literature to support some portion of the hypothesis. The reader will obviously come to his own conclusion.

Unfortunately, perhaps, this topic appears to have lost some of its glimmer and few researchers have persisted in their efforts to study it. Thus, most of our literature is approximately twenty years old.

In 1960 the issue of maternal adjustment was studied by Moll and Darley. They mailed the mothers' form of the Parental Attitude Research Instrument (Schaeffer & Bell) to twenty-six mothers of articulatory-defective children, thirty mothers whose children had delayed speech, and sixty mothers of normal-speaking children. All of the children were aged three to twelve. The adjustment scores for the twenty-six mothers of the articulatory defectives were inferior to those of the other two groups in subscales that cluster under the category of "excessive demand for striving." This finding seems related to the earlier one by Wood (1946), who reported that high social standards and skills were deviant areas of adjustment for mothers of such children. On the other hand, the instrument used is very comprehensive with many subscales reflecting other aspects of adjustment, and the mothers of the articulatory defectives were not significantly different from mothers of the other two groups on the majority of them. This shows that no general or pervasive personality disorder or maladjustment characterized their responses.

Other evidence for problems in emotional and personality adjustment in mothers of some articulatory-defective children and possible implications for this condition on remission of speech error was provided by Andersland (1961). She found that mothers of children who maintained some articulation errors over a five-year span and whose children were also most severely defective failed to score above the median on the total score from The Gordon Personal Profile (Gordon, 1963), while all mothers of normal-speaking children scored did so. Furthermore, she reported that these same mothers scored significantly poorer than many other mothers in items assessing ascendency, responsibility, and sociability on the Gordon Personal Profile. The emotional and personality scores on this instrument were significantly lower for mothers whose children had retained some portion of their articulation errors than for mothers whose children were normal in articulation five years earlier.

Finally, the PARI scale was also used by this investigator, and again the mothers of the most severely defective children scored worse on the subscale measuring "hostility." It appeared that severity of articulation impairment and retention of errors even after speech improvement and speech therapy were possible indicators of maternal adjustment difficulties. Andersland's finding linking degree of maternal maladjustment to maintenance of articulation errors was highly intriguing, but required confirmation by others for its acceptance.

In a report published a year later Dickson (1962) gave additional possible support for a portion of Andersland's study. Dickson studied the personality and adjustment of two groups of mothers, one whose children had outgrown their articulation errors by third grade and a second whose children had retained their errors. Using the Minnesota Multiphasic Personality Inventory (MMPI, Hathaway and McKinley, 1951) as his instrument, he reported significant differences on some subscales in favor of mothers whose children "outgrew" their articulation errors. Scores on the first three subscales primarily involved neurotic tendencies and "hysteria"; however, there was a general tendency for scores of mothers of children retaining errors to approach the critical range for adjustment on the MMPI.

In what might be the last study to appear in the literature dealing with the issue of maternal adjustment, the author and former colleagues determined the influence of maternal adjustment on the outcome of articulation therapy when mothers were intensively trained to assist in the corrective process (Sommers et al., 1964). To meet the design requirements of the research 144 such mothers, drawn largely from lower socioeconomic classes, were studied using the PARI instrument. Mothers completed the PARI individually in a large room under supervision. The distribution of scores on this instrument was studied, and the top thirty-five percent (poorest overall adjustment) and bottom thirty-five percent (best total adjustment) were included in the study of therapy effectiveness. Of interest is the fact that the group having "unhealthy attitudes" was so large in a sample of 144 mothers. These very high scores were in a range considered by the authors of the PARI to be clinically significant. It should also be noted that the "healthy-attitude" mothers were also extreme in their performances. The remainder of the mothers, not used as subjects in the experiment, had moderate-attitude scores, and this too was a sizeable group. These results tend to show that some larger portion of mothers of articulatory defectives, aged seven through ten, have scores reflecting near-normal, normal, or excellent adjustment as measured by this instrument, while a subgroup (larger than anticipated perhaps) reflects extremely poor attitudes and adjustment. Finally, it was observed that regardless of whether mothers had "unhealthy" or "healthy" adjustment scores, their children improved more in articulation therapy when speech clinicians trained them to assist in the process.

Although sparse in number, results from these studies tend to show some agreement and the likelihood of finding maternal maladjustment in some portion of this population may actually be quite high. Again, research on this issue has essentially stopped, and we need additional research evidence (using tighter research designs) before we can become comfortable about accepting this hypothesis. Very disturbing tactics were used in some of the reviewed studies, especially the completion of adjustment and personality instruments at home by mothers in three of them (Moll and Darley, 1960; Andersland, 1961; Dickson, 1962).

○ SOCIAL AND EMOTIONAL ADJUSTMENT OF THE ARTICULATORY-DEFECTIVE CHILD

Wood (1946) in his comprehensive study for parental adjustment decided to determine if the emotional adjustment of the articulatory-defective children resembled that of the parents. To accomplish this he administered the TAT (Thematic Apperception Test, Murray, 1943) the Pinter Aspects of Personality Test (Pinter et al., 1938); and a lesser known adjustment instrument, and he gathered extensive case history information on all children including descriptions of their parent/child interactions.

Half of Wood's sample were given the TAT. From the protocols it was concluded that thirty percent showed a lack of affection, sixty-five percent withdrawal tendencies and "dynamism" (feelings of frustration). Besides these findings, Wood maintained that they frequently reflected hostility, anger or aggressiveness, lack of belongingness, and anxiety in general. He also claimed that his case-history information corroborated these impressions.

Case histories reportedly also revealed some environmental factors of importance in understanding the adjustment scores of the children. Wood maintained that thirteen important factors emerged from them which included little recreational outlet for the parents, defective home membership, very severe child-discipline methods, and a lack of parental knowledge about coping with children's misbehaviors.

The classic, old study by Wood probably still constitutes the most comprehensive study of adjustment of articulatory-defective children and their parents. By today's standards it may be evaluated somewhat negatively, but this does not destroy it completely. For example, the children and their parents were special, clinical cases involved in an intensive therapy program at a summer camp. Thus, they may not be representative of the population at large. Furthermore, there is always a question concerning the accurateness of examiners in interpretation of some personality and adjustment scales which makes independent replication very important. Finally, if the study were done today, one might like to see more evidence of what these children were like in other ways, especially linguistically and perceptually.

Wood's findings related to emotional maladjustments in significant numbers of his articulatory-defective children were subsequently not confirmed by a number of early researchers who went directly into public-school classes, located the defectives, and used the California Test of Personality (1939) to get measures of their personality and adjustment. In

his 1956 review of the literature Spriesterbach concluded that the California test might be insensitive. For example, both Reid (1947) and Nelson
(1953) used the California Test of Personality to study school children
testing thirty-eight and thirty-five articulatory defectives and matched
controls, respectively. Subjects were in grades three, five, and seven in the
Nelson study and from grades one to seven in the Reid one. In both
instances differences in the adjustment ratings of the articulatory defectives
and control-group members were considered nonsignificant.

Interest in the identification of the degree of social and emotional
adjustment achieved by articulatory defectiveness has continued over a
great span of time. For example, Mildred Templin in 1938 reported that
a study of the aggressiveness of seventy-one speech-defective college
students and forty-nine normal-speaking ones provided data to show that
the thirty-seven speech defectives having articulation defects were significantly more aggressive than fifteen voice defectives, nineteen stutterers,
and forty-nine normals. Of interest was her finding of a slight tendency
for severity of articulatory defectiveness to be related to increased
aggressiveness.

The bulk of the literature appears to support the hypothesis that social
and emotional adjustment problems are more likely to be found in
articulatory-defective children than in normal-speaking ones. Even the
early review by Spriesterbach, which cited the negative and positive
evidence, gave evidence to support this statement.

Investigators have used a wide variety of tests and measures to evaluate
the social and emotional adjustment issue. These have included sociometric
scales, questionnaires, interview techniques, personality tests, and visual/
motor perceptual and memory tasks.

Perrin (1954) chose to use a sociometric questionnaire to explore the
social position of the articulatory-defective school child. A total of 445
children from grades one to six was studied. The social position or
acceptance of the articulatory defective by other children was found to be
generally poor, a condition found at each grade level but most pronounced
in the first grade where the chances of an articulatory defective to be a
social isolate was four times as great as normal speakers.

Parent and teacher opinion data were used by Kennedy (1951) to
investigate the issue. He used this approach to study and rate the social
adjustment of twenty-seven articulatory-defective children, and he concluded that twelve of them were moderately or seriously emotionally
disturbed to a noticeable degree.

A well-known clinical test, the *Bender Visual-Motor Gestalt,* was used by
Deming who considered it to reveal aspects of social and emotional
adjustment. Twenty functional, articulatory-defective, elementary-age
school children and twenty matched normal-speaking controls completed
the drawings. Deming interpreted their performances to reflect tendencies

to withdraw and show signs of social inadequacies. A similar conclusion was reached by Greenberg (1952) who used observational data-gathering techniques with intermediate-grade level children.

Using the digit-symbol subtest of the *Wechsler Intelligence Scale for Children* as a measure of anxiety, Trapp and Evans (1960) studied the performances of fifty-four eight- to ten-year old children. Subjects were of three types: normal speakers, mildly defective in articulation, and severely defective in articulation. The digit-symbol scores of the severely defective were significantly poorer than the scores of the mildly defective and normals and the latter two groups' scores essentially the same. The conclusion reached was that the anxiety level of only the most severe group in their sample was abnormally high.

An interview technique in which an open-ended questionnaire was used to gather information was used by Solomon (1961) to investigate the behavioral and personality traits of forty-nine first-grade children having normal speech, mild-moderate articulation defects, or marked-severe articulation defects. Nine areas of behavior and adjustment were evaluated including eating, sleeping, comfort patterns, tension, fears and anxieties, aggression, peer relations, and dependency. The combined group of articulatory defectives were significantly impaired in four of the above behaviors (sleeping, fears and anxieties, peer relations, and tension) plus overall adjustment. Finally, Solomon concluded that there was a tendency toward greater severity of the adjustment problem, the greater the severity of the articulatory defectiveness; but differences failed to reach statistical levels of significance. He noted further that the children with misarticulation tended to be passive, frequently internalizing their responses, have greater needs for approval, and show timidity.

Positioning human forms on a flannel board was felt by Lerea and Ward (1966) to provide good evidence of adequacy of social perception and adjustment. In the task involved the children were required to place five sets of human figures on a flannel board, the assumption being that "social schema" can be determined by the distance between the figures. Measurements obtained on the performances of twenty severe articulatory defectives and twenty normal-speaking controls showed significantly greater distance between the placed figures in the former group. The conclusion was that the social milieu of the articulatory defectives is also defective and perceptions are distorted.

Using a rating scale having four categories, oral-communication skills, social-acceptance characteristics, anxiety characteristics, and academic functioning, Sherrill (1967) evaluated fifty-three children having severe articulatory disorders and fifty-three matched normal-speaking control subjects. He found no differences in the ratings from peers and teachers comparing social acceptance, anxiety, and academic functioning but did, of course, find differences in the expected category of oral communication.

He went on to report that children most severely defective in articulation appeared to be less well accepted by others and themselves. According to Sherrill, children having severe defectiveness with either low-normal intelligence and/or low socioeconomic status seemed to be poorly accepted by others and by themselves.

In an investigation quite similar in purpose and basic design to the Perrin (1954) one, Freeman and Sonnega (1956) found no evidence that twenty-six third- and fourth-grade children who were attending speech-therapy classes were less accepted by their peers. A sociometric task, a "choose-the-friendliest-student-in-the-class" type, asked 133 children to respond to friendly, happy, welcomed, tidiness, enthusiasm, daring, good looking, and activeness in recitation. The negative findings are difficult to reconcile with the positive ones in the earlier Perrin (1954) study. The latter investigation was larger in scope and showed excellent internal consistency in its findings, since Perrin reported that at every grade level from one through six the articulatory defectives were socially less acceptable to their peers.

○ ACADEMIC PERFORMANCES OF THE ARTICULATORY-DEFECTIVE CHILD

Interest in the abilities of young, school-age children to learn basic skills, that is, reading, writing, and spelling has been weakly maintained over a span of thirty or more years. Of the three basic skills reading has been given the most attention, probably because of some stronger theoretical formulations related to both processes and possibly because it appears that articulatory-defective children of normal mental ability are more likely to manifest reading problems than writing or spelling difficulties. West (1969), for example, found that the chances of an articulatory-defective child's requiring remedial reading instruction in the Haddonfield, New Jersey public schools was almost three times greater than that of normal-speaking children from the same schools. The prevalence of writing problems in articulatory-defective children is unknown, and it may be that no problem exists in this skill area. Spelling errors have been linked by a few investigators to articulatory errors, but not by others, and the evidence is inadequate to form definite conclusions about any relationship (Bingham et al., 1961). Some exciting, new concepts and information, however, have emerged related to reading and articulation performances of children, and we maintain the optimistic view that the obscure relationship underlying both conditions may eventually be better understood.

articulation and reading

Vast numbers of American children have reading and speech problems. Estimates are that ten percent of school-age children suffer from reading difficulties (Gilliland, 1974) and about four percent have articulation disorders (Bingham et al., 1961). The percentage having both disorders is unknown.

Many speculations and some research evidence has supported ties between reading and speech (articulation defects) in young, school-age children. Unfortunately, none of the studies seeking a cause-and-effect relationship in articulation or reading has been successful in showing significant interactions between articulation and reading problems and possible etiological factors. Lacking any findings in which auditory skills, for example, are manipulated experimentally to study effects on articulatory and reading skills, we fall back upon investigations of relationships and draw inferences. This is the same exasperating research problem that makes cause-and-effect relationships nearly impossible to specify with any certainty. We cannot isolate functions such as auditory skills, like auditory discrimination, auditory short-term memory, auditory fusion of speech sounds, auditory blending, and others, and manipulate them experimentally on slow-developing skills, such as speaking, reading, writing, and spelling. Coupled with this limitation is the lack of longitudinal studies of etiological factors and their possible effects on the acquisition of articulation and development of reading skills. However, some possible etiological or related factors have been found to coexist in certain samples of articulatory-defective and reading-disabled children.

auditory, skills, articulation, and reading

Literature linking speech-sound discrimination, auditory memory, and auditory closure skills to articulatory defectiveness is presented in Chapter Two. Deficiencies in some of these same skills have been identified in reading-disabled children over a long span of time by different researchers. To document this the author will cite only a few examples for various auditory skills and urges the reader to refer to a comprehensive review by McGovern (1979).

One of the most thoroughly researched auditory skills and its relationship to reading disabilities is that of auditory discrimination. The germinal study by Monroe (1932) appeared to detonate a long string of additional ones (see, for example, Blank, 1968) in which investigators reported inferior auditory-discrimination performances in young, school-age readers. One prominent developer of an auditory-discrimination test (Wepman, 1959) found both articulatory-impaired and reading-impaired children deficient in speech-sound discrimination and concluded that this evidence implies a common link of defectiveness. Recognizing the limitation of tests and research designs employed, the author suggests that a great deal of the research relating auditory-discrimination weaknesses with poor reading skills in young children has shown a significant relationship.

However, one should question the belief that poor auditory discrimination must accompany all children's reading disorders, since some literature suggests that a population of reading-disabled children have deficiencies in other functions such as the visual/motor perceptual one rather than auditory skills (see, for example, MacGintie, 1967). In fact, a speech/language pathologist expressed the belief that the auditory perceptual hypothesis as an implication in children's articulation and reading problems is fallacious (Rees, 1973). According to Rees, the speech pathologist should assist in the remediation of reading problems by working on language. Development of the linguistic prerequisites for reading is accomplished by the speech/language clinician using the corrective techniques of the profession to improve articulation, and these serve effectively to teach the child the phonological linguistic awareness required to learn to read normally. Rees maintained that auditory discrimination and other related perceptual training is not required in order to improve articulation and reading. Some experimental evidence to counter Rees's opinion was cited by Barr (1974) in a strong attack against her negative views of auditory factors. Literature reviewed by McGovern (1979) appears to show many determined relationships between reading and auditory perceptual skills. Thus, Rees's opinion seems in opposition to a great deal of research literature gathered over many years.

Speech sound discrimination, articulation, and reading would appear to have two common denominators. The first of these is linguistic and the second is perceptual. There is some evidence that young, school-age children's speech-sound discrimination scores correlate significantly with their performances on certain linguistic measures (Marquardt and Saxman, 1972; Sommers, Erdige, and Peterson, 1978). These relationships are usually found in the moderate range, and it may be that the variance unaccounted for is partially unique to the different perceptual act required in perceiving finely decoded auditory stimuli (almost always minimal-pair words). Rule systems involved in word identification tend to improve this process and obviously basic linguistic functions. Generally, we would expect to find that the more meaningful the stimuli to be perceived, the greater the accuracy of perception and identification, since the meaningfulness of material has sometimes been linked to children's learning of speech and language (DeVilliers and DeVilliers, 1978; Miller and Johnson–Laird, 1976; Anglin, 1977; and Clark, 1973).

The two forms of auditory-discrimination difficulties that have been studied are the phoneme-specific type as reported by a number of investigators (Anderson, 1949; Aungst and Frick, 1964) and the general type unrelated to specific phoneme-production errors. As reviewed by Winitz (1969) and Weiner (1967) errors of both types are commonly associated with children's misarticulations below age nine, and additional research evidence of the inferior performances of articulatory defectives is constantly being provided. We have previously seen rather comprehensive evidence to show that significant relationships have been established between children's articulatory abilities and other linguistic measures. The precise nature of the relationship between speech discrimination, articulation, and reading remains obscure and probably vary by age, sex, intelligence, and language spoken.

In the normal course of events the child develops a high degree of competency with this speech and language prior to learning how to read. Children's linguistic abilities are generally adequate by age six to allow for the beginning of reading. Durkin (1972) asserted that readiness for reading is related most to the linguistic abilities of children. Liberman (1978) maintains that the young child beginning to read needs awareness of the phonetic structure in order to learn the alphabetic system of writing, since having this skill, he can segment words into the phonemic elements that the alphabet represents. Thus the visual symbols of words are identified via the phonological ones. This suggests that an intact phonological system is vital in learning to read well, but as stated earlier some children with defective phonology seem to become reasonably proficient readers.

The importance of good auditory abilities in learning to read was also stressed by Machowsky and Meyers (1975), who contended that normal auditory discrimination allows for the development of an inner model from which accurate phoneme/grapheme associations can be constructed. The development of an efficient process in which these associations are made is dependent upon the earlier acquisition of the basic perceptual skill of auditory discrimination of speech sounds. Apparently, by the age of five, six, and certainly by age seven auditory discrimination skills are well developed and capable of providing the underpinnings required to make this efficient association between the visual symbol and the stored auditory phonetic one.

short-term memory, articulation, and reading

Researchers have not been successful in mounting strong evidence of how deficits in short term visual and auditory memory skills affect articulation and reading or whether this factor is a common denominator for the existence of both conditions. Evidence linking defects in short-term memory to children's defective articulation has been inconclusive over a long span of time, and, interestingly, the topic never seems to wear out its popularity. Winitz (1969) reviewed much of the older research and found it difficult to sort in terms of factors which might account for negative and positive findings. Since his review, a number of additional efforts have been made to seek relationships between articulatory defects and short-term memory ones.

The newer literature appears to be about as troublesome to decode as the older; however, it also seems to have a little more consistency in its findings. In 1967 Smith reported that articulatory-defective children were significantly poorer in auditory digit-recall tasks than normal-speaking ones, but their performances on a visual task involving memory for beads were equivalent to the normal subjects. Recalling digits, while not completely devoid of meaning, is thought by some to reflect a lesser degree of linguistic involvement, thus making the task more dependent upon auditory memory *per se* than strong influences of linguistic ability.

The influence of auditory memory for speech was tested by Locke (1969), who reported that young children with high scores on an auditory-memory task learned to produce three non-English phonemes significantly better than those having poorer auditory-memory scores. Earlier, Epstein (1964) studied the abilities of delayed-speech and language-impaired children in contrast to normal ones on two auditory-memory tasks, one a meaningless syllable and the other a meaningful memory for sentences, and found their performances significantly poorer on both.

Deficits in the short-term auditory memory skills of college students were linked to articulatory defectiveness by Stitt and Huntington (1969) also. On memory tasks involving consonant-letter, vowel-sound, and tone those college students with misarticulations were significantly poorer than comparable normal speakers. Thus, their findings tended to suggest that short-term memory for speech and some nonspeech stimuli may be defective in this older age group of subjects who have retained articulatory errors. It once again should be noted that these researchers also found college aptitude and linguistic deficiencies in a significant number of these subjects.

The issue of linguistic inferiority as an explanation of the possible deficits of short-term auditory memory of articulatory-defective children was approached by Saxman and Miller (1973). These investigators chose to use three types of stimuli to test the short-term auditory memories of two groups of kindergarten children, one normal in articulation development and one impaired. Subjects had to recall digits, random words, and meaningful sentence strings. The performances of subjects from both groups were essentially alike on the digit and random-word recall tasks but significantly different on the memory for sentence strings with the normal articulating subjects superior to the impaired ones. This information appeared to oppose the findings from the earlier study by Smith (1967) and also one reported by the author and his colleagues (Sommers, West, and Cox, 1972). In the latter investigation of children of the same ages used by Saxman and Miller we found no significant inferiority on the part of children we considered as defective in articulation compared with others we termed deviant or superior articulators on a sentence-memory task. In their discussion Saxman and Miller cited an explanation that we offered for our negative findings which was a suspicion that our defective subjects were too mildly impaired to show differences on the sentence-recall task. It appears that the findings of Saxman and Miller were based upon children with more severe articulatory defects, and repeatedly in the recent literature, these types of subjects most often are found defective linguistically and perceptually.

Saxman and Miller conjectured that syntactical weaknesses in their articulatory-defective children weakened the chances for them to recall the lexical items, and this appears to be a reasonable explanation of their data. Perhaps revealing was their finding that sentence string-recall scores of their defective subjects were significantly correlated with their scores from a test of auditory comprehension of speech and also one of speech-sound discrimination. Newly learned material is easily forgotten and the overlearned, old material causes the interference that blocks new learning. They further stressed that weak auditory memory and recall skills for the new sound will not allow for adequacy of its use in conversational speech since sentential elements such as semantic, syntactic, phonological, and phonetic planning increase the probability that the error sound will be used. Evidence provided by Panagos, Quine, and Klich (1979) showing that children's articulation errors are systematically related to some of these same sentential elements bolsters Winitz's explanation of the auditory memory, recall, and interference hypothesis of sound learning. It does seem highly likely that these processes, sometimes difficult for normal children to master, have disastrous effects on the sound learning of mentally retarded and learning disabled, who often have auditory-memory deficits. Witness, for example, the great difficulty in correcting the misarticulations of many retarded children. Although getting many re-tarded children to articulate defective-speech sounds in small units of speech such as CV syllables is difficult at times, getting them to use newly acquired sounds in conversational speech is a formidable task indeed.

Winitz (1975) commenting on the role of short-term auditory memory as it influences articulation therapy, stated that this complex phenomenon becomes involved with the interference that children experience when competition occurs between their error sounds and their newly acquired ones. Presumably, memory limitation for newly acquired sounds prevents their accurate recall in various linguistic units and contexts, and old error sounds present strong competition.

auditory, sequential-memory skills

These abilities have been thought by some authorities to be very important to normal speech and language development (Huffman and McReynolds, 1968), and Witkin (1970, 1971) emphasized that short-term auditory memory is a needed requisite to adequate auditory discrimination of speech since the memory function is required to allow the individual to compare sounds. The auditory, sequential aspects of memory were stressed by Monsees (1968) as tied into the intelligibility of speech, and she provided data to support this contention.

The effects of rapid versus slow presentation of auditory and visual materials and accuracy of recall was studied by Piske (1978). Her experiment involved thirty children divided into three groups of ten subjects of normal, moderately defective, and severely articulatory defective. Using fifty one-syllable, singular nouns common to our language, Piske randomized the words making their presentation to the subjects meaningless when presented in sequential form for recall auditorily and visually under a slow-presentation rate and a fast one. Beginning with two words in a sequential order, she advanced until subjects reached a ceiling on each of the four presentations, namely, slow auditory, fast auditory slow visual, fast visual. Her results showed that both groups of articulatory defectives were significantly poorer to the normal subjects on the auditory memory tasks but not inferior to them on the visual tasks, thus supporting findings from the Smith (1967) study in which both types of short-term memory were compared. When rate was studied, the articulatory defectives were inferior to the normal speakers on both the slow and fast presentation of the auditory stimuli. She concluded that her data supported a short-term auditory deficit, regardless of speed of presentation of sequential words, which did not link in a definitive manner to a linguistic deficit *per se*, since words were presented in a random manner to obviate syntactical and semantic influences.

In a series of independent investigations the author (Sommers, 1980) has developed an auditory-visual sequential test of grammatical classes (nouns, verbs, adverbs, adjectives, and prepositions) and used scores on such tasks to predict various linguistic performances of both normal and speech- and language-defective children. In each investigation moderately high predictions were possible by using subjects' grammatical class sequence scores to predict those scores on language tests, both expressive and receptive in form, and tests of articulation. Other receptive, linguistic abilities are also predictable, as shown from combinations of scores on the grammatical class auditory-visual sequencing test, but expressive performances seem most highly related. The prediction of articulation errors, seen in all investigations to date, does show a strong relationship between such skills and those involved in an auditory-visual, sequential memory and organizational task. It is, therefore, the author's opinion that the auditory, sequential memory for linguistic material function is pivotal in articulation proficiency as well as in other related linguistic functions.

oral sensation and perceptual functioning

There appears to be a body of literature generated over the past fifteen or more years which confirms a weakness in some articulatory defectives to be successful in the correct recognition and discrimination of objects placed in their mouths. The size and shape of small objects has been varied by a number of investigators, and one or both of these dimensions not as adequately recognized or discriminated by articulatory defectives as normal-speaking subjects. As we shall see, other related perceptual activities that involve the tactile sensation and perception of the tongue of the defectives have also been studied by some and found to be deficient.

The important aspect of perceptual functioning for speech probably relates to the precision required for simultaneous integration of different sensory signals. For example, we are led to believe that articulatory control is monitored via feedback systems which are traditionally conceived of as auditory, tactile, kinesthetic, and proprioceptive. It has also been the opinion of a number of students of these complex processes that the relative degree to which any one of the four sensory/perceptual systems is operational in articulation relates to which speech sound is being produced. Locke (1969), for example, cautioned against articulation research that failed to control the phonemes studied as a source of variability claiming that each phoneme is likely to be uniquely different in its patterns of perception, feedback, and production. Some information that this might be true for the auditory aspects of functioning was earlier provided by Miller and Nicely in 1955 and Flanagan in 1965, while Grossman (1964) found differences for tactile information and McNutt (1973) found that teenage students defective in either /s/ or /r/ (but not both) had different patterns of sensory/perceptual and/or motor behaviors. This latter researcher was of the opinion that the oral sensations/perception needed to produce /s/ and /r/ are different, possibly because in /s/ production the tongue has a fair degree of contact with other articulators and the tongue-tip placement must be accomplished precisely, while for /r/ production the tongue has little contact with other articulators or structures of the oral cavity and may be reliant upon proprioceptive cues and auditory feedback for its accuracy of production.

In a series of related investigations Ringel and his colleagues (Ringel and Steer, 1963; Scott and Ringel, 1971; Putnam and Ringel, 1976) demonstrated that impaired oral-sensory function can cause disturbances in articulation. Normal speakers subjected to trigeminal nerve block demonstrated directional control over their articulators but reductions in their abilities to perform certain precise movements with speed and accuracy. Speech intelligibility was not necessarily affected but it was noticeably altered in form. These results may be considered as rather direct evidence of the need for intact sensory/perceptual functioning to be available if normal patterns of speaking are to be established and maintained. The commonly accepted influence of delayed auditory feedback to disrupt the articulation and other aspects of speech is strong evidence that disturbances in the auditory feedback systems are also potentially influential in causing a disintegration of the speaking patterns of many normal persons. Obviously, much of the impact of sensory/perceptual feedback systems and their integration of information upon normal articulation development remains unknown and largely unstudied.

The strategies for assessing oral stereognosis have changed from recognition to discrimination tasks. The tasks are three-dimensional based upon a motor exploration (largely tongue-tip) of the shape and size of small objects placed in subjects' mouths under the condition of having no visual clues available to help identify the objects by relating to similar ones or discriminating from another which is subsequently placed in the mouth. In discrimination tasks subjects probe the nature of the small, geometric testing forms for five to ten seconds and are asked if the two presented in sequence were the same or different. In the older strategy, the recognition task, similar, small geometric forms were used and the subject, who was blindfolded, was told to probe the nature of one form with his mouth and tongue, after which the blindfold was removed, and he was asked to locate the same form from a small collection of others placed before him on a table.

Accumulating over the past fifteen years, research evidence in which "recognition" and, subsequently, "discrimination" of these small oral forms have been tested has been supportive of the assertion that articulatory-defective children are weaker than normal-speaking ones (Hixon and Hardy, 1964; Aungst, 1965; Ringel House et al., 1970; Weinberg, Liss, and Hillis, 1971; Sommers, Cox and West, 1972; McNutt, 1973; and Rossman, 1970). A rather clear tendency has also been found by some researchers for the errors on such a task to increase as the number of erroneous speech sounds increases (Ringel, Burk, and Scott, 1970; Ringel, House et al., 1970; Fucci and Robertson, 1971). Thus, the child having the most severe degree of articulatory defectiveness may not be most suspect in his ability to perform such tasks adequately, but note that McNutt (1973) found that teenage subjects only defective in /r/ did more poorly on an oral-form discrimination task than normal, comparable speakers, while the scores of those having only /s/ errors were not significantly different from normal speakers. This suggests a lingering deficit that may have earlier related to a greater degree of articulatory severity in the /r/ defective subjects than in the /s/ only defective ones. A second hypothesis is that the sensory/perceptual feedback systems required to produce /r/ are differently impaired.

In summary, evidence to support the increased likelihood for general academic failures in articulatory-defective, young, school-age children is generally negative, but the investigations have been sparse in number. Children having severe numbers of misarticulations have been found frequently to show serious weaknesses in linguistic abilities and some perceptual functions. These deficiencies are characteristic of many children who require special tutorial or classroom experiences in order to succeed to some degree in basic-learning skills and conceptual/cognitive development. Children having milder degrees of articulatory defectiveness frequently move from one grade to the next without noticeable difficulty. Perhaps greater numbers of articulatory defectives may be underachieving in their general academic performances than normal-speaking children. The issue of underachievement is somewhat nebulous and difficult to determine, which may explain why studies of underachievement rather than failure to achieve have not been undertaken. Results from the investigation by Stitt and Huntington (1969) may be interpreted as showing some academic-skills weakness in college students who have retained articulation errors, a finding that suggests the possibility of some degree of academic weakness.

The issue of the presence of various types of auditory and oral-sensory perceptual impairments in some portion of articulatory-defective children now appears to be substantially stronger in its impact due to the evidence from many investigators using a variety of different tests and measures. Almost all of the independent research results to date that have explored linguistic factors related to articulatory defectiveness have found inferior performances of both statistical and clinical importance, and some investigators have reported that the greater the numbers of misarticulations the greater the likelihood for depressed performances on various types of linguistic measures.

Stronger support for the hypothesis of reduced oral-sensory skills in some articulatory defectives also appears to have emerged within the past decade. The reported evidence is largely consistent in support of this hypothesis with some investigations showing reduced abilities in older articulatory defectives, specifically teenaged persons who have retained articulation errors.

The relationship between auditory perceptual and memory factor and defective articulation remains strong, with most of the reported evidence showing significantly poorer performances by many subjects with articulation problems as the severity of the disorder increases. Many of the complex interrelationships associated with such findings need and deserve further study. The severely defective, articulatory-impaired child remains the poorest performer on many linguistic, perceptual, and auditory-memory tasks. Evidence to support the belief that subgroups of articulatory defective children exist showing various patterns across the perceptual, memory, and linguistic variables has been gathering, and it appears that the presence of specific types of correlates to articulatory defectiveness have already been identified. If such information is confirmed by other independent investigators, the next quest may be to determine if one form of intervention is specifically more effective with one subtype of articulatory defectiveness than another. If a state of matching of patterns of deficiencies and strengths with therapy approaches can be attained, we will, indeed, have made significant steps forward in the understanding and treating of such disorders.

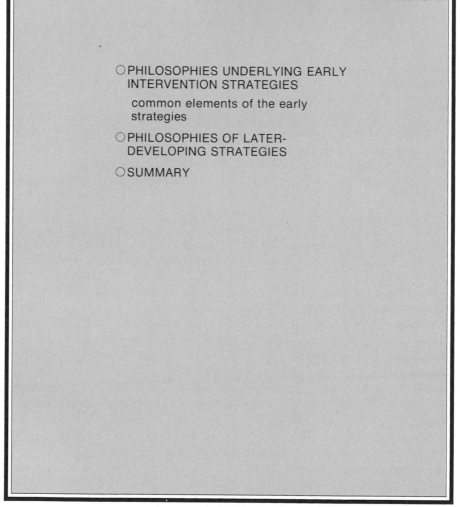

○ PHILOSOPHIES UNDERLYING EARLY
  INTERVENTION STRATEGIES

  common elements of the early
  strategies

○ PHILOSOPHIES OF LATER-
  DEVELOPING STRATEGIES

○ SUMMARY

Traditional and historical approaches to articulation remediation

○PHILOSOPHIES UNDERLYING EARLY INTERVENTION
STRATEGIES

Although many modifications of historical beliefs about the nature of articulation disorders and principles in their remediation have occurred, many theories have persisted and have stood the test of time. A small, dedicated group of early workers appear to have been instrumental in developing and promoting their philosophies and therapy principles resulting in improvement in the remedial process. A list of these "pioneers" and a glance at the trails they forged follows:

Martha K. Scripture Scripture was one of the very first "speech correctionists." She detailed many of her basic ideas and correctional strategies in a manual that she wrote in collaboration with Jackson in 1927. Much of the so-called "traditional" articulation-therapy approach seems to have emanated from this early publication. For example, she dealt with articulation disorders as phonetic problems and considered specific types of oral exercises to be most appropriate in therapy. She stressed the need for placement of the articulators and described many basic aspects of the phonetic-placement approach to articulation correction. Auditory identification and discrimination training was not focal in her work. The notion and value of working to get each defective speech sound into correct production in its isolated form stemmed from Scripture. Finally, her teachings and writing drew attention to the drill and exercise aspects which tended to highlight the structured and systematic nature of the articulation-therapy process. Scripture appears to have influenced the thinking of many later-developing authorities, particularly Charles Van Riper.

Charles Van Riper This authority completed a long and highly productive career in which he showed his special genius for developing and testing therapy strategies for speech disorders. The term "traditional articulation therapy" is most closely related to the types of strategies and principles first presented by him in 1939 in his classic book *Speech Correction: Principles and Method.*

Van Riper's influence on articulation therapy was pervasive, probably because of his clearly stated explanation of basic aspects of the process and his use of detailed illustrations for therapy procedures in case studies. In many of these clinical illustrations he displayed the specific technique and material required to master a skill needed to advance the client to a higher level of performance. In a sense Van Riper identified some of the basic weaknesses in the perceptual functioning of the articulatory-defective child, particularly in the auditory area, and specified a set of objectives and procedures to reduce the influence of such factors on articulation learning. His classical four steps in ear-training are well remembered by many present-day practitioners and served as procedural guides to this aspect of correction as well as a blueprint of some of the salient elements of the auditory-perceptual learning process in young children. In his therapy the clinician was to provide models of the target sound in the ear-training activities using isolation, stimulation, identification, and discrimination-training techniques. This emphasis was one of Van Riper's most important contributions to the thinking about the nature of articulation therapy.

The conceptualization of the relevant dimensions of the total program of therapy from sound defectiveness to full correct use in all types of conversational speech was his second major contribution. The therapy paradigm of development of the target sound in isolation (advocated earlier by Scripture), followed by correct use in increasingly longer and more complex linguistic units consisting of syllables, words, and sentences has largely persisted and can be seen in a number of the most modern approaches to correction.

The third area of important influence in articulation therapy made by Van Riper was his outline of what is required for a person to correct such problems. In his 1972 version of *Speech Correction: Principles and Methods* he described the process of training the defective to include

> —correct identification of the nature of the error and target sound
> —ability to scan and compare the defective's utterance with the target
> —modification of the error sound until correct sound production is attained
> —practicing the stabilization and habituating of the target sound so its correct production occurs automatically in all forms of speaking

It should be observed that the traditional articulation-therapy approach, most often associated with Van Riper, is largely phonetic, relies upon clinician modeling, and uses special therapy materials. The clinician motivated the client by educating him concerning the specific errors involved. Many aspects of the principles and particular techniques in other therapy approaches can be seen to be similar to those developed and tested by Charles Van Riper.

Sara Stinchfield—Hawk and Edna Young In 1938 these two professionals developed and promoted a method of articulation therapy they termed "motokinesthetic." Principles related to the approach have largely been used by persons who treat the articulatory defects of neurogenically impaired persons. Their writings and teaching probably influenced efforts to improve the articulation of many cerebral palsied persons.

In a sense the motokinesthetic approach is somewhat the ultimate of the general phonetic-placement concept. The stress placed on patterns of articulatory movements and the increasing awareness of kinesthetic cues to guide such movements made motokinesthetic different, however, from other less stimulating phonetic-placement techniques. The dynamic nature of speech was emphasized as the defective person was taught to recognize and then complete certain movements involved in producing speech.

Using pressure and touch the clinician teaches the client to feel the contact and pattern movement. The clinician's fingers are used to manipulate and stimulate such patterns. Devices of various types, such as tongue depressors, may also be helpful in stimulation and manipulation of articulators such as the tongue and jaw. Approaches involving the use of the brushing technique or icing to stimulate articulatory activity, which are still used today, undoubtedly rely upon some of the basic thinking of Stinchfield—Hawk and Young.

In the motokinesthetic approach emphasis was on the development of the target sound in isolation, and inherent in it was the belief that the accurate perceptual pattern of kinesthetic feedback would allow for a transfer of the correct sound into other units of speech and, ultimately, into conversational speaking. Unlike Van Riper's approach, ear training *per se* was not an important aspect of this method: motor programming using stimulation and sensation was its basic component.

Ollie Backus and Jane Beasley The importance of reducing psychological correlates to speech disorders, including articulatory defects, was stressed by Backus and Beasley, who felt that group approaches to correction would have greater impact on speech improvements, adjustment, and social-skills development. In their innovative approach they deliberately arranged group speech therapy so that many different types of disorders were represented in its membership. For example, they structured their groups so that the hard-of-hearing, persons with a cleft palate, the cerebral palsied, articulatory defectives, and stutterers were included. Development of confidence, social skills, increasing verbal output, and, to some extent at least, improved articulation were common goals of group sessions. No emphasis on systematic development of the target sound via phonetic placement, key words, linguistic cues, improvement of self-monitoring abilities or similar activities was made in their group approach. Rather, the activities centered around group projects designed to elicit sounds that members might misarticulate and provide practice from meaningful events to these words. Members of the group, presumably, learned from other members, were reinforced by them for improved or correct articulatory-production activities, and this practice and group reinforcement was considered powerful enough to support important improvements in the children's speech.

Again, the many traditional aspects of articulation therapy were not the focus of this approach. Group therapy benefits via changing perspectives, fear reduction, and positive identification were prominent goals used by Backus and Beasley to facilitate improved speech patterns including articulation. It should be acknowledged that group dynamics and other unstudied aspects of group-articulation therapy were first specified and manipulated by these early workers. The value of group interaction was brought to the profession's attention largely by Ollie Backus and Jane Beasley. Unfortunately, present-day clinicians have very limited information concerning how principles of group dynamics and interactions can positively affect the group-therapy process. Few have been interested in studying such factors, and we have not reaped the benefits of the power of some of them to assist us when group therapy is undertaken. Since most group therapy in the U.S. is provided for young articulatory defectives in school settings, this disorder, in particular, suffers from the dearth of information and techniques that might improve its effectiveness.

common elements of the early strategies

The author would like to emphasize that many elements of these four early approaches are in use today. Indeed, Van Riper (1978) appears to have modernized his "traditional" articulation therapy approach including such things, for example, as some linguistic considerations and perhaps reducing somewhat the total phonetic influence of his earlier writings. While the motokinesthetic approach stressed motor patterns, movement awareness, and touch to teach the client, Van Riper stressed the improvement of the person's abilities to "know the sound" via an auditory ear-training paradigm. However, common elements in the early approaches are as follows:

—Articulation disorders were phonetic in nature
—Defective speech sounds were to be developed first in isolation
—The importance of some perceptual training to teach sound learning was stressed by some
—Drills and practice were required for improvement

—Therapy devices and materials would facilitate sound learning and acquisition

—Both the clinician and peers could serve to positively reinforce correct sound production

—Most believed that once new sounds were learned in practice materials of various types carryover into spontaneous conversational speech would occur

○ PHILOSOPHIES OF LATER-DEVELOPING STRATEGIES

Building upon some of the common elements in earlier approaches to the correction of defective articulation, a number of individuals detailed specific differences in both rationale and procedure in later-developing strategies. One of the most influential of these persons was Eugene T. McDonald.

Eugene McDonald The Sensorimotor Articulation-Therapy Approach was conceived by McDonald, who drew on a body of information from motor phonetics to support its tenets. The dual concept of the articulatory function of an integration of sensory/perceptual performance and motor-movement patterns associated with speech sounds was explained by him as comprising the process. He promoted very successfully the concept of dynamism: articulating involved a series of skillful, overlapping, ballistic movements of the articulators. The process was continuous, related, and dynamic. He urged others to accept the concept of no medial position, that is, that consonants in our language serve to initiate or arrest syllables; and he relied on information from experimental phonetics and phonology to assert his view. He then developed the 'deep test' of articulation as a way of assessing the overlapping, ballistic function in speech without using spontaneous connected-speech samples to study it. His goal was to locate specific phonetic contexts in which the error sound may be articulated correctly; thus, the 'deep test' of articulation approached testing in a radically new manner. The results yielded what McDonald was after: a measure of inconsistency of error and the particular phonetic contexts in which some correct production was achieved.

Once the phonetic contexts in which there is some success in articulation of the error sound were located, McDonald was ready to begin his corrective efforts. Relying on the belief that the ballistic movements are basic in articulation and that these movements can best be identified in syllable form, McDonald recommended stages of nonsense-syllable imitation in which the clinician modeled the production. First, simpler bisyllables, such as /bibi/, were used to strengthen the client's awareness of speech patterns and motor movements. The sensorimotor-articulation approach educated the client to speech—its feeling, presence, and variation. Once rapid imitation occured and was evaluated by clinician and client, the phonetic contexts containing correct versions of the error sound were introduced and practiced in syllables of increasing complexity which were modified for changes in stress in a systematic fashion. The increasing skill of the client to use the error sound correctly in syllables was thought important to the enhancement of the use of the sound in other phonetic contexts in which deep testing found it to be in error.

Although McDonald described the relationship of articulation to other aspects of language, his approach to therapy was almost exclusively related to the motor-phonetic level of processing. His rationale for the value of auditory discrimination and other forms of auditory-perceptual training to improve the likelihood for success was to stress the accuracy of sound production which the client heard. More importantly, perhaps, was his heavy emphasis on the development of motor-speech patterns via the tactile and kinesthetic feedback systems. No ear training, as advocated by Van Riper and popular with many, was delineated as important to the corrective process when the sensorimotor approach was the choice for remediation. Not unlike other articulation therapy strategies, little information concerning the relative effectiveness of this approach to the correction of the defective articulation has been made available to the profession.

Edward Mysak The concept of the early authorities that sound learning was enhanced if the defective learned to identify the specific nature of the target and error sounds, described by Liberman et al. (1961) as "sharpening up the phonetic boundaries," was stressed in the writings of Mysak. Using theoretical information from Fairbanks (1954) and Van Riper and Irwin (1958) that concerned a servosystem theory of speech production and perception, Mysak focused upon the "activate error-sound sensitivity and error-sound measuring processes" and the related ones of "activate correct-sound seeking and approximating and correct-sound tracking" processes to guide his decisions about the nature of articulation therapy.

In his approach Mysak contends that the client needs to develop a "therapeutic error signal" (TES) which will guide future activities designed to get him to monitor the correct phoneme by the accurate identification of the target and error phonemes' specific sensory and perceptual parameters. Improvement in the client's visual, acoustical, tactile, and kinesthetic discrimination abilities comprises the vital element of Mysak's approach. Therapy appears aimed at the development of a powerful set of skills on the part of the client to accomplish this rapid, accurate discrimination and monitoring across a range of stimulus materials and linguistic units. The clinician chiefly provided examples of correct and incorrect productions of such varying material to give the necessary experiences to the client to make judgements followed by attempts to produce the target phoneme in various linguistic units. The approach was designed to develop correct sound production using feedback theory and signal detection concepts, and, as such, it represents a strong phonetic, perceptual orientation.

Mysak's ideas are reminiscent of older ideas of phonetic placement, ear-training, motor-kinesthetic training, individual application, practice, and modeling by the clinician. His ideas are not unique, but they do represent a strong, clear orientation concerning the value of strengthening the "phonemic boundaries" as a technique to improve acquisition of correct speech sounds.

Harris Winitz Probably the strongest proponent of the value of sound-discrimination training in children's acquiring of speech sounds is Harris Winitz. He has devoted a considerable portion of his career to researching sound learning as it can be enhanced using various types of auditory stimulation and speech-sound discrimination tasks. Much of his research was completed with Bellerose (Winitz and Lawrence, 1961; Winitz and Bellerose, 1962; Winitz and Bellerose, 1963; and Winitz and Preisler, 1967) and involved using various sound-discrimination strategies to teach non-English phones to normal-speaking children.

Much of his thinking and most of his articulation-therapy procedures are detailed in his publication *From Syllable to Conversation* (Winitz, 1975). Believing that the research literature associating speech-sound discrimination with defective articulation is conclusive and that the habit of misarticulating speech sounds results in reduced abilities to perceive differences between them, Winitz approaches training from assessment of the sound discrimination function as it relates to the specific sound-production errors of the child. He seeks phonetic contextual clues to understand more clearly what the exact nature of the sound-discrimination weakness may be as it relates to the production problem. Winitz provides instruction for using ten "sound-discrimination principles."

One of the principles advocated by Winitz involves teaching the child to discriminate between the error sound and the target sound—clearly not a new idea since early "traditional" approaches, such as Van Riper's, stressed this aspect of training. Winitz (1975) addressed the issue whether or not speech sounds, acquired with accuracy and skill in the clinical environment, will generalize to other spontaneous speaking situations. One of the more interesting premises that he established in this publication is that if the child sufficiently possesses error sounds that contain distinctive features, they will tend to generalize to connected, spontaneous speech without special production effort. According to Winitz, speech-discrimination training *per se* can accomplish this feat. This speculation appears to be unsupported by direct, clinical research, but seems supportable on an empirical basis, since most distinctive-feature systems assume both acoustical and motor commonality among speech sounds. Presumably, acquisition of features implies a readiness to generalize speech production, thus a technique such as speech-discrimination training is powerful enough to stimulate feature generalization which facilitates correct production of the error sound without the production-training aspect of articulation therapy. Under these conditions, phonetic-placement approaches would be unnecessary to achieve correct sound production.

Citing aspects of normal speech development, Winitz maintains that a strategy of merit that may be useful in gaining improved articulation in young children is to locate their defective sounds, to find common objects whose names contain these sounds, to engage the child in friendly play with the objects, and to stimulate the child with names of the objects but refuse to give the child any object in which he misarticulates the target sound. He suggests that an alternative strategy is to hesitate for awhile and then give the child the wrong object. This, in effect, he believes is a type of speech-sound-discrimination-training activity. It appears to this viewer that such a strategy might be effective if the child has good stimulability for the target sound(s), has some inconsistency in the production of the sound(s), and has a good temperament. A child with poor stimulability, consistently bad-tempered, might prove somewhat resistant to this particular type of tactic.

A principle of sound-discrimination training that Winitz recommends is to present sound contrasts to more difficult cases. This involves using progressions from easy discriminations to more difficult ones. An example of the type of approach he would recommend for a child substituting (t/s) reflects the following sequence of training:

1. /ta-ba/
2. /ta-ma/
3. /ta-fa/
4. /ta-la/
5. /ta-sa/

Training in more than one vowel context can be accomplished by modifying the above example so that step 2, for example, might be /ti-mi/, step 3 might be /tu-fu/, and so on.

Rather uniquely, Winitz maintains that training in sound discrimination begins with the error sound not the target sound, and he claims that beginning therapy on the target sound causes discrimination training to fail. In fact his perceptual training is focused almost exclusively on the child's discrimination of the error sound except for those portions that deal with his teaching the child to discriminate between the error sound as the child produces it and the target sound. Even under this condition,

Winitz seems to focus much more heavily on the child's learning the acoustical parameters of the error sound. The balance in emphasis, seen in other approaches, such as Mysak's feedback one, does not appear to be expressed in Winitz's descriptions of how sound discrimination should be taught.

While some speech clinicians might not choose to teach an articulatory-defective child to discriminate his errors at all, Winitz would amplify the process to include discrimination of words in running speech after accuracy has been obtained in isolated contrasts. He also suggests that speech production not begin until discrimination can be made well between the error and target sounds in sentences—an idea that hearkens back to some of Van Riper's early recommendations that the four steps in ear training normally precede efforts to gain correct production on defective speech sounds. Presumably, the ear training (or, in Winitz's case, solely sound-discrimination training) will either make the sound-production teaching unnecessary or facilitate it significantly so that acquisition is relatively simple for some children. Although this may be on the order of a speculation, there is some related evidence from sound-learning studies (Sommers et al., 1961; Winitz and Bellerose, 1972; Winitz and Bellerose, 1963; Winitz and Preisler, 1967), that speech improvement focusing on ear training, that is, identification of speech sounds, association of pho-neme/grapheme, and sound-discrimination training, will allow young, school-age children to make significantly greater improvements in artic-ulation than comparable control group subjects. Direct effort to get defective consonant sounds into production using phonetic placement and similar speech therapy techniques were not used in the studies cited. Thus, Winitz's belief that direct production efforts will not be needed to correct some portion of young children's articulation errors is partially supported by other experimental evidence.

Further refinement of the sound-discrimination training outlined by Winitz includes the importance of conceptualization in the articulatory-defective child's problem. Conceptualization is fashioned to be different from discrimination in that the latter is a perceptual task while the former is failure to learn rules concerning speech sounds. When a particular child shows evidence in his articulatory profile that he can discriminate certain sounds of the language correctly but continues to make errors, concep-tualization problems may explain the phenomenon according to Winitz. These problems limit accurate generalizations, thus training in the process is required to remedy the situation.

An example of such a problem would reside in a child who can be shown to discriminate certain sounds well but fails to produce them correctly in certain phonetic contexts. In what probably constitutes a common error pattern, a child shows evidence of being able to make the perceptual, acoustical differentiation between many of the speech sounds involved but is found to lack the use of the appropriate rule to conceptualize elements of the total process between certain stops and fricatives. Training, according to Winitz, teaches concepts or rules via grouping or sorting activities in which the child signals his response by raising either his right or left hand, for example, training to differentiate velar, alveolar, and bilabial stops, and the apicalveolar fricatives /s/ and /z/:

STIMULUS	LEFT HAND	RIGHT HAND
/t/	x	
/s/		x
/k/	x	
/d/	x	
/s/		x
/p/	x	
/z/		x
/b/	x	
/g/	x	
/s/		x

Using this system, place, manner, and voicing aspects of rule-governed articulatory defectiveness could be trained via the principles of conceptualization; in fact, voicing contrasted with voiced and other specific distinctive features could also be trained.

   Adele Gerber   A series of well-tested procedures incorporating the ideas of prominent authorities in articulation correction was presented by Gerber in her work, *Goal Carryover* (1973). This "eclectic" series of procedures has been tested both within the public school setting and in the university speech and hearing clinic over a period of fifteen or more years. Noticeably, the emphasis in her work stresses the specific differences in children's misarticulations and perceptual awareness of two troublesome speech sounds, /r/ and /s/. From the clinician's viewpoint, her description of the procedures required for the correction of these two speech sounds represents the most detailed set of procedures available since the earlier writings of Charles Van Riper.

   Gerber appears to represent the view that articulatory defects in children can be explained by both phonetic and phonemic principles. Her writings reflect a respect for the phonetic nature of speech sounds and the importance of phonological/linguistic aspects of some children's defectiveness. In particular she stresses the importance of phonetic-placement techniques for more difficult articulatory defectives, highly structured, step-by-step procedures that early in the therapy paradigm use the nonsense syllable to facilitate early, sound-production skills and later in therapy contribute to the possibility of caryover into spontaneous speech. The use of linguistic principles in the late stage of therapy contribute to the inclusion of newly developed speech sounds into the total language performance of the child. As such, Gerber's approach to articulation therapy for young children appears to represent a most comprehensive one for clinicians to evaluate. She directs her attention to two of the most difficult stages of articulation for many children who are more severely defective: the early sound production stage and the troublesome carryover one.

SUMMARY

Articulation therapy techniques and principles have been discussed for fifty years or more, and many of the very early ideas have persisted. Early approaches and later developing ones have generally been committed to a blueprint of events that involves three phases of effort. In the first stage the individual learns how to produce the target sound. Teaching the correct form of a target sound can be accomplished rapidly and easily under some conditions, particularly if the individual errors in its production inconsistently and/or shows good stimulability for its correction. When these conditions do not exist, production of the target sound may be more difficult requiring more time and intensive teaching strategies. Early approaches tended to suggest that phonetic placement activities are particularly valuable for those who experience little or no ability to produce the target sound without this assistance. This notion persists in some of the later developing approaches also (for example, Gerber's approach).

In the second stage of therapy, sometimes referred to as the "establishment" one, the clinician strengthens the ability of the individual to use the target sound skillfully in increasingly more difficult units, namely, from the sound in isolation, to the sound in syllables of increasing complexity, to individual words, and finally into phrases and sentences.

In the final stage, sometimes called "habituation" but well recognized by clinicians as the carryover one, many therapy approaches fail to direct specific attention to the needs of the individual for support to accomplish this. One of the few to pay special attention to this formidable aspect of the corrective process is that advocated by Gerber (1973). As stated earlier, it is this writer's belief that the first stage can be difficult for some more severely involved persons, the last stage can be a major challenge under some conditions, but the second or middle stage of articulation therapy may be relatively easy and predictable.

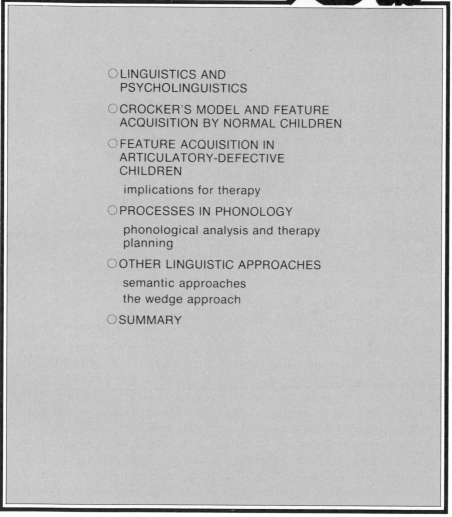

Linguistic concepts and articulatory remediation

○ LINGUISTICS AND PSYCHOLINGUISTICS

Classically, linguists have been largely concerned about those universal variables which underlie man's acquisition and use of language and similarities and differences in languages as a function of historical, ethnic, geographical, and racial influences. Seeking "truth," linguists have dedicated themselves to detecting and verifying the existence of "rules" which explain how man has been able to develop and use the extraordinarily complex yet naturally adopted linguistic system of his society. Linguistics as a discipline has not been concerned with the failures of individuals to learn rule systems or the impact of handicapping conditions on linguistic learning; rather, linguistic scholars and investigators have sought factual information to develop theoretical constructs which help to explain historical antecedents of languages, stages in normal acquisition within various cultures and societies, and the purposes of language.

The authoritative linguist Noam Chomsky (1969) has postulated the existence of a competency model of linguistic functioning which explains aspects of the phonological and grammatical components of language. When a functional, underlying rule system guides an individual's linguistic behaviors, the term "competency" is thought to be warranted to describe the condition. Children's abilities to produce speech sounds are seen as natural competencies; however, experience and learning are thought to provide the necessary factors for correct rule development and use.

A major application of this competency model of language acquisition has been applied to developmental phonology. In particular, those supporting a generative phonology, namely, a sequence of rules which tend to follow and support each other to explain phonological development and which rely heavily on distinctive-feature concepts, have contributed to our understanding of how and why normal and speech/language-impaired children use the phonemes of their language. Many of those cited earlier who openly support the use of a phonological model strongly suggest that speech/language clinicians look at the child's acquisition of rules in articulation learning instead of concentrating on phoneme acquisition *per se*.

With the advent of the psycholinguist, attention was directed at the use of basic information from the field of linguistics to understand how individuals apply linguistic rules and systems within societies. These specialists have stressed modern applications and problem solving, rather than historical understanding, and, in so doing, have worked to stimulate the development and application of linguistic theory and principles to problems such as phonological disorders in children.

Some prominent psycholinguists who have sought to apply linguistic theory and principles to the analysis and remediation of phonological disorders are Menyuk (1968), Crocker (1969), Compton (1970), and Ingram (1976). A related group of professional workers, largely trained and educated in the framework of the speech/language pathologist, have emerged and become involved in the introduction of linguistics concepts and principles to the process of remediating young children's speech disorders. Some of them, more professionally mature than others, such as Winitz (1975), McReynolds and her colleagues, Hueston and Bennett (1971; 1972), and Pollack and Rees (1972) have advocated reasonably widespread use of distinctive-feature analysis, inspection of rules that children either fail to use or misuse, and studies of linguistic processing to yield efficient and effective ways of correcting phonological disorders. Others, newer on the scene, such as Costello (1975), Bountress (1979), and many others, have become contributors to and hawkers of the limitation of "traditional" articulation-therapy approaches for children having multiple misarticulations. They have served as powerful advocates for approaches in which the phonemic features can be manipulated to allow distinctive features to generalize into children's phonological systems and make the corrective processes more efficient and more effective. (Available research to support this contention will be reviewed later in this chapter.)

While almost all early developers of distinctive-feature systems ignored any applied value of such systems to the remediation of phonological disorders in children (Jakobson, Fant, and Halle, 1952; Miller and Nicely, 1955; Chomsky and Halle, 1968), the application of these and other similar theoretical constructs has been urged by Compton (1970) and Crocker (1969).

○CROCKER'S MODEL AND FEATURE ACQUISITION BY NORMAL CHILDREN

Crocker (1969) contributed an exciting model for the development of children's phonology based upon the acquisition of features and advocated its use in the analysis and remediation of phonological disorders. He presented an informative case study of a young child who presumably "failed" to respond to traditional articulation therapy, but excelled with the use of distinctive features and other linguistic analyses to guide the corrective process.

Only Crocker (1969) has provided us with a model of distinctive-feature evolution that explains how bundles of features develop and ultimately result in phonemes. This model and the rules established by him have been viewed as a plausible explanation of how normal phonological development occurs in American English-speaking children. Research evidence to test Crocker's 1965 model has been theoretical and tangential rather than direct-hypothesis testing. Since it uniquely shows the evolution of consonants based upon the Jakobson, Fante, and Halle (1952) feature

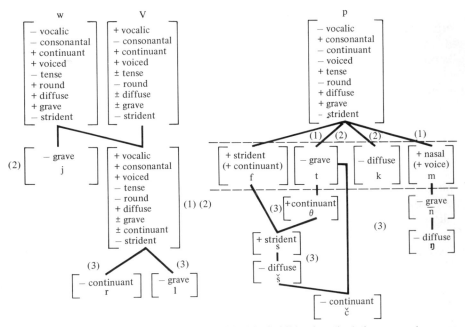

FIGURE 4–1 Diagram of the Phonological Model of children's articulation competence as it develops from prime feature sets, through the formation of base sets, to terminal feature sets. (From J. Crocker, "A Phonological Model of Children's Articulation Competence," *Journal of Speech Hearing Disorders* 34:207, 1969. Reprinted with permission.)

system, the model offers a tool for the enterprising speech/language clinician to understand the difficulties some children have in the development of normal articulation. It is also valuable for its rule systems, which allow one the opportunity to see how features are systematically combined to make new phonemes and classes of phonemes. Moreover, from a view of what may be the normal acquisition process, comparisons can be made of the feature and rule systems of articulatory-impaired children. It also represents a theoretical set of constructs which may encourage additional research into features and their application to therapy.

Crocker (1969) postulated three general rules which govern phonological development since they allow features to combine and separate:

> *Rule one:* Combine primary-feature sets with base sets
> *Rule two:* Combine secondary-features with base sets
> *Rule three:* Combine secondary-feature sets with secondary-features sets

To implement the use of the three general rules above, he grouped the features into two distinct categories: first, distinctive-feature classes, and, second, distinctive-feature sets. Distinctive-feature classes consist of

> *Primary features* To establish a class of sounds, that is, consonants, vowels, nasals, liquids, glides, and stridents, the following features are required: ±vocalic, ±consonantal, +nasal, +stridency.
>
> *Secondary features* These are: ±continuant, ±diffuse, ±voiced, and ±grave.
>
> *Cognate features* Cognates are sounds identical in features except for voicing. For example, /t/ and /d/ are identical in feature composition except that /t/ is −voice and /d/ is +voice.

Crocker conceived distinctive-feature sets to consist of prime sets, derived sets, base sets, and terminal sets. In essence he meant that each sound with each unique combination of features comprise a set. Three types of feature sets play different roles in the phoneme-acquisition process:

> *Prime-feature sets* This is a set of features needed to start the process, since all phonemes develop from one of three types of prime features sets. The three types are

> *Base-feature sets* From these sets additional sets develop. All base sets are *not* prime sets, but all prime sets are also base sets.
>
> *Terminal sets* No further feature sets can be developed from terminal sets.
>
> *Derived sets* This term is used to describe all other sets.

Figure 4–1 is a diagram of the Crocker model. From this model one can see that phonology develops by combining primary or secondary features with prime-feature sets to form derived sets, which may be base or terminal. The three sounds resulting from each of the three prime-features sets are /w/, /vowel/ (written as V), and /p/. For many children experience with the feature combinations contained in these three basic sounds apparently can be gained in early infancy, since they have been noted in the babbling states of development (Irwin, 1948). As Crocker pointed out, many of the common substitutions that children make, such as p/f, f/s, t/k, and others, are predictable, developmental errors, since these errors are fundamentally rule governed.

In his original work Crocker provides us with a number of examples of how his three basic phonological rules can be used to evolve speech sounds. We will look at only one example here, and the reader is urged to study the original material for others. In this example we will see how the rules are used to evolve the important and difficult /s/ sound. This, according to Crocker's interpretation, is a four-step procedure. In the first step, using rule one (combine primary-features sets with base sets), the +strident feature is combined with the prime base-feature set /p/ to form the new set /f/ (thus showing how /f/ is derived from /p/). In the second step rule two (combine secondary features with base sets) is applied when −grave is combined with the prime base-feature set /p/ to form the new set /t/ (thus, also showing how /t/ develops). In step three we see that rule three (combine secondary-features sets with secondary-features sets) is used as +continuant feature is combined with −grave to form the set /θ/ (thus showing how /θ/ is developed also). In the fourth and last step, aimed at development of /s/, rule three is again used when the +strident feature and the −grave feature distinction are combined to form another set −, which is our target sound, /s/.

In summary the Crocker Model of Articulatory Competency for consonants is both a practical tool and a theoretical set of conceptualizations concerning phonological development. Rules from the system are capable of assisting us to understand some of the patterns of articulatory defectiveness that we see in young children. The model has face validity and is capable of making predictions such as those related to types of substitution patterns that children make most frequently. The model also is apparently capable of taking into account current information about sound and feature acquisition in normal children and, furthermore, can account for the developmental sequence and orderliness of almost all sounds.

Two of the investigations that have yielded developmental information concerning distinctive-feature acquisition in normal, young children were reported by Menyuk (1968) and Prather et al. (1975). Agreement in the feature acquisition of Japanese and American children was reported by Menyuk (1968). Using features from the early 1952 Jakobson, Fant, and Halle system (many included in the later 1968 Chomsky and Halle system), she found that the earliest developing features in both Japanese and American young children were: nasal, grave, voice, and diffuse with continuancy and stridency developing last. Data from the Prather et al. (1975) investigation of the articulation development of normal children, aged two to four, essentially agreed with Menyuk's earlier findings, thus showing that many features are developed and acquired to high levels of acquisition very early in life and these features correlate very highly (as they must) with the order of speech/sound acquisition.

○FEATURE ACQUISITION IN ARTICULATORY-DEFECTIVE CHILDREN

Ideally, speech/language pathologists (SLP) can benefit from an understanding of the acquisition of features by normal children, as well as contrasting information about feature acquisition and use in speech/ language-impaired children. However, studies of feature acquisition in articulatory-defective children are not plentiful. Menyuk reported that the feature of stridency was the one least maintained by articulatory-defective children, while the features of voicing and nasality were most often maintained. Stridency is characteristic of many later-developing and troublesome phonemes (such as /s, z, tʃ, ʤ,/) perhaps making both the production and perception of such phonemes more difficult. Indeed, Menyuk (1968) studied the abilities of both children to produce phonemes containing stridency and adults to recall stridency in a task that she contrived. Stridency was the most difficult to produce in its phonemes as well as the most difficult feature studied for adults to recall.

In her observation of feature acquisition and use by normal children Menyuk (1968) also described the importance of one-feature errors as they contributed to misarticulations:

> Distinction between sounds which differ from each other only in one feature (place of articulation) seems to cause the greatest difficulty both in recall by adults and production by children. The one other feature distinction that is frequently not observed is continuancy. The tendency then, seems to be nonobservation of a single feature differentiation in the most frequent consonant substitutions of the child who is developing language normally. For example, we find substitutions such as 'tar' for 'car', 'dis', for 'this', or 'fink' for 'think'. In each of these substitutions all the attributes are maintained except for one each instance (i.e., place, continuancy, stridency).

A comprehensive study of distinctive-feature acquisition in articulatory-defective children was completed by Gowman and Sommers (1979). Using the Chomsky and Halle 1968 system and a method for determining feature acquisition developed by Sommers et al. (1978), ninety children's performances were investigated. Thirty children were four years of age, thirty five years of age, and thirty six years of age. Within each of the three age groups, ten children has mild, ten moderate, and ten severe overall degrees of articulatory defectiveness. Two features of the thirteen in the Chomsky and Halle 1968 system were not studied since they involve only vowel sounds (round and tense). The remaining eleven features comprised twenty-two units, since each feature is binary and marked as + if present and − if absent. Almost all of the ninety children, regardless of age or degree of overall defectiveness, had complete or very adequate (eighty to one hundred percent) use of the following features:

- −vocalic
- −continuant
- −coronal
- +back
- +high
- +voice
- +anterior
- +nasal and −nasal
- +consonantal and −consonantal
- +low and −low

Certain features comprised a common core of difficulty for the four-, five-, and six-year old children, although their relative percentages of acquisition varied from one age level to the next. The nine features combinations that made up this collection and the average percentage of acquisition for all subjects were as follows:

+ strident	52%	− strident	48%
+ continuant	65%	− voice	34%
+ coronal	60%	− anterior	19%
+ vocalic	48%	− back	27%
		− high	31%

These results show that certain features were difficult for children to produce correctly in combination with others. Correct deletion of some features from certain phonemes was also a problem. We suspect that a lack of proper rule use or a misuse of phonological rules accounts for the difficulty; however, underlying this may be a perceptual/motor encoding-of-speech difficulty—at least for some portion of the total sample of ninety four-, five-, and six-year old articulatory defectives. Interestingly, age-level reflected feature difficulty well with a few exceptions. At the six-year level, the acquisition of −voice doubled compared with the two younger age groups, but remained less than fifty percent. Six-year old subjects also showed impressive gains in all four feature combinations but little increase in acquisition in the −ones, except for −voice. As Menyuk had found earlier, + and − stridency were found to be troublesome at all age levels, and this was the only feature showing a lack of good acquisition in both its binary forms.

An explanation for nine combinations of the eleven features studied in the Gowman and Sommers (1979) investigation being most difficult for four-, five-, and six-year old articulatory defectives to acquire can be found in the nature of those consonant sounds. (Of course, we all recognize that features only exist in individual phonemes; thus, eventually one returns to this basic unit of speech for understanding why they fail to be acquired and/or how they are misused.) Judging by data from Menyuk (1968) and Prather et al. (1975), these nine combinations of features should be linked to late-developing speech sounds, and the late-developing ones are those most frequently misarticulated by speech-defective children. Was this the case? If so, what speech sounds accounted most for the loss of the nine feature combinations?

The results of the analysis in Table 4-1 strongly support clinical experience and findings from investigations in which the ten most difficult consonants for American children have been identified. Indeed, distinctive features using the Chomsky and Halle 1963 system do reflect that losses of correct feature use (as small as nine combinations of a possible twenty-two for consonants) lead to the difficulties that four, five, and six year old children have in their production of ten prominent speech sounds. These data validate distinctive features using this system, since they show the

TABLE 4-1

FEATURES POORLY ACQUIRED	SPEECH SOUNDS									
	r	l	s	z	ʃ	tʃ	ʒ	f	θ	dʒ
+ strident			X	X	X	X	X	X		X
+ continuent	X	X	X	X	X		X	X	X	
+ coronal	X	X	X	X	X	X	X		X	X
+ vocalic	X	X								
− strident	X	X								
− voice			X		X	X		X	X	
− anterior	X				X	X	X			X
− back	X	X	X	X	X	X	X	X	X	X
− high	X	X	X	X				X	X	
total	7	6	6	5	6	5	5	5	5	4

precise correspondence between either lack of feature use or misuse of features translated directly into the most commonly defective consonants in young children's speech. In this sample of ninety children having varying degrees of articulatory defectiveness, a small number showed evidence in the feature-acquisition analysis of atypical development, with patterns of later-developing features being used adequately but with inadequate use of earlier developing ones. Most often members of this small group came from those children having the most severe problems and frequently displaying what Renfrew (1966) described as the "open-syllable syndrome," a condition linked to more general linguistic impairments by some investigators and perceptual/neurological immaturities by others.

Children reflecting aberrant use of distinctive features and thus phonological rules have been described by Ingram (1976) as 'deviant.' Those who show patterns of delayed feature development, with feature use predictable and constant but arrested, have been categorized by Ingram as 'delayed'! Within our sample most of the children could be considered 'delayed' in feature acquisition rather than 'deviant.' This finding concurs with Leonard's (1973) report in which he found seventy percent of 200 children to show developmental delays in feature acquisition. It was Leonard's opinion that deviant-rule use could more commonly be seen in younger than older children. To study this he located four-, five-, and six-year old children from his sample and determined the percentage using what he termed 'deviant feature rules.' His conclusions are summarized in Table 4–2.

The reader can see from the rules written by Leonard that the common element in most of them is a loss of the +continuancy and +stridency features when paired with certain other features three times and when occurring alone twice. Both continuancy and stridency are commonly found in later-developing fricatives, and +continuancy and −stridency are found in /r/ and /l/. Furthermore, most of the examples that we shall see later of therapy applications using distinctive features teach continuancy or stridency, thus showing that these features are commonly troublesome for some significant portion of the articulatory defectives. A review of the specific sounds that accounted for the rules written by Leonard using the Chomsky and Halle 1968 system revealed a common element in all of them. For the most part the present author and a colleague found that these "deviant feature rules" were probably highly related to what many more severe articulatory-defective children do to compensate for the loss of ability to product later-developing speech sounds: they substitute sounds that are easier to produce and which occur earlier in the developmental sequence. The predictions that Crocker (1969) made from his model also show this as the most likely condition.

Weber (1970) presented a brief account of the errors in articulation

TABLE 4–2
Percentage of Children at Three Age Levels Found to Use Deviant
Feature Rules

RULE		AGE 4 (N 36)	AGE 5 (N 43)	AGE 6 (N 28)
[+ coronal, + strident] → { − strident, [null] }		33	23	14
[− vocalic, + contin.] → { − continuant, [null] }		28	07	11
[+ strident] → { − strident, [null] }		19	09	07
[+ coronal, + contin.] → { − continuant, [null] }		19	05	07
[+ contin.] → { − continuant, [null] }		17	05	07

made by eighteen children, ten of whom were in the first grade and eight others in grades one to three. All were considered to be within normal limits intellectually, to have normal hearing, and to show moderate-to-severe articulation disorders. In his summary of their most salient "deviant" patterns of articulation Weber frequently cited errors of using stops for fricatives, place for stops, fricatives often forward, substitutions of w/r and w/l, and occasional errors of voicing. Examination of the feature-acquisition data from the Gowman and Sommers investigation (1979) will support the conclusion that what Weber was describing may have been the relatively normal feature use of children having more severe degrees of articulatory defects. That is, the lack of + stridency and − continuancy plus the influence of a lack of the + coronal features can account for many of the errors involving the use of stops for fricatives in the Weber report. The use of glides for liquids, as seen in w/r and w/l errors, is very common in young children and also reflects a pattern of features inadequacy that represents what many of the ninety subjects in the Gowman–Sommers investigation did when producing /r/ and /l/. Our data also show that voicing is a more troublesome feature for young articulatory defectives to master, a finding which may imply that such problems rather than reflecting "deviancy," as in some of his subjects Weber believed, may merely reflect the types of errors seen in defective children generally.

Singh and Frank (1972) presented data from ninety children attending a university speech clinic and typically six years of age but ranging from three years, six months to ten years. A feature analysis was completed on each child, and the exact number of times that consonant sounds were substituted for each other was recorded and summarized as shown in Table 4–3.

The predictions that Crocker (1969) made from his model concerning which sounds would most likely be substituted for others fit nicely into the Singh and Frank (1972) data presented above. Furthermore, three of the four features not used correctly by Leonard's subjects were found by the author and Gowman to be in the troublesome list of features, suggesting that these deviant feature rules may not be all that deviant. When the rules Leonard specified for these subjects were analyzed, the prominent substitutions which characterized the data were stops for fricatives t/s, d/z, θ/s, p/f, and many other combinations and liquids for glides, for example, w/r and w/l. Although the possible combinations are limited and strange phenomena, such as nasal for fricative substitutions, could have been made by some of Leonard's subjects, these other possible, really deviant patterns are rarely if ever seen; and it is difficult to imagine that the number of subjects showing deviant-feature rules in his data was actually doing so. The greater likelihood is that many of the subjects showed rather predictable substitutions, particularly since they were younger and severely impaired in articulation. Under these conditions, the term "deviant" would seem to be overused with many children showing delayed development.

While deviant patterns do exist, they are not common, and children manifesting them may be atypical of the larger group of articulatory defectives. An example, whom the author considers to have a deviant phonological disorder, is J.P., aged five years, four months. This child's articulatory profile shows numerous omissions of consonants in the syllable-arresting position, some vowel distortions, and a pattern of substitutions not commonly seen in children of his age.

Set one: Substitution pattern: k/s, k/tʃ, k/ʃ, k/f

FEATURE ANALYSIS

+ strident	− strident
− high	+ high
− back	+ back
+ coronal	− coronal
/s, tʃ, ʃ, f/	/k/

Rule one: Voiceless strident sounds are produced as voiceless velar stops.
Set two: Substitution pattern: d/t, b/p, g/k, z/s

TABLE 4–3
Substitutions of Consonant Sounds

SUBSTITUTING PHONEMES

REPLACED PHONEMES

	θ	v	s	z	ʃ	ð	k	g	f	d	n	t	m	ŋ	p	b	TOTAL
t	19	0	33	7	31	2	46	0	20	1	0	X	0	0	0	0	159
d	2	5	0	27	3	45	4	46	1	X	3	5	0	0	0	0	141
b	0	84	0	0	0	0	0	0	0	0	0	0	4	0	3	X	91
f	74	2	7	1	4	1	0	0	X	0	0	0	0	0	0	0	90
θ	X	0	47	25	11	0	0	0	1	0	0	0	0	0	0	0	84
s	5	0	X	15	31	0	0	0	9	0	0	0	0	0	0	0	60
v	1	X	0	2	0	24	0	0	0	0	0	0	0	0	0	0	27
p	0	0	0	0	0	0	0	0	10	0	0	0	0	0	0	3	13
ð	0	1	0	9	0	X	0	0	0	0	0	0	0	0	0	0	10
m	3	0	0	0	0	0	0	0	3	0	4	0	X	0	0	0	10
n	0	0	0	0	0	0	0	1	0	5	X	0	1	3	0	0	10
k	0	0	0	0	0	0	X	2	0	2	0	1	0	2	1	0	8
g	0	0	0	0	0	0	1	X	0	1	0	1	0	0	0	0	2
z	0	0	0	X	0	1	0	0	0	0	0	0	0	0	0	0	1
ʃ	0	0	0	0	X	0	0	0	0	0	0	0	0	0	0	0	0
ɔ	0	0	0	0	0	0	0	0	0	0	0	0	0	X	0	0	0
Total	104	92	87	87	80	73	51	49	44	9	7	6	5	5	4	3	706

FEATURE ANALYSIS

− voice	+ voice
/t, p, k, s/	/d, b, g, z/

Rule two: Voiceless cognates are replaced by voiced cognates.
Set three: Substitution pattern: f/l, v/r

FEATURE ANALYSIS

+ coronal	− coronal
− strident	+ strident
/r, l/	/f, v/

Rule three: Glides are articulated as labio–dental fricatives.

These three sets or substitution patterns in J.P.'s phonology contribute greatly to his very poor intelligibility. In the first set he has four feature errors; in the second, one error; and in the third, two errors. Almost by definition, we would expect to find that the greater the number of feature errors the greater the loss of speech intelligibility. We might also be willing to assert that the more deviant the phonological disorder the more multiple-feature errors to be found in sets. However, there appears not to be any perfect relationship between numbers of features in sets, loss of speech intelligibility, or even degree of deviancy. It is clear from Menyuk's (1964) data and from that of Singh and Frank (1972) that one-feature-change-errors most often occur in children's substitutions so that this might be construed as a norm for many young, articulatory defectives. However, the point is that unusual, one-feature errors can wreak havoc with speech intelligibility and reflect bizarre performance. In J.P.'s case this is illustrated by the replacement of voiceless cognates by their voiced counterparts. This one-feature change is deviant behavior in the five-year old child, since voicing errors on consonants disappear in normal pho-nological development very early, perhaps seldom seen after three years of age (Prather et al., 1975). His articulating of f/l and v/r reflects a highly unusual set—one seen very infrequently even in much younger children, and this two-feature change also contributes greatly to his loss of speech intelligibility. From this orientation one might suggest that one of the characteristics of "deviant" articulation would be a disproportionate degree of loss of speech intelligibility for the listener, who would not find it easy to encode the strange transmission perhaps due to a lack of experience with anything like it.

implications for therapy

The phonological rules that children can demonstrate in their distinctive-feature use have been considered to be important determiners of the need for therapy. Strange and infrequent patterns of feature use, in particular, have been cited by Weber (1970), Menyuk (1964), and Leonard (1973) as signs that a child's phonology is disordered (or, as Weber and Leonard described it, "deviant"). Presumably, children with delayed feature acquisition and thus inadequate articulation, may gradually improve and develop normal articulation but at older age levels than normal children, while the "deviant" child may require therapy in order to master his phonology. Unfortunately, this is an assertion, and we have no research evidence to support this view. While the assertion may eventually be found to be correct, it may be determined that some portion of the "delayed" group will also require therapy. This seems likely since older children and adults having misarticulations usually have only one defective speech sound, which is /r/ or /s/, and this implies that many of the features are adequately represented in other consonants that are produced correctly. Thus, a great deal of accurate feature-rule use *per se* does not seem to be a precursor of normal articulatory ability. Problems of this type are often referred to as "phonetic" rather than "phonemic" to show that they are probably more perceptual/motor difficulties than linguistic problems. There is no reason for denying speech therapy to children regardless of whether their phonological development can be considered related to either phonetic or phonemic factors or both, and no one has advocated that only one type of articulatory disorder deserves to be treated.

○PROCESSES IN PHONOLOGY

Although we have become rather accustomed to associating distinctive-feature concepts with phonological analysis and children's phonological disorders, the concept of 'processes' in phonology and their application to analysis and remedial strategies have not been stressed until recently. One reason for this may be that older, articulatory-defective children, such as young, school-age children, who have traditionally received the bulk of corrective service for such disorders, almost always have mastered most of the process variables in phonology but have not necessarily mastered distinctive features. Among some with strong orientations toward linguistics, such as Bloom and Lahey (1978), studies of phonological learning have moved from the single phoneme or speech sound as the basic unit of analysis, to distinctive-feature concepts, to the word as the basic unit. Process variables, indeed, are viewed only in the word context, and it is the belief of some that a universal ability found in children is to simplify speech until the child's words eventually match their adult models (Ingram, 1976). At the moment, in the author's opinion, there is no reasonableness to the view that only the word needs to be studied and that processing variables must be dealt with to the exclusion of the study of speech sounds in isolation, syllables, and the powerful interaction of distinctive features in speech production. We do need to examine the 'process' variables in phonological development and see if they are capable of helping us understand and deal with phonological disorders more expertly.

Being basically phonological constructs, the 'process' variables would be expected to and do have some rules which guide their functions. Two types of rules are commonly specified:

1. *The Substitution Rules.* These rules are thought to segment specific phonemes produced by children who have tried to imitate the speech of adults.

2. *The Phontactic Rules.* These rules are context sensitive ones and reflect the influence of speech sounds on one another as seen in syllable contexts in words.

The various types of phonological processes most often described consist of the following:

Final consonant deletion. This consists of the omission of final consonants, for example, [bv] for book

Assimilation. This process shows the influence of speech sounds on the production of other sounds in the utterance.

   1. front assimilation, for example, [git] for keep

   2. back assimilation, for example, [gæk] for cat

Cluster reduction. This process simplifies consonant clusters by avoiding the production of one or more of them when clusters are produced.

   1. one consonant is deleted;

      a. liquid reduction, for example, deletion of /r, l/ as seen in /pis/ for please

      b. /s/ reduction, for example, deletion of /s/ as seen in [ti] for still

      c. nasal reduction:

         1. for voiced stops, delete the stop; for example, [bæn] for band

         2. for voiceless stops, delete the nasal; for example, /[dʌp]/ for dump

   2. a schwa is inserted between two consonants, for example, [pəle] for play

Voicing. This process consists of the voicing of all initial consonants and unvoicing of all final consonants, for example, [gəʊ] for cow and [pɪk] for pig

Fronting. This represents a preference for alveolar and dental consonants over velar and uvular consonants, for example, [dnn] for gun

Deaspiration. This refers to a failure to aspirate, for example, [pəɪ] for [phəɪ]

Spirantization. This occurs when stops are substituted for fricatives and affricatives in the final position, for example, [wat] for watch

Stopping. In this process stops are used for fricatives and affricatives in the initial position, for example, [pəɪ] for fire and [pɪt] for fish

Reduplication. This occurs when repetition of the first syllable results in simplification, for example, [sisi] for sister

Weak-syllable deletion. This occurs with the deletion of unstressed syllables in a two or more syllable word, for example, [bəʊ] for about

The process aspects of children's phonology obviously interact with distinctive-feature acquisition. For example, when 'stopping' (a process) occurs in a child's speech, the likelihood is that the loss of +continuancy (as seen in Chomsky and Halle's 1968 system) in fricatives where they are replaced by −continuant stops drastically reduces the use of the +continuancy feature. Another example to show how process factors may affect distinctive-feature use is related to the process variable of 'fronting,' in which alveolar and dental consonants are preferred over velar and uvular consonants. This results in the loss of the +back feature, since many of the back consonants are replaced by those coded −back. The process 'voicing' seems most directly related to distinctive-feature loss of + and − voicing. Other process variables in phonology are not so easily related to distinctive-feature use. In summary, the process variables attempt to explain the strategies that young, normal children use to master their phonology and prevent their overall linguistic capabilities from being overtaxed. Most involve reduction of complexity of the speech signal; and while not monotonically related to distinctive-feature competencies and performances of children, many processes have influences on feature use, and the converse may also be true to some degree. The precise nature of the relationships between these process variables and distinctive-feature use in children's developing phonology remains for future scholars and investigators to determine.

The extent to which very young, normal children use certain types of phonological processing was investigated by Edwards (1980). She studied the processing abilities of six children, aged one and a half to two and a half, over a seven-month time span sampling their performances eight to twelve times to get sufficient data. All six subjects used the same nineteen processes, but a total of thirty-three processes were discovered. To account for their common elements Edwards devised a classificatory scheme that consisted of two elements. The first she termed *process persistence,* and the second *process strength.* The former related to the length of time a certain process occurs, and the latter to the number of times it occurs.

While data from the Edwards (1979) report showed that subjects' processing varied considerably, some summary information revealed that patterns could be delineated. In the category of process persistence six types were identified as being most affected. These six are summarized as follows:

PROCESS	PERCENTAGE	EXAMPLE
1. stopping	100%	jacket - - -
2. depalatalization	94%	fish - - -
3. alveolarization (of dentals)	90%	feather - - -
4. final devoicing	84%	shoes - - -
5. gliding	81%	"*G*" - - -
6. dedentalization	78%	T.V. - - -

All six subjects were found to use these six persistent processes much of the time over the seven-month period of the investigation.

A similar analysis completed by Edwards also reflected the process strength patterns of the children. Again, she identified the six most influential ones:

PROCESS	PERCENTAGE
1. depalatalization	64%
2. alveolarization	51%
3. final devoicing	55%
4. dedentalization	27%
5. stopping	22%
6. gliding	70%

These findings reflect that very young children's processing is heavily influenced by common occurrences, and the most frequently occurring ones also last the longest. Many others were found from time to time in the speech of these children, so individual variation was also taking place. Edwards also observed that various combinations of processes can operate to affect individual sound production. Further, the influence of the lexicon of the child and phonological processing was revealed in the children's performances, since she observed that as new words were added to their spoken language, they frequently underwent a type of processing with a pattern of activity unique to a specific lexical item.

Attention directed most recently at phonological processing and its intrinsic role in language development has resulted in a systems analysis devised by Shriberg and Kwiatkowski (1980). This system, termed the Natural Process Analysis, uses spoken samples of children's speech to investigate eight processes thought by the authors to be natural ones which commonly occur in preschool and young, school-age children. The intention is to provide a reliable and meaningful analysis of the process errors of speech defectives to help guide therapy decisions. Among these decisions are those concerning which processing errors to correct and the specific speech sounds contained in such errors. The choice about which processing errors require remediation is also guided by the loss of speech intelligibility resulting from their use. No specific therapy technique *per se* is recommended as part of this analysis system.

phonological analysis and therapy planning

Those interested in using phonological concepts to improve their therapy might choose to locate phonological rule systems by studying feature use, to study phonological processes using phonetic transcription of spontaneous speech samples, or to do a comprehensive series of both features and processes. The resultant corpus of data would need to be evaluated in terms of patterns of behavior which conceivably could be used to pick targets and goals for the therapy process (see Compton, 1968). (There would be a need, for example, to illustrate how rules can be developed and the influence they have on therapy targets and goals.) There is no information concerning the common phonological core that exists when feature use and processing errors occur in the same segment of speech; thus, there is a need to interrelate this type of information at the level of the individual child. It is possible that features reflect performance while processes reflect a general type of linguistic competency; and we do expect and will find some degree of overlap but no complete correspondence between the two.

Most of the reported therapy experiences have stressed the assessment of feature use by young children with multiple sound errors. As we noted, some very recent efforts have been made to show how processing errors can be assessed and used as guides for making therapy decisions (Shriberg and Kwiatkowski 1980); however, this work is in its infancy, and we have little research information showing its efficacy.

Sound and Feature Generalization   The importance of generalization in articulation learning has surfaced. Particularly appropriate at the moment is response generalization, that is, increase in the frequency of a

bit of operant behavior following reinforcement also results in the increase
of the frequency of similar responses. The form of response generalization
best studied in articulatory disorders is sound generalization beginning
with the 1967 study by Shelton, Elbert, and Arndt. In this experiment,
seven children who misarticulated /s/, /z/, and /r/ were given training for
eleven weeks to correct /s/ but no therapy for /z/ and /r/. While /z/
improved along with /s/, /r/ did not, presumably because they are too
dissimilar (in terms of features, at least), and dissimilar events are slow to
show generalization effects. A further test by Shelton, Elbert, and Arndt
(1967) in which /r/ received training while /s/ and /ʃ/ did not, showed that
while /r/ production improved, improvements on /s/ and /ʃ/ production
failed to occur. In a small study done with the author, Cox (1974) found
that four children misarticulating both /ʃ/ and /j/ improved in their
productions of /j/ when /ʃ/ was trained but no training was provided for
/j/.

The literature to show that distinctive features *per se* generalize in
therapy is not so clear, although some studies' results have been interpreted
to show that features may generalize across phonemes in which they are
missing; for example, train + stridency in /f/ and then probe /s/, /ʃ/, and
/tʃ/, which are left untreated, and find stridency developing. To what
extent feature generalization is akin to or part of the explanation for the
more plentiful studies showing that sound generalization occurs is not
known, but some significant interaction seems plausible. Perhaps we are
talking about manifestations of the same phenomenon.

Articulation Testing and Features Published reports of feature assessment and planning in articulation therapy are not bountiful. Most of
them reflect very similar philosophies, assessment procedures, and therapy
strategies. Following is a review of a number of the reports seeking
likenesses and differences and hopefully giving the reader some details
concerning the rationale for these approaches and some popular strategies.

An authority who influenced the feature approach to therapy planning
is McReynolds. In concert with others (McReynolds and Huston, 1971;
McReynolds and Bennett, 1972) she provided the initial impetus to the
use of features in articulation therapy. Later she and Engemann (1975)
provided a workbook in which feature analysis was described in great
detail along with some general recommendations about therapy.

Some of the basic aspects of determining feature acquisition and use
concern securing an adequate sample of speech. McReynolds and Engemann (1975) specify the use of the McDonald Deep Test (1964) with
sufficient study of the types of substitutions use for defective phonemes
to obtain a valid and reliable sample from which to derive the degree of
error or failure of use of each of the thirteen features in the Chomsky and
Halle 1968 system. To accomplish this all consonants are deep tested to

insure that the total performance of the child is taken into account—a procedure requiring an average of forty-five minutes when four preschool subjects were studied (Sommers, Milikich, and Savage, 1980).

Once the articulation sample is completed, McReynolds and Engemann instruct the reader to complete nine additional steps to determine the percentage of error for each feature. These steps include many scoring forms and worksheets for transcribing each phoneme as correctly produced, substituted, or omitted; comparison of each test phoneme's distinctive features with the substituted one(s); numbers of times each substitution or omission was used in the contexts tested; recording of total number of times each feature was correctly omitted; and then a summary of information on worksheets to obtain the number of possible occurrences of each feature, which is then added to the number of correct occurrences. Finally, the percentage of feature error is determined by dividing the total of correct occurrences by the total for possible occurrences for each (+) and (−) aspect for each feature. The percentage is then computed by subtracting this number from one hundred.

The entire process of complete deep testing of all consonants and the computational procedures have been found to average two hours and fifty minutes when applied to the articulation of young, moderately severe articulatory-defective children (Sommers, Milikich, and Savage, 1980). A short-cut procedure developed by this author was also tested on the same subjects and found to reduce the time required, on the average, by one hour. The percentage of feature error found using the short-cut system was almost identical to that obtained using the McReynolds and Engemann (1975) complete analysis system.

Procedures for determining feature use were also described by Costello (1975). She recommends that the analysis begin with the Fisher–Logemann Test of Articulation Competence (1971) in order to locate specific error phonemes. Than she checks the findings from this testing by giving the Goldman–Fristoe Test of Articulation (1969). Information about articulatory performances is gathered across all the subtests, which, interestingly, include the Stimulability Subtest and a test of articulation in spontaneous speech, the Story Portion. All of this aspect of testing she calls the "pretreatment phase." Following this the "baseline data" phase is completed by obtaining scores on each error phoneme from the McDonald Deep Test of Articulation (1964).

To determine which features to enter into therapy, Costello's choice of a feature system was the one devised by Singh and Polen (1972). This system distinguishes twenty-two English consonants using a binary coding of zero and one to indicate the perceptual dimensions of a feature, thus seven features correspond to fourteen articulatory components capable of distinguishing the twenty-two consonants. The seven features of this system contain five that are in the Chomsky and Halle 1968 one, namely, front/back, nonnasal/nasal, stop/continuant, nonsibilant/sibilant, and voiceless/voice. Two other features in the Singh and Polen system are nonlabial/labial and nonsonorant/sonorant, and they deserve to be defined. The nonlabial/labial feature is defined as one adding the lips to the place of articulation, and the nonsonorant/sonorant one distinguishes consonants which have either a restricted or unrestricted airstream. All glides and nasal consonants have the sonorant feature, since they have an unrestricted airflow; and the remaining consonants are all characterized by the nonsonorant feature.

Costello appears not to have a feature-acquisition method *per se;* rather, she has a rapid system of locating the predominant feature errors. This system of analysis requires that the Singh and Polen features be applied to a child's substitution errors only to identify the lack of use or misuse of features. It is accomplished using one data form in which the examiner writes the seven features across the top of the page and the error phonemes and their substitutions are placed vertically in the far left column. Following this, the feature-by-feature analysis is performed comparing the substitution to the error phoneme. Finally, all discrepancies are circled to show the features that account for each error phoneme. Costello suggests also that the examiner should look carefully down each of the columns to seek significant or consistent feature errors, that is, ones which are responsible for several phoneme errors.

The Costello approach, which should be efficient enough to allow the clinician a basic evaluation of feature use, is incomplete. It fails to take into account feature loss in omissions, other sounds that may be substituted for error phonemes, for instance, substitution by the child of p/s for t/s sometimes, and the number of times that feature errors occur in phonetic contexts. Regardless, it is basically adequate for decisions about what features to train in the portion of children who tend to be consistent in their patterns of phoneme errors.

Feature Information and Therapy Planning Once feature-acquisition information is completed and data are available concerning substitution patterns and omission errors, phonological rule determinations can be accomplished by the clinician. A question of some importance is: When is a rule a rule? *Webster's New World Dictionary* (1978) defines this particular type of rule as "a valid generalization." If this dictionary definition is applied to the development of phonological rules based on feature analysis, what does it take to establish "a valid generalization"? Clearly, one would not think that a singular occurrence for the use of stops for fricatives, for example, that t/s would allow for a valid generalization that the rule is: articulate voiceless stops as voiceless fricatives. How many such occurrences within a class of sounds should occur before a phonological "rule" is established? Perhaps if there are five probabilities and three of the five show the same pattern, we have a simple majority and it spells "rule." From a statistical point of view, however, three out of a total of five is nonsignificant at the .05 level of confidence. The problem is unresolved and deserves attention if clinicians are going to increase their skill and spend more time uncovering the phonological disorders of children. In the interim, common sense suggests that a conservative approach be used prior to the announcement that phonological rules characterize the behaviors of some children.

If valid rules can be found to describe a child's phonological disorder, can these rules be used to make precise and efficacious therapy decisions? Compton (1970) has claimed that this is so, and he attempted to explain to his audience how two children were improved as a result of rule understanding. Unfortunately, Compton had no control group or other nonrule treatment group in his small investigation; therefore, we remain unsure about whether his decisions based upon phonological rules really were an effective way to go about the corrective process. We would like to believe that rule development or discovery will be a valuable therapy aid that many clinicians can master and use to assist them in the corrective process.

Under the condition that the clinician does not develop (or fails to locate in some children) valid phonological rules that show regularity but are deviantly used or inadequately used, what value is there in doing an analysis of the extent to which a child has acquired correct use of features? We need to address these issues carefully, since all require time and effort. It is also clear that much that has been attempted in the use of features to improve therapy has been based upon the concept of feature acquisition and the importance that correct feature use has in the total speech production process. Following is a review of some of the rationale for feature therapy and an exploration of some of the recommended approaches.

After the articulation testing has been completed, Pollack and Rees (1972) suggest that an analysis of the sample be used to supply answers to these questions:

1. Is a feature absent from the child's repertoire?
2. Does a feature appear in combination with one or more other features, but not in combination with a different feature?
3. Are all the features present, but inappropriately incorporated into the child's phonemic system depending on positional variables of the phoneme within a morpheme or word?
4. Are all the features important to a specific phoneme present in one phonetic context but absent in another?

Presumably answers to these questions may guide us in how to group and order features in therapy.

Guidelines presented by McReynolds and Engemann (1975) to assist the clinician in the selection of features to be trained are as follows:*

1. If feature error is twenty-five percent or less, the feature is thought to be established in the child's repertoire.
2. Features in error at the forty to fifty percent level probably reveal one or more patterns:
   (a) consistent use in some phonemes in which it is present, but not in others in which it is normally present
   (b) correct use of the feature in either the releasing or the arresting position in words (deep test), but not in both
   (c) use of the features in sometimes appropriate phonetic contexts and sometimes inappropriate
3. Inconsistent production of the feature can be seen in errors of approximately sixty-five percent. If the error is to this extent, the feature has not been stabilized; therefore, it should be considered for training.
4. If the feature errors are eighty percent or greater on any feature, it has not been acquired adequately. Errors of this magnitude deserve a high priority for training.

The above guidelines have been empirically developed; some definitive research to validate their use has yet to be accomplished. Other suggestions from McReynolds and Engemann state that a feature or features in error at the eighty percent level or greater should be given top priority for training. If no features are this severely affected, those at the level of fifty to sixty percent may be chosen for therapy. Further assertions are that the purpose of training is to stabilize features across phonemes in which they are missing, get the feature into word positions in which it is not used, and correct feature use in inappropriate context by exhibiting an appropriate context.

The major strategy in feature therapy, originally advanced by Mc-Reynolds and Bennett (1972), is to select a feature for training and then find a phoneme pair to train the feature contrast. The basic element of this contrast training is to get the child to produce two consonants that contrast the feature being trained, for example:

/t/ (− continuant) contrasted to: /s/ (+ continuant)

Thus, a target phoneme (here /s/, which possesses the (+) aspect of continuancy) is paired with a phoneme in which the other (−) aspect of the feature is produced. In this example two features are actually con-

---

* McReynolds, L.V. and K.L. Engemann. *Distinctive Feature Analysis of Misarticulation.* Baltimore: University Park Press, (1975) p. 103. Reprinted with permission.

trasted simultaneously, namely (+) and (−) continuancy and (+) and (−) stridency, a condition that might spur any generalization occurring across features in the target phoneme.

In their 1972 study McReynolds and Bennett found that by training +stridency in the context of /f/ they obtained generalization to some extent to /v/, /tʃ/, /s/, /z/. They used /θ/ as a control to see that only the feature being trained was changing during training. They reported that the degree of generalization was greatest in the /f/, /s/, and /tʃ/ phonemes. Also reported was some degree of generalization in the training of +voicing by contrasting /ba/ to /pa/ and in acquisition of +continuancy in the context /ʃ/. These investigators also suggested that the consistency of feature error be considered when choices are made as to which features to correct, and they additionally suggested that phonemes having only a few feature errors might be better choices for early intervention.

In a study of feature manipulation as an adjunct in articulation therapy Costello and Onstine (1976) also reported favorable results. They investigated the use of /s/ and /θ/ to teach a child the +continuancy aspect. This feature was only partially present in the child's repertoire. Again, contrasting as a technique was used with both /s/ and /θ/ contrasted with /t/, which is of course −continuancy. While they reported that posttherapy testing showed improvement for these treated phonemes, improvements were noted to be comparable or nearly so for untreated phonemes sharing the feature +continuancy in error. Costello and Onstine claimed that feature training was more efficient in number of required therapy hours because of the number of phonemes improved simultaneously, although this conclusion was unsupported by either control groups of untreated children or other experimental groups who received other approaches to therapy.

Popular Feature-Therapy Programs The program that was used in the McReynolds and Bennett experiment to determine if features generalize has been a model for others and perhaps can be considered a model one for feature-generalization therapy. Although it is available in the original source, a detailed presentation here may highlight aspects of therapy based on features. This program consisted of three elements in the typical operant paradigm fashion, namely, antecedent events, responses, and consequent events.

McReynolds and Bennett used two types of antecedent events consisting of a pair of nonsense pictures and a pair of verbal nonsense syllables. The nonsense pictures were black geometric line drawings on white posterboard. The nonsense syllables were either CV (consonant/vowel) or VC (vowel/consonant) syllables. Choices of vowels in the syllables were dependent upon the phase of the training, and four different vowels were used (/a/, /i/, /æ/, and /u/).

In their operant approach they also used two consequent events, both positive reinforcers:

1. tokens (marbles and chips)
2. verbal praise ("good," "that's right," "fine")

To reinforce a correct response a marble was dropped into a container. At the end of twenty training sets, the marbles in the container were removed and counted. If enough marbles were found to meet the criterion, the child was able to exchange them for a poker chip. The child was able to exchange poker chips for toy objects when enough of them were accumulated. Verbal praise was used along with the tokens in phase one of the training (FR–1 schedule), and this continued until later in the program at which time the schedule of reinforcement changes to the FR–3 type. In the final phase of training the verbal praise was discontinued but marbles were continued on an FR–3 schedule.

Their program contained three phases and a pretraining one used to get the child conditioned to the task. In the pretraining phase the child was taught the token system to point to easily identified pictures which were named by the clinician. (Pointing is used to eliminate the possibility of the clinician's reinforcing incorrect verbal responses.) A criterion level of eighteen to twenty correct pointing responses was established, and when the child reached this level of responding, he received a chip which could be exchanged at the token store.

Following successful pretraining, the training sessions were begun. In each session the child was presented with six sets of twenty trials. After each trial, the clinician totaled the number of correct and incorrect responses and recorded it on a data sheet. At the end of each set, the number of correct responses was converted to a percentage correct score and also recorded on the data sheet. This tabulation allowed the clinician to know whether the criterion level had been reached and to present the child with a chip if the level had been achieved. In the event that the criterion level had not been achieved, the set was repeated prior to moving ahead in the program.

Since this program stressed generalization, it was designed to test for this phenomenon. Under the condition of using an FR–1 schedule of reinforcement, transfer could not be tested until the end of the twenty trial set. But when the FR–3 schedule was used, transfer was tested, because, as McReynolds and Bennett pointed out, if the subject receives feedback on the accuracy of his response, he is being trained and not tested.

In their program there also was a probe, the McDonald Deep Test, the purpose of which was to check for transfer of phonemes in nonsense syllables to words. Also evaluated using this instrument was correction of untrained phonemes for evidence of feature generalization.

The program described above was established in three phases:

> *Phase One.* In this phase the child learned to produce either the (+) or (−) aspect of the feature in the context of a phoneme. For example, if a child lacked the feature of (+) stridency, he would receive training on /s/ since this phoneme contains the (+) feature. As McReynolds and Bennett indicated (and as is very obvious), one cannot train a feature except in the context of a phoneme. Therefore, to manipulate features one needs to manipulate phonemes, which is why the strategy of contrasting phonemes is most often used to train features.
>
> *Phase Two* Nonsense syllables were used, and the child was taught to produce the feature in a phoneme in the initial (arresting) position.
>
> *Phase Three* Nonsense syllables were used, and the child was taught to produce the feature in a phoneme in the final (arresting) position.

To show examples of therapy procedures within phases the following was presented:

Phase One

The first step in phase one consisted of the clinician's holding up the appropriate picture and saying, "say /s/." If a correct /s/ was made by the child, a marble was dropped into the container. If the /s/ production was incorrect, the clinician put the picture down, waited ten seconds, then repeated the stimulus presentation. When the twenty trials were over, the clinician counted the marbles and informed the child whether he had earned enough to get a chip, after which a new set was begun until six sets of twenty trials were completed. Subsequently the child could trade in the chips for toys.

In the second step of phase one, the child continued to imitate the clinician, but reinforcement was changed from FR–1 to FR–3. The criterion for success was the same as in step one (ninety percent), but to receive a chip the child needed only pay with six marbles.

In the third step of phase one the child was required to perform spontaneous productions of the target sound. This was accomplished as the clinician held up the nonsense picture and asked "What is this?" Again, if a correct response was made, the child received one marble. Verbal praise was now discontinued. To advance to the next step, the child had to meet or exceed the criterion level of ninety percent on two sets of trials.

The only difference between step three and step four of phase one was that the FR–1 schedule was discontinued and marbles were awarded on an FR–3 schedule. The criterion level was now set at ninety percent for three consecutive sets of twenty trials.

When the criterion level of step four was achieved, the materials were removed; and the clinician administered the McDonald Deep Test to probe for generalization. As noted earlier, two types of generalization were studied. If generalization probing shows transfer to eighty percent or more of the items in all test phonemes, training for the feature can be discontinued; but McReynolds and Bennett reported this degree of generalization to be very uncommon.

Phase Two

In this phase the child received experience with both the (+) and (−) aspects of the feature. This was accomplished by having the clinician hold up one of the pictures, produce the CV nonsense syllable associated with the picture, and wait for the child to imitate her production. Training continued from imitation to spontaneous production. The schedule followed the pattern of beginning with FR−1 and moving to FR−3, and the major difference in this phase was the requirement that the child correctly produce two phonemes. A probe for transfer used generalization items which were readministered. Steps are repeated using additional syllables containing different vowels but the same target phoneme if the eighty percent criterion level is not met.

Phase Three

This was the same as phase two, except the emphasis was on correct production of the VC nonsense syllable. A new phoneme pair was introduced for contrasting in the event that the feature had not generalized after the four vowel contexts had been trained in both the initiating and arresting positions. For example, in the different pairs with (+) stridency, /s/ and /z/ might have been used, and the same procedure was followed in training the second pair as in training the first pair.

In summary the operant, distinctive-feature program reported by McReynolds and Bennett systematically used speech-production activities with little or no auditory, sound-discrimination learning as its vehicle for contrasting phonemes. Feature differences were highlighted and then tested systematically to determine if one or both of two related types of response generalization had taken place.

Although based on case study information, the reported results of such a program have been thought by some to be good evidence that phonemes can be corrected effectively and efficiently if training is designed to stimulate feature generalization, while others perhaps continue to wonder whether many features can generalize without the entire bundle of features being affected, resulting in sound generalization and a correct form.

The McReynolds and Bennett program was advanced by Costello (1975) to allow for inclusion of the new phonemes into spontaneous, conversational speech. Furthermore, the authors included branching steps needed at times for reluctant learners. They also advocated the use of thirty-minute therapy sessions four days weekly. A breakdown of their recommended program and its constituent parts consisted of

PHASE	RESPONSE REQUIREMENTS
1	*Goal:* Target phonemes in isolation *Mode:* Imitative and spontaneous
2	*Goal:* Target phonemes in releasing position, NNS *Mode:* Imitative
3	*Goal:* Target phonemes in arresting position, NNS *Mode:* Imitative
4	*Goal:* Target phonemes in releasing position, words *Mode:* Imitative and spontaneous
5	*Goal:* Target phonemes in arresting position, words *Mode:* Imitative and spontaneous
6	*Goal:* Target phonemes in releasing and arresting positions, words in phrases *Mode:* Imitative and spontaneous
7	*Goal:* Target phonemes in releasing and arresting positions, words in sentences *Mode:* Imitative and spontaneous
8	*Goal:* Target phonemes in releasing and arresting positions, words in story form *Mode:* Delayed echoic
9	*Goal:* Target phonemes in releasing and arresting positions, words *Mode:* Spontaneous, conversational speech

Since the carryover stage has been considered by many experienced speech clinicians as the most difficult one to achieve, a program that advances the generalization phenomenon further toward the terminal phase seems most valuable. In phase nine of Costello and her colleagues' program one would still be concerned about the use of the corrected phonemes in spontaneous, conversational speech within the child's habitual environment be it the clinicial setting, the home, or the school; and few articulation-therapy programs spell out these final steps that are required for some portion of the speech defectives to gain final and total correction.

Some of the principles of feature programs were applied in an attempt to improve the articulation of retarded children by Mayberry and Nissen (1974). Nine mentally retarded girls with a mean age of sixteen years and mean IQs of thirty-six served as subjects. Three were untreated controls, three received a more traditional whole-phoneme approach, and three served as the feature group, who received special training to acquire the continuant, voice, strident, high, and anterior features from the Chomsky and Halle 1968 system. Subjects received twelve consecutive days of group therapy for periods of fifty minutes. The selected target phonemes were /ʃ, tʃ, θ, ð/.

The authors described their therapy for both the traditional, whole-phoneme approach and the feature-group approach as a modified "stimulus shift" method in which each step alternated between echoic and nonechoic responding. In the echoic stage a picture was paired with the clinician's model. In the nonechoic stage the same picture served as a stimulus to evoke the correct phonemic response from the subject. Beginning with the target sound's production in isolation, work continued to production in the initial and final positions in words, then on to the production of these words in carrier phrases. Before therapy began, subjects were introduced to training words, five in which the target phoneme was in the initial position and five in which it occurred in the final position. These same ten words were used throughout all the therapy stages.

The described procedures were essentially the same for both experimental groups; the basic difference was that the whole-phoneme group members were taught each target phoneme separately following each of the stages. The feature-group members, on the other hand, were taught the selected features and then all of the target phonemes together at each stage. An operant-oriented paradigm was used with the criterion for proceeding to the following stage set as eighteen to twenty correct responses or ninety percent.

Although some of the details specifying exactly how the phonemes were taught together at each stage for feature-group subjects were not described in the original work, some information concerning how the five features were trained is available. For example, presence or absence of the voicing, continuant, and strident features was paired with pictures and the vowel /a/. If voicing was a target feature, the subject learned that when the vowel /a/ was prolonged, the (j) voicing target sound preceding was voiced, for example, /ja/. When the vowel was of short duration (or even normal duration apparently), the subject learned that the preceding target phoneme was voiceless, for example, /ʃi/. In a related way, auditory and visual cues were used to teach these three subjects the nature of the continuancy and stridency features. For the features of high and anterior, pictures were used to show the location as well as the clinician's demonstration of tongue positions characteristic of these features.

For subjects in both experimental groups, verbal praise was used as reinforcement. FR–1 was given during the first session and then on an intermittent schedule for the remaining nine sessions.

The three subjects who received the whole-phoneme therapy received no special-feature training, and the sequence of training for them was one phoneme at a time. For this group, therapy began with /ʃ/, which was presented in isolation to be imitated as its production by the clinician was accompanied by a point cue—clinician pointed to her mouth then to the subject's. The second stage consisted of training to the criterion level eliminating the clinician's model. Imitated correct production of /ʃ/ in the initial position of the five training words paired with their pictures comprised the third stage. Finally, in the fourth stage, the clinician's model was discontinued, and the subject was required to respond correctly to the picture stimulus.

The results of the Mayberry and Nissen experiment, while hardly conclusive, indicated that the untreated control subjects did not improve their articulation of the target phonemes over the span of the study. Changes occurred in the three whole-phoneme group subjects, and changes occurred in the three-feature group subjects to a greater extent; but the differences between the improvement in the two groups failed to reach the .05 level of statistical significance. When viewed in terms of generalization, all subjects in the two therapy groups correctly articulated a mean of 7.5 previously misarticulated phonemes in various positions in words used in the Fisher–Logemann Test of Articulation Competence. Thus, no generalization to untreated phonemes could be credited to the feature-training group approach compared with the more traditional, whole-phoneme one.

Other Feature Approaches In a test of the ability of features to generalize Rossetti (1979) constructed and administered a program to twenty-four children, twelve in each of two age groups. The younger age group consisted of children aged four years, six months to five years, six months, and the older children were aged six years, six months to seven years, six months. All had articulatory errors but normal hearing and normal-range oral/peripheral speech structures. Subjects were given the Photo Articulation Test (1955) and a feature analysis using the Miller and Nicely system (1956). The sixteen consonants that can be analyzed using this early system were studied. (The Miller and Nicely system was capable of analyzing only sixteen consonants and consisted of five features: voicing, nasality, duration, affrication, and place; it could not accommodate laterals, semivowels, and some other classes of sounds.)

Rossetti's study was of basic interest since he was attempting to see if speech stimulation using the minimal, distinctive-feature contrast principle could be capable of making significant improvements in children's use of features. But the thrust of his effort was different: He wanted to see if features, using the five-feature system of Miller and Nicely, could be trained to a ninety percent criterion level and then reflect the results of this training by a significant reduction in feature confusions on features not included in his training program.

To accomplish his purposes Rossetti trained the place and affrication features and measured the generalization effects to the voice, duration, and nasality features of the system. He devised a training program which consisted of minimal-pair items for each subject. Subjects were expected to produce a randomly chosen member of each minimal pair at a ninety percent level of performance for each of three presentation modes. In the first mode a clinician produced the contrast pair followed by a subject; the second mode consisted of the clinician/subject production ratio of three to one, and the third mode a five to one ratio. The minimal-pair items used to train each of the two features are portrayed as follows:

FEATURE	MINIMAL PAIR ITEMS TRAINED		
Place	Sack–shack	thin–fin	date–gate
Affrication	bat–vat	tick–thick	the–"D"

After the subjects evidenced ninety percent correct production rates for these minimal pairs in each feature category for all three modes, the investigator administered the Photo Articulation Test as a post measure, and he reevaluated their feature use. His results reflected significant reductions in confusion for both the younger and older subjects in voice and duration errors when only the features of place and affrication were subjected to training. (Errors on nasality were too infrequent to show significant reductions from *pre* to *post*). The results of this unique experiment reflect that speech stimulation and the perceptual/production contrasts of speech sounds lend themselves to a type of generalization with children of the type studied. It seems likely that many had promising stimulability scores on many of these defective phonemes studied, as well as some degree of inconsistency of phonemic errors; important details of this type are missing from this study and make its provoking findings somewhat limited in their own generalizability.

An enterprising approach to failure training with a dysfluent child was presented by Weisberg (1973). Some portion of dysfluent children have been observed to reflect deviant or delayed articulatory development, and Weisberg's orientation was to improve articulation and hope that the dysfluent speech problems will disappear (an old idea with senior speech pathologists, but certainly never put under good scientific scrutiny). To accomplish this feat she evaluated a five-year old girl at a college speech clinic who had a history of convulsive episodes, "stuttering behaviors," unintelligible speech, and slow language and motor development compared with her two siblings. A distinctive-feature analysis employing procedures detailed by Compton was applied to the results of the Hejna

Articulation Test and recorded samples of spontaneous speech. This analysis showed that the child did not use fricatives, affricatives, and sibilant phonemes, thus losing the +continuant feature.

Therapy decisions included the choice of /f/, since it was considered normally developed at age five and easily imitated and it contained the +continuant feature. The consistency of correct production of /f/ was found to be three percent using the McDonald Deep Test. The following is a basic description that Weisberg followed to train features and thus help correct the defective phonology. This is presented in considerable detail since techniques and procedures for the use of feature training are often not delineated in detail and often resemble those of traditional approaches to remediation.

According to Weisberg, the subject was instructed to produce a "long" continuant sound, which was /a/, /i/, or /m/. At the same time, she was moving a toy car on the table. Then she was instructed to produce "short," interrupted sounds, such as /b/, /p/, or /k/, as she moved the toy car on the table. The clinician manipulated a small, rubber policeman which directed the movement of the toy car under each condition of "long" or "short," and the subject learned to continue to produce the sound until the policeman raised his hand to signal "stop." The subject was then reinforced for each correct response of both vocalizing the continuant sound and moving the toy car appropriately following the policeman's signal.

In a related training activity a small, furry, windup toy dog with a wagging tail was used to teach the feature. This toy dog danced and moved his tail when wound, and the clinician controlled him by holding his tail firmly. The child, told to produce short and long sounds, learned that the dog stopped dancing when an interrupted sound was produced but continued when a long sound was produced. The child was reinforced for each of her correct vocalizations to keep the toy dancing.

In the next stage the child was instructed to produce the target phoneme, /f/, and it was now used in contrasting exercises. After mastery of this phoneme's production at the ninety percent level, the therapy advanced to the next stage.

In this stage the clinician introduced a procedure involving the use of index cards having line drawings which represented words that contained the target phoneme in either initial or final position, thus creating a series of different nonsense compound words, for example, leaf/fish, puff/face, root/feet, tough/phone. Pairing of words beginning with /f/ with words ending with /f/ was accomplished because the clinician had found this to be a facilitating phonetic context. The child was instructed to imitate the clinician's production of the nonsense compound words as the pairs of cards were presented. To help the child "feel" the target phoneme, visual, kinesthetic, and tactile cues were used during this stage.

After successfully accomplishing the above set of procedures using the cards, the child was instructed to produce the compound words without imitation. Once this was accomplished, the nonsense compound words were separated into single, meaningful words; thus, the child could produce /f/ without imitation in the initial and final positions.

In the final stage the subject was presented with utterances containing many /f/ and /v/ phonemes and asked to imitate them. This was followed by a procedure that consisted of asking the child a series of questions requiring responses containing /f/ and /v/ to get spontaneous responding in a conversational mode.

After about eight weeks of therapy Weisberg reported that /f/ had stabilized in the initial position and was often produced correctly in the medial position. The child's stuttering blocks had decreased to a large extent. Furthermore, /v/ was reported to be emerging in her spontaneous speech without any specific training.

Six weeks later (a period of no therapy) no stuttering was present. Her target sound /f/ needed some work to stabilize production in the final position. The feature + continuant was found to generalize to /v/ and also to /θ/ and /ʃ/. Weisberg concluded that the distinctive-feature approach was highly efficient with this five-year old girl.

○OTHER LINGUISTIC APPROACHES

Unlike approaches to articulatory remediation developed by speech pathologists, the ideas of linguists concerning teaching correct phonology stress the use of words not sounds in isolation or syllables. Some descriptions of phonological corrective techniques will include the teaching of phonemes to establish contrasts needed for further development (Haas, 1963; Ingram, 1976), while others ignore them completely.

Careful study of the word processing of young, severely defective children is recommended by Ingram (1976) who states that two types of word analysis may be required: 1) study of processes in operation, and 2) use of homonyms. The third aspect of study he recommends consists of an analysis of the accuracy of use of individual phoneme (linguists call phonemes "segments" at times), since a lack of phonemes of specific types cause the child's phonological contrasts to be weakened. To obtain his data for analysis Ingram would phonetically transcribe portions of the child's utterances—an approach that is characteristic of all linguists who have written material related to analysis and correction.

One of the goals advanced by Ingram (1976) is to stabilize the young child's speech. This relates to reduction or elimination of the different forms of processing errors that the child produces, for example, labial assimilations, syllable deletions. He advocates the careful identification of these errors, picking a target processing error and reinforcing its presence while ignoring other types of errors used for the same word. Presumably, the child will learn to produce only one form of process which then makes its removal over time easier to accomplish.

A second goal established by Ingram (1976) is to eliminate homonyms if, indeed, the child uses them to represent certain words or classes of words, like nouns. Most clinicians have faced the problem of "breaking the code" that some young, severely impaired children use to simplify their communication, but this problem is rather rare in most older articulatory defectives. To eliminate what is troublesome, Ingram would teach the child to make distinctions. By selection of processes to be eliminated one at a time, Ingram provides the distinctions needed to destroy the widespread use of homonyms. As can be seen in this branching network, the young child's use of [dado] for butter, ladder, letter, spider, water, and whistle is systematically modified through teaching. In particular, the processes of alveolar assimilation, glide stopping, and vowel neutralization are eliminated while concurrently the use of the homonym [dado] is also eliminated. (See Fig. 4–2.) This clever tactic which incorporates two factors to gain correction seems to show a high degree of usefulness for children of the type described by Ingram.

The third therapy goal also involves the use of a wide variety of words to teach phonemic contrasts. Ingram would analyze utterances to locate which consonants and vowels are in the child's repertoire and view these, as Haas (1963) suggested, by place of articulation. To establish a basic set

FIGURE 4–2 An example of the Selection Processes for Elimination of Homonyms. (From R. Ingram, *Phonological Disorders in Children*, New York: Edward Arnold Publishers, 1976. Reprinted by permission.)

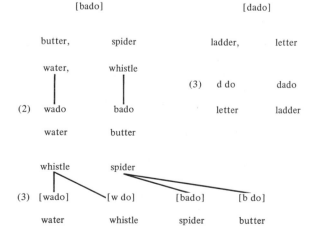
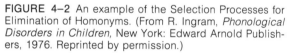

of consonants Ingram evaluates the labial, alveolar, palatal, velar, and glottal contrasts used by the child seeking the presence or absence of place contrasts. The relationships between place of articulation, processes, and class of error (glides, fricatives, etc.) are considered in order to pick targets for contrast training.

Contrasting was the basic technique involved in the feature approaches to articulation therapy that we reviewed earlier. Unlike Weber (1970), for example, who used contrasting across patterns of feature errors and used sounds in isolation, syllables, and words as training stimuli, Ingram would apparently teach all contrasts in word form. The speech–language clinician might use other techniques, such as phoneme-discrimination training (Weber, 1970; Winitz, 1975) and the method of approximations or phonetic placement to speed the correct acquisition of the target phonemes, while doing therapy in which contrasting was the principal method. (Interestingly, the inclusion of these traditional "tools" of articulation therapy in the published, operant programs is virtually nonexistent except for Weber's mention of phoneme-discrimination training.)

semantic approaches

One of the earliest advocates of meaning as a basic tool in the articulatory-corrective process was Cooper (1968) in his *Method of Meaningful Minimal Contrasts*. Citing evidence, such as results from the Grey and Stunden (1961) study, in which phonetic discrimination of speech-impaired and normal children was enhanced when the meaningfulness of the stimuli was increased, Cooper provided a convincing argument for the use of meaning in articulation therapy. The crux of his thinking is as follows:

> Such evidence suggests a new methodological approach to articulation therapies in which meaning is used as a variable. *Meaning* is here defined operationally as the conditioning of a referent to an utterance so the subject will reliably point to the referent with the utterance as a stimulus. In general, the method is based on the principle that in paired contrasts of the articulations of defective and standard utterances of words where the defective utterance is conditioned to a new meaning, children will tend to alter the articulation of the defective utterance.*

In further discussion of the role of meaning in phonological acquisition Cooper emphasized that a child's language develops from a dynamic process that involves increasing differentiation of utterances in the context

---

* R. Cooper, "The Method of Meaningful Minimal Contrasts in Functional, Articulation Problems," *Journal Speech Hearing Association* 10, 17–22 (1968). Reprinted by permission.

of increasing differentiation of events. He went on to explain:

> However, I believe, the impetus to word differentiation lies in the child's
> compulsion to use different words for different events when these are
> perceived as different. A child will thus utter the words for *mother* and
> *father* in a way that both distinguishes between these two noble creatures
> as well as approximates the articulation for the words used in his
> environment. At first gross sound differentiations are made by the child
> with gradual demand for finer discriminations as the number of words
> in his vocabulary increases. These discriminations appear to arise out of
> two kinds of pressure: the need for linguistic differentiation and the need
> to conform to social requirements. An example of the linguistic need is
> the minimal contrast found in the words /kæt/ and /æt/. An example of
> the social need is the rejection of /kæ/ or /tæ/ as a substitute for /kæt/.*

Implementation of the Method of Meaningful Minimal Contrasts requires that the clinician study the child's utterances to locate targets. After
choosing a target word (which is usually a noun), the clinician then
fabricates a nonword to represent it and associates the *nonword* with a
picture or an object. The next step consists of teaching the child an
imaginary set of concepts related to the nonword, for example, "This is
/tæt/. You can build a castle with it." Thus, various meaningful associations
are used to contrast the correct form of the word with the nonword. For
example, using a toy cat the clinician might say "This is a cat." "You can
give milk to the cat." Contrasting continues until the clinician knows that
the child has a clear distinction between the nonword and the target word,
after which the child may self-correct the t/k substitution in the word "cat."
If a direct attack on the defective phoneme does not occur, the clinician
may have to resort to phonetic-placement techniques to get production.
Cooper has said that after one paradigmatic pair is taught successfully,
others may be entered into therapy, and the child may progress at a faster
rate across them. He maintained that his method is more efficient than
other methods for younger children who have omission and substitution
errors, is less boring for them, and is a more natural way of learning
language since it does not require mechanical, tiresome drills and does
use the natural conceptualization process to accomplish its goal of
correcting defective articulation.

Another heavily semantic-oriented approach, quite different from the
Method of Meaningful Minimal Contrasts of Cooper, has been described by
Hillard and Geopfert (1979). The notion of using meaning in articulation
therapy is hardly new. One of the tenets of the Backus and Beasley
approach to group speech therapy was to use words commonly needed by
individuals within their groups as practice items. This, with amplification,
is the thrust of Hillard and Geopfert's *The Semantically Potent Word Approach*.

* Ibid.

This method is multiphonemic in nature. Basic to it is the belief that if one can gather for individuals functionally useful words, words which are "semantically potent," therapy for articulation defects will be more effective and efficient. Presumably, semantically potent words will reflect personal needs, motivations, and interests; and since they will be used to a greater extent than other words, phonemes correctly articulated in them in practice will have more opportunities to be used in the same meaningful, phonetic contexts. Thus, a core of training words is used to practice articulation, and the authors point out that each misarticulated phoneme is taught so that whole-word accuracy is achieved.

To select semantically potent words clinicians observe carefully the words used during play and in verbal interaction with others. Words can also be provided by teachers and parents. Words are then categorized into twelve groups:

1. *protection words,* for example, don't, stop, help;
2. *bathroom words,* for example, bathroom, wash, brush;
3. *location words,* for example, there, this, that, here;
4. *emotion words,* for example, love, mad, like;
5. *attention words,* for example, look, watch, hey;
6. *personal words,* for example, child's name, age, boy/girl;
7. *action words,* for example, go, run, push;
8. *preschool words,* for example, juice, play, scissors;
9. *refusal acceptance words,* for example, no, yes, more;
10. *social words,* for example, please, thank you, okay;
11. *family words,* for example, sister/brother, pet's names, favorite foods;
12. *words parents request,* for example, refrigerator, crying, cereal, school, etc.

The program presented by Hillard and Goepfert is basically operant. It begins by the clinician's selection of five words from each child's core of words, and a pictorial representation is made for each of them. In a stage called "relating part to whole" the clinician presents the child with each picture and discusses what it is that the picture represents; conditions under which the child has used the word, including where, when, and persons with whom the child might be speaking; and the child's idea of why this word is important. The child's life experiences comprise a common core of interest throughout the program.

Using a method of imitation, the clinician teaches each of the five semantically potent words in three steps:

1. One phoneme in each word is selected for training.

2. A picture is placed in front of the child, and the clinician might say, "I'm listening for /d/, say 'don't'."
3. Under the condition that the child is not successful with imitating the target sound in the word, alternative strategies can be followed:
   a. imitation of the sound in isolation and instruction on placement of the articulators
   b. imitation of the target phoneme at the word level before proceeding to the next core word

Rules are now used to make decisions concerning therapy practices. Using a reinforcement schedule (FR–1) and an echoic method, the child is required to produce eighty percent of the target phoneme in two consecutive training sessions under two conditions used to formulate new decisions:

1. If no other misarticulations are in the target word and the target phoneme reaches or exceeds the eighty percent correct-production criterion, either advance to nonimitative word training for the corrected word or start a new word into imitative word training.
2. Under the condition of having other misarticulations in the target word and having the target phoneme reaching criterion, begin instruction on each of the remaining phonemes in the word in a singular fashion and following the above procedure.

In the "nonimitative word training" stage the clinician begins by discussing with the child his or her ability to say the target words which are at this level of training. This is followed by three steps:

1. A FR–2 schedule is used, and the clinician explains to the child how it will operate.
2. The clinician places a picture in front of the child and asks the child to name it.
3. If an inaccurate articulation of the target word occurs, the clinician says to the child, "Say it your new way." If the response is incorrectly produced again, the child is instructed to imitate the clinician's production of the word.

When the criterion of ninety-five percent whole-word accuracy is realized during one training session, the child advances to the "sentence-imitation level" for this target word.

At the sentence imitation level pictorial clues are eliminated, the schedule of reinforcement moves to FR–3, and the clinician requests that the child repeat a sentence containing the target word. (The authors caution that the sentence be relevant to the child's world.) The criterion at the sentence-imitation level is one hundred percent correct production in two consecutive training sessions. After attaining this level, the child is encouraged to take the picture of the target word home.

The last stage, "retell story," is designed to reinforce the child's use of a target phoneme in words other than the semantically potent ones used in therapy. Four steps are recommended:

1. One phoneme is chosen by the clinician who instructs the child to try and use it correctly in the retelling of a story.
2. The child is informed that other words contain the same sound as in the semantically potent word.
3. The child is told that he will hear a story told by the clinician which will contain words having the target sound. As the clinician tells the story to the child, she/he places a chip on the picture containing the target sound.
4. The clinician now asks the child to retell the story. The chip on the picture corresponding to the target sound is earned by the child if the word is articulated correctly.

When the child demonstrates the ability for ninety-five percent correct phoneme production in one story retold on two consecutive days, the criterion has been reached, and the emphasis in therapy shifts to a different phoneme in the stories.

Hillard and Goepfert did not provide controlled experimental evidence for the effectiveness of their approach. However, they did cite pre- and post-therapy phonemic error scores for five children ranging in age from three to five, who attended a university speech and hearing center. Phonemic error scores were gathered using the retelling of stories technique which, unfortunately, was not as successful in getting spontaneous speech from the subjects as the investigators had hoped, and they found it necessary to have the children imitate short segments. Thus, "the assessment was more imitative than spontaneous."

Their five subjects received two hours of individual therapy for ten weeks. Little information was provided to assist us in making better judgments of their Semantically Potent Word Approach applied to the subjects' phonological disorders, such as, feature use, processing errors, and rule structures or to their phonetic abilities, such as, stimulability scores for defective phonemes. Twenty hours of individual articulation therapy accomplished differently may have resulted in comparable or greater improvements than these investigators reported. Again, while the idea of using words from a child's personal environment is hardly new, the approach does have a pronounced emphasis on meaning and sets of procedures.

the wedge approach

The author's Wedge Approach to articulation therapy, which has been described elsewhere (Sommers and Kane, 1974), has been further tested and refined. A number of preschool children having severe articulation disorders have been subjected to this approach in a university speech clinic over the past eight years, and these experiences have resulted in modifications. The approach is not basically linguistic; rather, it represents an effort to use distinctive-feature and phonological-rule concepts with more phonetic, research-tested measures of speech, namely, consistency of misarticulation and stimulability performances, to develop a multisound (or phoneme if you prefer) approach to therapy, which is basically accomplished in an operant model of learning. Research evidence to show the efficacy of using trained parents (largely mothers) to assist in the corrective process for articulation disorders (Fudala et al., 1972, Sommers, 1962) is also supportive of the Wedge Approach for its inclusion of mothers (and maybe fathers?) to strengthen the method in all stages of therapy—not just in the carryover stage in which many early authorities claimed parents can be helpful adjuncts in the therapeutic process for articulation disorders.

The older notion that articulation therapy should proceed one sound at a time while dying slowly, was first challenged by the Wedge Approach, which the author has used and taught to former staff members (school clinicians) for many years. The sound and feature generalization studies now seem highly supportive of the fact that many children's misarticulations are rule-governed events with clusters or patterns of perhaps confusions characterizing their existence. Thus, in some cases at least, a type of confusion matrix may best represent what some children do to attempt to communicate. An understanding of the exact nature of these events and the skills of the child to cope with them plus the assistance of parents in the process may be the most productive way to gain correction. The Wedge Approach, no panacea, is intended to take into account these relevant variables and plan a continuous approach to therapy: it is not a special set of different therapy techniques; it is an approach.

The Wedge Approach will be illustrated in a clinical example. Principles underlying the choices made will be explained as we go along. We will show in some detail how specific information is gathered concerning our subject's stimulability performances and his pattern of distinctive-feature acquisition and use. The Screening Deep Test of Articulation will yield his percentages of consistency of error, and it will be administered and scored in the normal manner. As we plan therapy for Jack, aged five, who has a pattern of delayed articulatory development, we will attempt to weigh the value and impact of stimulability and consistency measures, feature acquisition and use, and any phonological rules that are operating to maintain his defectiveness. We will also cast our therapy in an operant model, determine the need for a probe of auditory, sound-discrimination training, and use a variety of production techniques as required to advance the child's skills. Since many clinicians are not conversant with how stimulability scores are gained (particularly on the noncommercial Carter–Buck Prognostic Test, which has been the basis for the research showing the predictive validity of this factor), an example and description of how to do this is included. Likewise, we will work some examples of a short-cut method of distinctive feature analysis devised by the author. Stimulability testing can be accomplished reliably (Miller, 1978) and fairly rapidly; and, with practice, the time required to complete a reliable feature analysis can also be reduced.

Stimulability Assessment To obtain stimulability scores on a child's misarticulations, the Carter–Buck Prognostic Articulation Test (Carter & Buck, 1958) is administered. All that is required to complete this testing is a set of nine pictures, three testing sounds in each position in words— the initial, medial, and final—, and the record form.

The first step in the assessment is to get measures of the extent to which the child misarticulates a sound in each position. This is traditional, spontaneous, picture-articulation testing. If the child has difficulty identifying the picture, leading questions can be asked to elicit a response. It is imperative that the tester not give the child the word to imitate since this procedure would invalidate this portion of the test. Errors can be recorded on the record form as substitutions, distortions, or omissions; however, in stimulability testing the only thing of importance is whether the sound is misarticulated.

In the second step, the clinician tests each of the sounds in error on the spontaneous picture test in the positions in which it was misarticulated. Thus, if a child misarticulated /s/ in all three medial positions and in all three final positions on the spontaneous portion of the test, only these contexts would be tested on the imitation-of-nonsense-syllable portion.

TABLE 4–4
Part 1. Spontaneous-Picture Portion

	INITIAL				MEDIAL				FINAL		
	Sub.	*Dis.*	*Omm.*		*Sub.*	*Dis.*	*Omm.*		*Sub.*	*Dis.*	*Omm.*
santa	X			ice cream	X			house			X
saw	X			bicycle	X			horse			X
soap	X			gas station	X			bus			X

TABLE 4–4, Cont.
Part 2. Nonsense-Syllable Imitation

	INITIAL				MEDIAL				FINAL		
	Sub.	*Dis.*	*Omm.*		*Sub.*	*Dis.*	*Omm.*		*Sub.*	*Dis.*	*Omm.*
si	X			isi	X			is				X
s				s	X			s			
sa				asa	X			s				X

The child must be given explicit instructions when taking the nonsense-syllable portion of the test. The instruction is usually, "Tommy, look at me and listen very carefully to what I say and then you say it just like mine." This structure is important in order to get the best possible imitative performance from the child.

Just as each picture was given only once with no feedback from the tester on the accuracy of the child's response, so in the nonsense-syllable imitation each syllable is said once for the child, and the child responds only once to each stimulus. Scoring the errors as substitutions, distortions, and omissions is permissible but not of any particular value. The important thing to remember is that to be scored "correct," the response must be absolutely correct.

An example of the scoring for the testing of one sound, /s/, is given in Table 4–4.

The following simple procedures allow for a computation of the stimulability percentage for each sound tested and also for the child's average performance across all of his defective sounds. The scoring steps to compute the stimulability percentage for any sound are:

1. Determine the total number of errors on the picture test (maximum is nine).
2. Determine the total number of errors on the nonsense syllables for the sound tested (maximum is nine).
3. Subtract the number of nonsense-syllable errors from the number of errors on the picture portion and divide this number by the total number of errors on the picture test.

For our example of the child tested for /s/ stimulability we see:

SPONTANEOUS PICTURE ERRORS	NONSENSE SYLLABLE ERRORS	DIFFERENCE
9	6	3

Stimulability Percentage for /s/ = ⅜ or 33.3%

Generally, stimulability scores across phonemes are averaged, and this statistic comprises an index which may be useful for case selection. Depending on the age of the child and the particular research report considered, a "low" percentage score ranges from zero to twenty-five, and a "moderately low" one from twenty-five to forty percent. Scores of these magnitudes have been found to indicate need for articulation therapy. Scores of sixty percent or greater are usually considered favorable signs that articulation therapy may not be necessary or that if the sounds are entered into therapy, they may be amenable to rapid, initial improvements (Carter and Buck, 1958; Sommers et al., 1967).

Feature Analysis The basic, shortcut procedures in this method are related to two major economies. First, the long method of McReynolds and Engemann feature analysis specifies that the clinician must deep test all consonants to insure that a thorough assessment is made of feature use. The author does not feel that this very time-consuming effort is often justified, and, indeed, the correspondence between deep-test scores and actual misarticulations in children's connected, spontaneous speech is suspect. We have found with four-, five-, and six-year olds (Sommers, Milikich, and Savage, 1980) that ten minutes of conversational speech in which the child does most of the talking tends to show excellent identification of many phoneme errors, and phonemes not heard to be in error are almost never found misarticulated on a deep test of articulation. Phonemes of low frequency of occurrence in children's speech, such as /v/, /θ/ and some others, may require a storytelling approach or some type of picture articulation testing to insure that they are not misarticulated to supplement the conversation speech sample. The ten minutes used to obtain this sample and any other probing required on infrequently produced phonemes appear to shorten the feature analysis by an hour or more on the average, and our data show the results to be highly comparable when the long method and the shortcut system are compared.

The second area of savings is in time and paper. Only the form presented in the example below is actually required to make the determinations of feature acquisition for the twelve-feature Chomsky and Halle 1968 system. Since few errors occur on many features for numbers of young children having multiple misarticulations, some feature determinations can be made in less than three to four minutes. We will now see how this shortcut system works to give us acquisition data.

To complete the analysis we need to use the Chomsky and Halle 1968 feature chart found in Chapter One. It is obvious looking at the substitutions for the error sounds that two features badly in error are +strident and +continuancy; but there will be others, and anytime there are omissions of phonemes we will suffer some feature loss across all those in the bundle that comprises the error phoneme. We could begin by taking

TABLE 4–5
Short-Cut Method of Feature Analysis

Example: Four-year old male. A good spontaneous speech sample showed a large number of errors but only on sibilants.

SCREENING DEEP TEST POSITIONS

Error Sounds	Initiating Position	Errors	Arresting Position	Errors	Total Number of Phonetic Contexts in Error
/s/	/t/	10	/t/	10	20
/z/	/d/	10	/d/	10	20
/ʃ/	/t/	5	omission	5	10
/tʃ/	/t/	10	/t/	2	14
			omission	2	
/dʒ/	/d/	8	omission	5	13
/j/	/d/	5	omission	10	15
/ʒ/	/d/	10	/d/	5	15
			Total =		107

the first feature from the system, the vocalic one, and compute its (+) and (−) components doing all twelve features (+) and (−) until we finish with (+) and (−) coronal.

For illustrative purposes we will do one quickly that is only in error because of omissions. While feature use is one hundred percent for both (+) and (−) vocalic since all error sounds are consonants, feature use for (+) and (−) consonantal will be slightly reduced by errors of omissions. All of the error phonemes are (+) consonantal except /j/ which is (−) consonantal. We will now compute the percentage of correct feature use for the (+) consonantal component. The tabled data show that there was a loss of five phonetic contexts on /ʃ/ due to omissions in the arresting position, two on /tʃ/ in the arresting position, and five on /dʒ/ in the arresting position. Total loss due to omissions, therefore, is twelve contexts. The possible number using the Deep Screening Test would be twenty-one phonemes with the (+) consonantal feature × twenty contexts for each phoneme or a total possible of 420 contexts (the seven error phonemes plus fourteen others not in error). From this total of 420 maximum possible the twelve lost due to omissions is subtracted, leaving 408. To get the percentage of correct use for (+) consonantal we divide the total number possible into the total number correct; hence, 408/420 = ninety-seven percent correct use of (+) consonantal.

To compute the (−) consonantal we do the same thing, except that the one phoneme in error that is (−) consonantal must be considered, and this is /j/. There are ten omissions in the arresting position for this error phoneme. Maximum possible is three × twenty, since only /h, w, and j/ are (−) consonantal in the list of consonants in the system (features contained in vowels are ignored in our computations). The total of ten lost is subtracted from the maximum possible of sixty (three × twenty), giving us fifty correct. Dividing fifty by sixty gives us the correct percentage of acquisition for (−) consonantal of eighty-three percent.

For purposes of providing a further example, based upon a troublesome feature, (+) strident, we will compute one more of the twelve consonant features. The feature (+) strident occurs in the system in eight phonemes and seven of these (all except /j/ which is −strident) have feature losses on (+) strident, since the phonemes substituted for these seven are all (−) strident; and we have some loss due to omissions. By subtracting the fifteen contexts that are not relevant since /j/ is (−) strident, our total phonetic context loss drops from 107 to ninety-two. The eight phonemes in the system that are (+) strident gives us a maximum possible of 160 (eight × twenty). The number correctly produced then is 160 minus ninety-two, or sixty-eight. The percentage of correct acquisition for (+) stridency is then computed to be 42.5% (68/160). Now we could continue and complete (−) strident taking into account a small loss for the (−) strident one error sound, /j/, compute the percentage of correct use and do all the remaining features in the Chomsky and Halle system.

Having completed the stimulability, consistency, and feature evaluations of Jackie's speech, we could likely benefit from two additional measurements. The first of these is an assessment of Jackie's general ability to discriminate speech sounds, and the second is the important, tape-recorded sample of his spontaneous, connected speech. The auditory, sound-discrimination test might be the Wepman (1959), but the author prefers the old nonsense-syllable one developed by Templin (1938). The outcome of this assessment was a score of eight pairs misdiscriminated—a finding suggesting poor performance. Inspection of the pairs in error showed a general pattern, not one solely related to those sounds that he misarticulated. Thus, early in therapy at least, there is reason to believe that sound-discrimination training may be required for good results along with, of course, sound-production training.

Aspects of Jackie's articulatory performances based upon the Screening Deep Test of Articulation and the Carter–Buck Prognostic Test are summarized in Table 4–6.

By inspection of the above phonetic analysis one can discern three distinct patterns of misarticulation, which, to some extent at least, are verifiable because of feature commonalities and rules that we can write specifying their nature. The first pattern consists of the substitutions of f/θ, θ/s, and θ/z. The second pattern is t/ʃ, t/tʃ, d/dʒ, and d/ð. The third pattern is w/l and w/r. We can see how these errors and patterns of errors

TABLE 4–6
A Summary of Jackie's Total Articulatory Profile

ARTICULATION ERRORS		STIMULABILITY	CONSISTENCY OF ERROR
Initiating Position	*Arresting Position*		
f/θ 10 contexts	f/θ 8 contexts	22%	90%
θ/s 7 contexts	θ/s 7 contexts	50%	70%
θ/z 7 contexts	θ/z 6 contexts	45%	67%
t/ʃ 6 contexts	t/ʃ 5 contexts & 4 omissions	33%	75%
t/tʃ 10 contexts	t/tʃ 5 contexts & 4 omissions	11%	95%
dð 10 contexts	d/ð 10 contexts	0%	100%
d/dʒ 10 contexts	d/dʒ 6 contexts & 3 omissions	11%	95%
w/l 10 contexts	4 omissions	40%	70%
w/r 10 contexts	4 omissions & 6 vowel distortions	0%	100%

tend to show a regularity of rule use as we look at prominent features in terms of degree of acquisition and use.

Following the examples given earlier in feature analysis using the shortcut method, we can note that small numbers of omissions will reduce slightly the presence of features that are rarely a problem such as (+) and (−) voicing. We can also see that (+) and (−) low and (+) and (−) back are one-hundred percent acquired and used appropriately, and all features are represented. The features of greatest difficulty for Jackie were determined to be:

FEATURE	PERCENTAGE ACQUIRED
+ strident	47 percent
+ high	63 percent
+ continuant	67 percent

Features not listed above were either one-hundred percent acquired or had very small losses and were basically very well represented in the child's repertoire.

If we were planning a direct attack on Jackie's problem using a feature approach, we would choose to work to develop (+) stridency and to get generalization not only on it but on (+) continuancy as well, since both features would be contrasted simultaneously if /t/, for example, would be contrasted with /s/.

To support the author's assertion that three patterns of phonological error can be identified we can develop some rules to express relationships.

Rule One

For the substitutions in the first pattern of f/θ, θ/s, θ/z we see:

+ strident	− strident
/s,z/	/θ/

The rule is: Jackie articulates alveolar fricatives as voiceless labio–dental fricatives. Related to the misuse of + stridency is an error in the − stridency component in which the + strident /f/ is substituted for the − strident /θ/. Thus, a major component in pattern one is confusion concerning the use of stridency, although we also can see one error in the use of + coronal in the f/θ substitution and one error of voicing in the θ/z one.

Rule Two

For the substitutions in the second pattern of t/ʃ, t/tʃ, d/ʤ, and d/ð we note:

± continuant	− continuant
+ strident	− strident
+ high	− high
− anterior	+ anterior
/ʃ, tʃ, ʤ/	/t, d/

Here we observe two places of articulation changes and two manner changes. The rule is: Fricatives are articulated as alveolar stops.

Rule Three

In the substitutions involving the two glide sounds, /r, l/, we find that /w/, a liquid, replaces both of them in the initiating position. The rule is: Glides are articulated as liquids.

We have now identified three patterns of phonological impairment. The basic method underlying the Wedge Approach is to weigh the relevant variables and decide how patterns or sets can be attacked using "key" target phonemes to lead the way. Just as an oak log can be difficult to split using a single steel wedge but come apart easily when two or more wedges are used, so can the multiple phonemic errors of many young children "come apart" when different "wedges" are used in the corrective process. The belief that phonemes (and maybe features) can be stimulated to generalize to others that are very similar to them is basic to the Wedge Approach, although the basic notions for this approach developed earlier from clinical experience.

Planning Therapy   For purposes of illustration, therapy for Jackie's articulation problems will be projected for sixteen weeks with two, thirty-minute sessions provided for him weekly. The length of each session will be kept within a range of thirty to forty-five minutes depending on the need to get closure on a step in therapy, his interest and motivation, the need to do special assessing (probes), and other factors. Ideally his mother (or father, but, again, this is difficult to arrange) will attend every session and be trained to assist in the corrective process, so that this condition is best achieved in an outpatient clinical program to which usually a parent most often brings the child.

If Jackie is enrolled in a kindergarten class and receives articulation therapy from a clinician working in the schools, some parents can be urged to attend and participate in one session weekly or perhaps once every two weeks. Experience in many areas of the country shows that some parents of children having more severe speech problems will make this effort if they are convinced their attendance and participation will help their child. An effective clinician working in the schools probably has a set of special strategies that are used to explain the need for parental involvement and make the offer for the establishment of an amiable partnership.[1]

Prior to the treatment phase the various diagnostic studies were completed. During the first one-hour diagnostic session, the ten-minute, connected, spontaneous-speech sample was obtained, sounds in error noted, and some additional checking done using a spontaneous-picture articulation test. The Screening Deep Test was given on sounds noted to be in error (in Jackie's case nine sounds). This exhausted the one hour. During this time, however, the clinician obtained the primary baseline probe, that is, the articulation of the child's error sounds in connected, spontaneous speech; obtained the consistency measures desired; and also generated the phonetic contexts in error from which the feature analysis is done. The secondary probe measures for the treatment phase of the effort were also obtained, since these will be screening deep-test scores on error phonemes.

During the second one-hour diagnostic session, all of the remaining data were gathered. An oral/peripheral speech examination, taking five minutes or less, showed that his dental occlusion was normal, tongue movements horizontally and vertically were adequate, two-, and three-step

---

[1] Some may consider what has been presented in the preliminary assessment stage and what will be presented in the therapy stages as "utopian." If parents cannot become actively involved, the program changes somewhat but goes on. If feature analysis cannot be done and considered, then quicker measures of stimulability and consistency perhaps can be used. In other words, while not totally practical for some practioners, the Wedge Approach and assessment procedures can be streamlined even to the extent that its principles and basic concepts can be used with children such as Jackie, who are seen in group rather than individual articulation therapy.

oral, volitional movements could be made successfully, his tongue withdrew on the midline, and his palate retracted, elevated, and sustained when he phonated /a/ normally with palatal retraction on the midline. Lip and jaw movements were normal.

Next, the Templin Nonsense-Syllable Sound-Discrimination Test, which required fifteen minutes, was administered. The Carter–Buck Prognostic Speech Test was then given on error phonemes, and this required thirty minutes. His hearing had previously been screened audiometrically and found to be within normal limits bilaterally, and the school psychologist had determined that his intelligence was also within normal limits earlier. The remaining ten minutes of the hour were spent talking to Jackie's mother about his speech development, his interests, and his social–emotional adjustment. The clinician planned to talk further about these factors as they progressed. The treatment phase of the program was ready to begin, but the clinician had the task of doing a careful analysis of the data and casting it into a blueprint for correction.

Therapy for Jackie The following principles will characterize our use of the Wedge Approach with Jackie:

> *Principle one* The patterns of sound defectiveness in many severely defective young children represent a series of confusions concerning the perceptual, motor, and linguistic aspects of stages in normal development.
>
> *Principle two* A multisound approach, which stresses choosing a target sound to comprise a "wedge," is capable of fostering generalization involving a pattern or family of errors.
>
> *Principle three* Target sounds that will be easily acquired will have good stimulability and low consistency-of-error scores.
>
> *Principle four* Phonetic placement and traditional techniques for sound acquisition in isolation and in syllables will be useful to teach sounds that fail to generalize and which may show low stimulability and high consistency-of-error scores.
>
> *Principle five* Choice of secondary error sounds as targets in therapy depend upon their dissimilarity to the primary target sound of the pattern in terms of distinctive features, including acoustic aspects of features; likelihood of generalization to others in the pattern not influenced by the primary target sound; and probability of easy acquisition as revealed in the stimulability and consistency measures.
>
> *Principle six* Auditory discrimination of speech sounds will be used if necessary; and when accomplished, the unit for its training will be identical to the unit of sound-production training occurring at that time. For example, if /s/ is trained in CV syllables, /s/ will also be trained in CV syllables for sound discrimination.
>
> *Principle seven* The parent can be effectively entered into the therapy process from the beginning and serve continuously to reinforce learned responses and provide a powerful vehicle for stimulus generalization.

Principle eight Using an operant articulation therapy paradigm, the child will guide the teaching/learning process, and decisions in therapy cannot be precisely made in advance of measurements of critical behaviors: Only a blueprint can be constructed by the clinician.

Stages of Therapy In the first stage of therapy the clinician has decided to attack Jackie's first error pattern, which is delineated in Table 4–7. The attack on this pattern pinpoints the θ/s substitution as the best choice because of the high probability that the child might generalize from a correct /s/ production to a correct /z/ production without any special training on /z/. The substituted sound of /θ/ is common to both errors, indicating perhaps that place confusions and poor discrimination of the phonetic differences among the class of sounds represented in this pattern are contributing to the problem. This is also true for the f/θ substitutions, since the frequencies relating to auditorily discriminating between these two sounds is similar (both spread energy on a broad, high frequency spectrum). The hope is that elimination of the confusion of /θ/ would allow the perceptual and production nature of this sound to become known to the child, and the substitution of f/θ might disappear without direct intervention.

The primary target sound /s/ has also been chosen, because it had the best stimulability score and the lowest consistency of error score in this pattern (fifty and seventy percent, respectively). This should increase the ease of gaining a correct form of /s/ early in therapy.

Stage one The primary goals of stage one therapy are as follows:

1. Train /s/ discrimination and production in isolation; and train /s/ discrimination in CV, VC, and CVC nonsense syllables.
2. Establish /s/ production to high levels of performing using both echoic and nonechoic stimuli.

TABLE 4–7

A Summary of Jackie's Articulation Errors and Measures of Stimulability and Consistency for Error Pattern Number One

ERROR SOUND		STIMULABILITY	CONSISTENCY OF ERROR	
Initiating Position	*Arresting Position*			
f/θ 10 contexts	f/θ 8 contexts	22%	90%	
θ/s 7 contexts	θ/s 7 contexts	50%	70%	WEDGE #1 ←
θ/z 7 contexts	θ/z 6 contexts	45%	67%	

3. Develop first a visual then an auditory only discrimination of /s/ from /θ/ and /z/.

4. Choose a "wedge" or target sound from the second pattern (stops become fricatives) and teach its production.

5. Get the mother working effectively with the clinician to reinforce newly learned skills.

Stage one will consist of eight therapy sessions over a span of four consecutive weeks. Procedures are as follows:

Step One

Reinforcement for correct /s/ responding = FR−1; criterion level for step is ninety percent.

1. Jackie is told a short story about hunting in the woods leading to the introduction of /s/ as the "snake sound."

2. He is instructed that he can win a prize if he learns to find "snakes," and for every nine snakes he finds he gets a pea. When he acquires fifty peas, he gets a chip; and after getting five chips, he gets to select a "prize" (a balloon or other inexpensive toy).

3. Jackie is instructed to watch the clinician's face carefully to see what a snake looks and sounds like after which he is told, "Clap your hands when you catch me making a snake."

4. The clinician produces a string of five /s/ sounds in isolation to stimulate him with the nature of the sound. Every time he claps to show its presence, he receives verbal positive reinforcement ("good").

5. After success on procedure four, Jackie is told that he must clap when hearing the "snake sound" again, but this time to be careful because some other sounds will be heard. The clinician presents random vowels in isolation with ten /s/ sounds in isolation interspersed among them, and presents him with a pea for each correct discrimination of /s/. When a ninety percent level is attained for three strings of discriminations that contain ten /s/ sounds, the discrimination aspect is completed for the sound in isolation and production work receives attention.

6. At the end of this discrimination of /s/ in isolation, Jackie's mother witnesses some of his successful discrimination, reinforces him with verbal praise, and is then given a list of long vowels in which /s/ has been embedded and instructed how to play the "find-the-snake" game at home. The clinician observes her do this and offers some suggestions for home practice.

Step Two

This is an echoic, production step beginning with /s/ in isolation. The ninety percent criterion level is maintained and the schedule is FR−1.

1. The clinician instructs Jackie to watch his/her face and "make snakes

the way I do." The clinician provides an /s/ stimulus in isolation at a slow rate of presentation (one /s/ every three seconds). When a correct /s/ production is made by the child (totally correct, not an improved approximation), "good" is used as the reinforcer, and if he gets nine out of ten in a series correct, he receives a pea. After three strings of ten each have been produced by Jackie at the ninety percent criterion level, this part of the procedure ends; and his mother is brought into the session to observe his success and reinforce correct responses simultaneously with the clinician. (Make mother a big discriminative stimulus (SD), since in her presence Jackie has a higher probability of emitting correct /s/ sounds.) The clinician checks the mother's ability to detect correct /s/ productions from Jackie's /θ/ substitutions and then allows her to conduct the activity. The mother is then instructed to practice it "once or twice a day until the next session." The clinician also suggests that it might be nice if "daddy" could observe and see how well Jackie can make his snake sound. (Make father a big SD also.)

2. The criterion level achieved in part one is checked at the beginning of the next therapy session, and if reached, procedure two is begun. If not reached, training on part one's procedure is again accomplished until the ninety percent criterion is regained after which part two begins. (This practice of checking gains made against criterion levels in preceding sessions is constantly used in the program to insure stability and step-by-step modification of behavior.)

An exact repeat of part one is done except that the /s/ stimuli are presented echoically by the clinician at a rate of one per second. If the same criterion is reached in this session, the clinician introduces the first probe to determine what form of syllable to be taught in step three. (No word probe is done at this time, since it seems likely that generalization of a correct /s/ to words would not occur after only a few therapy sessions.)

The syllable probe at this point is presented echoically. Accuracy of imitation of CV, VC, and CVC syllables is determined by the clinician's modeling of five lists of syllables in which each type of syllable (CV, VC, CVC) is randomly interspersed in each list of twelve syllables. No reinforcement is given for correct-syllable imitation at any time in the probe. After five lists of twelve are presented, the data are analyzed to determine which position Jackie has the most success imitating, the next-best type, and the worst. The next therapy step will train the syllable type having the best performance as determined by this probe; thus, the order for training syllables has been established by using information from the probe.

Step Three

In this step and many subsequent ones, the practice will be to provide some degree of training on both production and discrimination activities. As Winitz (1975) has maintained, sound-discrimination training without production training may be influential in some children's generalization to correct forms, particularly if features are very similar and if stimulability is favorable. As the reader may recall, Jackie's general sound-discrimination score on the Templin Nonsense-Syllable Test (Templin, 1943) was poor, thus suggesting that this weakness might deserve attention in therapy. However, his responses to sound-discrimination training at this point in therapy have been very encouraging, and the extent to which such training is warranted must be evaluated continuously in the therapy program. Such training may show value in terms of stimulating sound (or feature) generalization to certain phonemes which were never entered into sound-production activities. In step three, therefore, we will try to get /θ/ and /z/ into the discrimination phase along with /s/ and advance /s/ production through CV, VC, and CVC syllable imitation. We will also train Jackie to discriminate between and recognize the phonemes and graphemes for /s/, /z/, and /θ/ plus the long vowels of ā, ē, ī, ō, and ū. We may need the visual modality discrimination to assist the auditory one, and we may find that this aid reduces some confusions about the ethereal nature of auditory input alone.

Using an FR–1 schedule of reinforcement (because we are still trying to stabilize Jackie's productions of /s/ in a basic unit) and holding to the original ninety percent production criterion, we will train him to produce CV syllables containing the long vowel sounds, first echoically and then using a "stimulus shift" to the written syllable. The procedures and requirements for CV syllable production in this portion of the step are identical to those detailed for parts one and two of step two. Therefore, he is trained to produce /s/ correctly ninety percent of the time at a slow speed and ninety percent of the time at a much faster speed, the method of stimulus presentation being echoic. In the event that he cannot meet the fast-speech CV imitation at the ninety percent criterion level the clinician has the option of returning to the slow-speed level, repeating it, and then trying the fast speed again. Or the clinician may branch off by establishing an intermediate speech level followed by the fast speed or, if there is a phonetic context difficulty by eliminating the specific vowels causing the problem, and may then gradually reintroduce them after a high degree of success has been realized.

Phoneme—grapheme training will be conducted. Jackie is shown a large letter S printed on a piece of oak tag paper. He is informed that this is the "snake" and asked if it looks like one coiled up. The letter O is then printed on another piece of oak tag paper. With the schedule set at FR–1 and the criterion set at one-hundred percent, the clinician instructs him to point to the one that he/she is saying. Two sets of ten trials each are used, and the stimuli are presented randomly. The letter I is now introduced (because its visual configuration is quite different from O and S. The procedures are repeated. When all three sounds are recognized without error, the phoneme—grapheme associations have been established.

The next procedure consists of a random visual presentation of the graphemes for the vowels O, I, and S. The stimuli are presented in a random order, and Jackie responds by producing the sound in isolation. Three sets of ten stimuli each are used for training, ninety percent criterion is used, and FR–1 is continued with the word "good" used as the reinforcer. (At this point in therapy the clinician discontinues the use of the pea, the chip, and earning a prize; and all subsequent positive reinforcemrnt is verbal, for example, "good," "fine," "great."

Following success on the previous procedure, the clinician instructs Jackie that two letters can be pronounced together, and she/he prints the CV, SĪ on an oak tag card. While looking at the printed syllable, Jackie is instructed to model the clinician's production of it five times; then he is instructed to "read it" each time the clinician flashes the card. After five correct responses, the clinician repeats the above procedure using the second CV, SŌ. The two cards are then placed in front of Jackie who is told, "Point to the one I say." After ten consecutive correct responses each reinforced with "good," "fine," or "great," the remaining two vowels, E and U, are trained using identical procedures. The final procedure in the phoneme–grapheme training is the child's spontaneous production of all five CVs when the clinician presents the cards randomly over three sets of ten simuli with the criterion set at ninety percent and FR–3 now used. At this point, Jackie's mother has observed the last activity and is instructed to do it with him in the presence of the clinician. Subsequently, Jackie takes the CV cards home and practices once or twice daily with his mother.

Training on VC syllables with the long vowels is now accomplished following the procedures for CV. When Jackie reaches the spontaneous-production criterion for all five VCs, the CVC combination is trained.

Beginning with the VC syllable, sound-discrimination training is provided. Jackie's initial training is visual–auditory. The clinician presents him with five sets of ten CV syllables. Within each set of ten, five begin with /s/, three with /t/, two with /f/, and one with /θ/. Jackie is instructed to clap his hands when he hears the syllables beginning with the "snake sound." He is also told that he and the clinician will play a game in which he will receive one point for each correct response but lose a point to the clinician every time he claps by mistake. (The clinician is certain that Jackie will win, since half of the responses in each set begin with /s/, and Jackie's discrimination abilities have been improving.) After the three sets are completed, the scores are totaled and Jackie earns a piece of sugarless chewing gum. Discrimination training is repeated using the same procedures except the visual modality is taken away by the clinician's holding a piece of paper in front of her/his face. These two procedures are then repeated for the VC and CVC syllables.

His mother observes and is told by the clinician that Jackie's production and discrimination of /s/ in syllables has stabilized. The clinician requests that his mother buy him a scrapbook in which she and Jackie will find things that begin with the "snake sound," such as the picture of a saw. The clinician requests that his mother not drill him on these words but let him have fun finding, cutting, and pasting them in his book. His mother is also instructed by the clinician not to correct Jackie's /s/ errors when he talks for the time being, because it is too hard for Jackie to change his conversational speech at this time. Note that the emphasis here is to foster word generalization from syllables without having the clinician do it in therapy. Therapy for /s/ will be drastically reduced at this point, but /s/ will be probed by the readministration of the Screening Deep Test. Also please note that the discrimination training for syllables deliberately contained three sounds that are substitutions for error sounds, /f/ and /θ/, in pattern one, and /t/ in pattern two. This was designed to peak Jackie's perceptual awareness concerning the nature of each of these.

Once the clinician is confident that /s/ perception and production have reached an adequate level of stability, the "wedge" for the second phonological pattern is introduced. This pattern is delineated in Table 4-8. As noted earlier, the /ʃ/ sound was chosen to serve as the "wedge" for this pattern because its stimulability and consistency scores were the best of the error sounds. It will be contrasted with its substitution, /t/, in production and discrimination training. The tentative plan will be to get /ʃ/ into rapid production, probe for generalization of the other error sounds in the pattern, and if nothing favorable happens, teach /tʃ/ hoping that its improvements will generalize to /ʤ/ since they are cognates.

To continue with step three Jackie is trained to produce /ʃ/ in isolation echoically using the simple procedures of step one for /s/ training. Because his stimulability and consistency scores show that he has some knowledge of this sound, production is successful. In the beginning the clinician told

TABLE 4–8

A Summary of Jackie's Articulation Errors and Measures of Stimulability and Consistency for Error Pattern Number Two

ERROR SOUND		STIMULABILITY	CONSISTENCY OF ERROR	
Initiating Position	Arresting Position			
t/ʃ 6 contexts	t/ʃ 5 contexts and 4 omissions	33%	75%	WEDGE #2 ←
t/tʃ 10 contexts	t/tʃ 5 contexts and 4 omissions	11%	95%	
d/ð 10 contexts	d/ð 10 contexts	0%	100%	
d/dʒ 10 contexts	d/dʒ 6 contexts and 3 omissions	11%	95%	

him about a noisy child in a movie theater who was told by all the other people around him to "be quiet" by placing their fingers on their lips and making a noise. Jackie imitated the clinician's production of the "be-quiet sound" the first time it was attempted; he was successful under fast and slow speeds and moved rapidly into the nonsense-imitation stages. Subsequently, he was taught the grapheme as SH to contrast it with the single letter S. In responding ninety percent of the time or more to rapid presentation of cards containing the /s/ grapheme and the /ʃ/ grapheme, with FR–3 used, Jackie was found to make highly accurate productions of each sound and the phoneme–grapheme association appeared acquired at this level.

Next Jackie is trained to produce /z/ in isolation echoically using the simple procedures of step one for /s/ training, the FR–1 schedule, and the ninety percent criterion level. The "bee sound," /z/, is entered into discrimination training allowing visual cues and trained against /s/ in isolation. Jackie is instructed: "Drop the penny in the box every time you hear me make the 'bee sound'." Random presentations of /s/ and /z/ are given in three sets of ten stimuli each, FR–3 is used, and ninety percent maintained. Following this training, the /z/ grapheme is introduced using the printed form on an oak tag card. Jackie is told to say the sound presented to him when /s/ in isolation is shown on one card and /z/ on another in random order. Three sets of ten presentations are made, and FR–3 is used with ninety percent.

In the final procedure of step three the /θ/ is taught. The clinician dubs this "the wind sound—Hear the wind, Jackie?" Note that Jackie obviously needs no training on production of /θ/, since he uses it in the θ/s and θ/z substitutions. Discrimination training of it against /s/ and /z/ and later /f/ hopefully will reduce confusion and sharpen his perception of the sound. The grapheme association and discrimination procedures will follow; and, finally, there will be a discrimination activity involving /s/, /z/, and /θ/ in isolation with visual cues removed and discrimination done with auditory information only.

Jackie's mother observes, does the /s/, /z/, and /θ/ discrimination training under the clinician's supervision, and is requested to do it once or twice daily until the next session. After a review of Jackie's /s/ pictures in his notebook and a trial run to see if VCs containing /s/ could still be produced, the clinician also recommends that mother and child begin finding pictures of words with the "snake sound" at the end as in "bus." *Note:* Pictures of /z/ words will not be requested and this sound will receive little attention except in discrimination training. Again, the hope is that as /s/ improves, /z/ will mirror these changes. Pictures in the notebook may be required later for /θ/, since /f/ substitutes for it and this substitution seems to be stubbornly related to word associations, for example, "fink" for "think" and "fumb" for "thumb."

Stage two This stage is five weeks in duration and spans ten therapy sessions. At the beginning of stage two, a primary probe will be made to check Jackie's articulation in spontaneous, conversational speech. A ten-minute or longer period will be devoted to talking about his favorite TV programs. A tape recording will be made, and the clinician will note at this time the status of the primary sounds that have been trained so far (/s,ʃ/); interest is high, however, in the status of all errors. A careful study of the tape recording may be important to guide the steps in therapy in stage two. There will also be an increasing use of Screening Deep Test probes in this stage and throughout the remainder of the therapy, since generalization may occur at this level and not be seen in spontaneous, connected speech for some time. Of course, comparisons of both types of measures will be made with the pretherapy scores which serve as baseline measures.

The therapy goals for stage two are as follows:

1. Enter into sound-discrimination training /f/, /t/, and /w/ at the syllable level.
2. Teach /θ/ production in words via the home-training program.
3. Train Jackie to self-monitor his speech using a method of "right/wrong, correct-me training."
4. Increase the effectiveness of family members to foster generalization at home and elsewhere.

Step One

Three sounds substituted for error sounds, /f, t, and w/ are entered into discrimination training one at a time. It can be seen that all three patterns are now represented. In pattern three the /w/ was substituted for /l/ and /r/. Placing it into a discrimination phase is the first attack made, but as yet we have not developed a "wedge" sound for this pattern. We will deliberately withhold any production work on the wedge sound for pattern three until accurate discrimination is made for almost all substitutions and many of the error sounds and we have good evidence that both /s/ and /ʃ/ are generalizing into words.

Sound-discrimination training follows procedures previously presented in step three of stage two, except that the grapheme is taught first for each sound followed by a pair-discrimination activity (t−f; t−w; w−f). After each combination can be discriminated at the ninety percent criterion level of three ten-stimuli presentations, with visual cues allowed, the clinician readministers the task but holding a paper in front of her/his face to eliminate the visual-discrimination aid. In both instances FR−1 is used, and the task is a discrimination of whether the two sounds in each pair are the same or different. Jackie's response is signaled by nodding his head "yes" or "no." After the ninety percent criterion level is met, with auditory clues only, the three cards used to teach graphemes are presented to him in a random order, and he responds by producing the sound represented on them. Again, FR–1, ninety percent, and verbal praise are used. Jackie's mother is instructed to use the cards and do the discrimination activity once or twice daily until the next session.

Step Two

This is a multiple-discrimination phase. All sounds that have received discrimination training (/s, z, θ, f, ʃ, t, w) are presented rapidly by the clinician with no visual clues allowed. Jackie is told to clap his hands when he hears, for example, the "angry cat sound." Each sound in turn is presented ten times in random strings of all other sounds, namely, /s, w, t, z, f, θ, ʃ/. FR–1 is used and the ninety percent level must be attained for each sound, all sounds being entered into the task. The same procedures are now used in a CV, VC, VCV discrimination task. For example, "Clap your hands when you catch me making the bee sound (sæ, tæ, wæ, θæ, ʃæ, zæ, fæ). After correct discrimination in the CV example given above, identical procedures and requirements train VC and CVC syllables.

At this point in therapy a probe for generalization is made on /s/ and /z/ using the Screening Deep Test. Evidence shows that the baseline measure of 14/20 errors has dropped to 1/20 errors; for /z/, generalization also has taken place, the baseline measure of 13/20 having declined to 5/20. The decision is to avoid working on /s/ and /z/ words in any form and let the pictures for /s/ in the notebook serve as the stimuli for further learning.

A second set of deep-test probes studies the status of /ʃ/ and /tʃ/. Changes in /ʃ/ are dramatic, the baseline measure being 19/20 errors and the probe showing 1/20. For /tʃ/, highly consistently defective at the baseline period and poorly stimulable, no changes are found on the probe. The decision is to allow the notebook—picture program for /ʃ/ to be continued, not to work on words with this sound in the clinic setting, and to consider the strong possibility that improvements on /ʃ/ may be too slow, affecting /tʃ/, or may not happen at all. Thus, /tʃ/ may need production training. After acquisition, it might generalize to the defective /ʤ/.

A final probe using the deep test was made for /θ/. Although it was emitted accurately in Jackie's spontaneous speech when the written syllables were used as stimuli, the probe was disappointing with all original eighteen errors remaining. The decision was to use the home program consisting of pictures in Jackie's notebook depicting words that begin with /θ/.

Step Three

This is a word-discrimination stage for /s/ and /ʃ/, which may be expanded to include (θ/, since words in picture form will begin to be practiced at home. (It is what the author calls "right/wrong, correct me training.") The task is designed to teach the contrast between the substituted sound and the error phoneme in a meaningful context with speed and accuracy followed by the child's correction of the error presented for which, of course, he is reinforced. The clinician instructs the child:

> Jackie, watch me and listen to what I say. I will say some words that you know. Some will be bad words because I didn't say them right. Some will be good words that I did say right. Clap your hands if you catch me saying a bad word; then you say it right. If you catch me and correct the word, you get a point; but if you clap after I've said a good word, I get a point and the one with the most points wins.

With FR–1 in use the clinician presents strings of words containing /s/ interspersing an error on selected words, which are randomly ordered in a series, thus: bus, face, mouse, houθ (for house). When Jackie discriminates the error, evidenced by hand clapping, he corrects the "bad word" and earns one point. Stimulus words are changed to provide training in the initial, medial, and final positions (or initiating and arresting, if you prefer). The criterion is reached when ninety percent of the words in error are discriminated and corrected by Jackie. Training of the same type is now accomplished for /ʃ/ words. In the final phase of this task /s/ and /ʃ/ words are entered into the same series, and Jackie must discriminate and correct errors on both, for example, soup, θun (for sun), pass, bicycle, toud (for should).

Jackie's mother is instructed by the clinician in how to play this discrimination and correction game at home with Jackie using pictures in his notebook. The clinician demonstrates to Jackie's mother how to point to an /s/ or /ʃ/ picture and say it either correctly or incorrectly (using Jackie's exact substitution, of course). After pictures of words beginning with /θ/ are added to his notebook, this same type of practice is done with him at home by his mother. After Jackie's mother offers the statement that her husband is seeing changes in Jackie's speech at home, the clinician makes a strong request that the father attend some therapy sessions and serve to reinforce Jackie's accomplishments. During the latter portion of stage two the father makes some appearances, and Jackie is pleased, showing an eagerness to respond and demonstrate what he has learned to do.

Stage three This consists of four weeks of therapy and eight sessions. A primary probe is again used to study his spontaneous, connected speech talking about his new ice skates, sledding, and the snowman that he and his brother made in their front yard. The sample is revealing: It shows that many /s/ words in various positions are being correctly used, and this seems true for /z/ as well. All /ʃ/ words in the sample are correct, but those containing /tʃ/ and /dʒ/ are almost totally incorrect. The few words containing /θ/ are partially correct (fifty percent), while /r/ words are consistently in error. Articulation of /l/ is mostly the w/l substitution, and the /d/ error is consistently in error.

The clinician makes the decision to teach /tʃ/ because the results of his probe and a second one using the deep test are not promising. The decision to attack wedge three directly is also made, since, although the substituted /w/ is well discriminated by Jackie, no changes have occured in /l/ or /r/ production. The baseline data on /l/ and /r/ error scores, stimulability, and consistency suggest that /l/ is by far the best choice. The clinician's experience tells her/him that /l/ is most often an easier sound to teach and that once into correct production may generalize to the prevocal /r/, particularly since the substituted sound, /w/, is common to both /l/ and ./r/ errors. The decision is also made to put /l/ and /r/ into the sound discrimination activities, since Jackie is accurately discriminating all the sounds that have been trained and shows the capacity for even further discrimination training.

Step One

Finding no reliable phonetic context in which /tʃ/ is articulated correctly, the clinician uses phonetic placement techniques to try to achieve production in isolation. Jackie is instructed to "make the train sound" by the clinician who shows him in a mirror how to close his teeth, produce a series of /t/ sounds in rapid order, and move his lips forward. After a period of time and the clinician's instruction and modeling, some nearly correct /tʃ/ sounds are heard; and the clinician uses the method of approximations to modify the somewhat distorted sound to its correct form. Once correct /tʃ/ production can be made without looking into the mirror, Jackie is placed back on the operant program and receives production training using the same criterion, schedule of reinforcement, and techniques used in stage one, step two to get /s/ into production. This involves the echoic and nonechoic correct responding to the sound in isolation and syllables.

Discrimination training using /t/ in contrast to the newly developed /tʃ/ is provided. First /tʃ/ is trained using vowels (as in stage one, step one); then, after the success needed to advance, discrimination training in having Jackie nod his head "yes" or "no" is accomplished for the same/different paradigm. The clinician presents in random order four combinations to discriminate: /t–t/, /t–t/, /tʃ–tʃ/ and /tʃ–t/. With FR–1 set, the criterion is established at ninety percent correct responding over four consecutive sets of ten stimuli each.

With the long vowels previously learned, "stimulus–shift" is accomplished using an oak tag card on which the grapheme CH is printed. The procedure for recognition of the grapheme consists of pointing to the one syllable in which it is contained. All five vowels are used in training, and Jackie proceeds through CV, VC, and CVC recognition training, his response to the spoken syllable of the clinician being to point to the card having the /tʃ/ syllable printed on it. FR–3 is used and the criterion over thirty stimulus presentations is maintained at ninety percent. Subsequently, /t/ is printed on a card by itself. The card is given to Jackie, who is asked to make the sound in isolation.

After this, the three syllable cards are constructed consisting of the five long vowels and /t/. The procedure for syllable recognition for /tʃ/ above is repeated for /t/ until the criterion level is reached. The next activity is rapid recognition of randomly spoken syllables for both /tʃ/ and /t/. Pointing responses are used, FR–3 and ninety percent criterion level maintained. The final procedure in this phase of training is to train Jackie to sequence two or more syllables randomly spoken by the clinician, for example, tā chē and chō tū. When the criterion level has been met, with FR–1 used (because task is more difficult at first), the sequential training is repeated except that Jackie has to imitate two (or more if he has succeeded with two) syllables with correct articulation of those containing /tʃ/.

Step Two

Wedge three is inserted into phonological pattern three. The /l/ sound is chosen rather than /r/ for various reasons cited earlier. At this point in therapy, no great emphasis or time committment would be made getting /l/ into production: The sound was stimulated to see if it would respond, and the forty percent stimulability and seventy percent consistency scores appear to offer promise that it would. *Note:* The author's opinion is that /l/ is a difficult sound to teach in isolation, and, in fact, production in isolation tends often to distort its true auditory coloring. Training in syllables appears to be a more natural speaking process for this sound. Therefore, Jackie is trained using CV syllables and children's songs.

Discovering that Jackie learned some simple children's songs at home and in nursery school, the clinician sings "Here We Go 'Round the Mulberry Bush" substituting the CV /lʌ/ for each word. After this, the child is told to sing the song with the clinician using the /l/ syllable for words. The clinician observes that in about half of the words sung, the /l/ is correct. Conditioning then follows using these procedures: With FR–1 and a ninety percent criterion level, Jackie is asked to sing the song using /l/ syllables rather than its words, but to sing it rather slowly (clinician demonstrates desired speed). The clinician uses "good" when syllables are heard that begin with a correct /l/ and nothing when the /w/ is substituted. The criterion level is 80 percent or 16/20 words sung in one of five trials. Another song in Jackie's repertoire, "London Bridge," receives comparable training up to criterion. Jackie's mother is informed concerning the purpose of the singing exercise, practices it with Jackie in the presence of the clinician, and promises to "have fun with him" at the piano singing other songs that he enjoys substituting /l/ syllables for words.

Step Three

In this step /r/ is introduced as "the rooster-crowing sound." *Note:* At this time, no production work on /r/ is planned, due to other emphases in therapy and the poor prognosis for its development based on stimulability and consistency testing. Production work on /r/, if required, will be in the last stage of therapy or delayed for some time. The same decision is made for the /d/ substitution in pattern two for comparable reasons and also because this particular sound is one of the last to be mastered in the language (Prather et al., 1975).

Sound discrimination training for /r/ begins with its being pitted against consonants which are many distinctive features apart, and training is first done in isolation. Jackie is instructed to drop a marble in the box every time he hears "the rooster crow." Random presentation of /s, t, tʃ, f, ʃ, and θ/ are provided by the clinician with /r/ placed in different positions within the strings. FR–1 is used as is the criterion of ninety percent with visual clues allowed. Visual clues are dropped and the task repeated. After this is achieved, discrimination training proceeds from consonants to vowels, /w/ and /l/. First high front vowels are discriminated in isolation from /r/, namely, /i, ɪ, e, ɛ, and æ/ using the same procedures and requirements for success. This is followed by discrimination of /r/ from the central vowels (ə, ʌ, a). For this procedure the criterion level is reduced to eighty percent due to the increasing difficulty of the task. For the back-vowel (u, ʊ, o, ɔ, ɒ) discrimination and /r/ task, the eighty percent level and FR–1 requirements are also used due to the increasing difficulty of discriminating these vowels (some of which Jackie uses in the syllable arresting position for vocalic forms of /r/).

Discrimination training of /r/ moves to opposing it against first /l/, then /w/, and finally against both of them. The clinician, using a card with a picture of a rooster on it, prints the grapheme R for Jackie. The card is held up, and the clinician produces the sound five times in isolation. Then the /l/ card with the L grapheme are placed next to it, and the clinician presents randomly either /l/ or /r/ in isolation. Jackie points to the one spoken. The schedule is set at FR–3 and ninety percent criterion level over three consecutive sets of ten presentations each. The above task is repeated using the long vowels and CV, VC, and CVC syllables printed on cards. The exact discrimination procedures for /r/ opposing /l/ are repeated for the discrimination training that follows /r/ and /w/. After Jackie meets the criterion level for this task, all three cards are used, and he is required to point to the card containing either /l/, /r/, or /w/. As before, FR–3 and ninety percent are maintained.

During part of a session in which the above training is conducted, Jackie's mother observes. After his success with the last discrimination task, she is instructed to repeat one set of stimuli with Jackie in the clinician's presence. The cards are given to Jackie to take home for daily practice with his mother.

The "right/wrong, correct-me training" described in step three of stage two is repeated at this point except that it now includes correct and error words containing /tʃ/ and /θ/ as well as the two sounds trained earlier, /s/ and /ʃ/. Because of the increasing difficulty of the task, FR–1 is set and eighty percent criterion is selected.

The final training activity in stage 3 consists of a production–stimulation task. The clinician directs Jackie to watch her/his face carefully and repeat CV syllables. High, low, front, central, and back vowels are now used, and all of the error sounds, except /z, ð, ʤ, and r/, are trained. In the first phase of this training individual syllables are randomly presented for imitation once every three seconds. In the second phase they are presented one per second. With FR–3 the criterion for forty CV syllables is set at ninety percent. The above slow then fast procedure is subsequently used with VC and CVC of the same vowels meeting the same requirements and conditions of training.

Stage four This is the final three weeks or six therapy sessions. A primary probe and a series of secondary probes are used to set the goals and make decisions. Ten minutes or more of connected, spontaneous speech is taperecorded relating to Jackie's birthday party and presents. There is strong evidence that phonological patterns one and two are literally coming apart. In pattern one /θ/ is heard articulated correctly three times out of four, and /s/ and /z/ are in error only two or three times each out of fifteen to twenty responses. Pattern two is also showing its demise, since /ʃ/ occurs five times and is correct five times, /tʃ/ is heard six times and is correct in five of these occurrences, and /ʤ/ only occurs once but is correctly articulated. Pattern three evidence indicates that /r/ is consistently misarticulated but /l/ is spoken ten times and is correctly articulated in five occurrences.

Screening Deep Test probes are now made to check progress against the baseline measures for /ʤ/, /l/, and /ð/. Results of the probe for /ʤ/ show only two errors out of twenty, both in the arresting position. Although only three phonetic contexts are in error now in the arresting position for /l/ production, five of the ten responses in the initiating position remain as /w/ substitutions. For /ð/ the probe shows some change from baseline.

Some correct responses are found (three in each position). These probes show that generalization is taking place, obviously faster on some sounds than others.

Based on the above information, the clinician sets goals for the final stage of therapy. These are as follows:

1. Provide a limited amount of word training for /l/.
2. Put /d/, /ʤ/, and /ð/ into some discrimination training.
3. Do some trial production training on various types of /r/.
4. Continue to improve Jackie's self-monitoring of his speech.
5. Prepare a set of instructions for Jackie's mother for home practice after clinical speech therapy has been concluded, and present her with pretherapy, posttherapy improvements.

Step One

To stimulate correct /l/ production the clinician uses picture cards containing noun objects beginning with /l/. Placing Jackie so that he can see both the clinician's face and his own in a mirror, the clinician places a picture on the table in front of him and asks him to say "lī lī." After this is successfully accomplished, the clinician picks up the picture of a light and places it on the mirror with tape. With Jackie watching her/him in the mirror, the clinician says "lī lī light" rapidly five times. Jackie is then told to repeat this utterance. (*Note:* Jackie has learned to use /l/ in CV syllables by practicing the singing exercise, and the purpose of this technique is to take advantage of the syllable production and both visual and auditory clues to eliminate his tendency to use w/l in words.)

Ten /l/ words are trained this way with FR–1, criterion ninety percent, and each set of ten words is presented three times. Subsequently, the same activity is repeated, except that the stimulus modeled for Jackie is the repetition of only one syllable before the word, that is, "lī light." Then the syllable is gradually removed and Jackie is instructed to watch the clinician's production in the mirror and then do his own, the emphasis being on correct /l/ tongue position and a slow, carefully monitored start into the word. Jackie's mother is requested to help him find pictures of objects beginning with /l/ for this notebook, and she demonstrates her knowledge of the technique of getting correct /l/ production in words to the clinician who requests daily home practice.

Step Two

The common substitution of /d/ for /ʤ/ and /ð/ is attacked more directly via discrimination training. The procedure involved is discrimination in isolation (/d/ against /ʤ/ and /d/ against /ð/). These basic simple techniques are identical to those used in early stages of this program.

Again, the graphemes are associated with the phonemes in each case and used for discrimination training, first in isolation and later in the series of syllables using the long vowel sounds. Having been successfully trained to discriminate many sounds at this point in therapy, Jackie's training is rather easily completed, the approach, once again, being visual/auditory training followed by auditory alone.

Step Three

Although no correct form of /r/ has been found in any probe, the clinician decides to look further for a facilitating phonetic context. Jackie is asked to imitate sound productions of initial prevocal /r/ in isolation and blends, and words and syllables containing the two types of vocalic /r/ sounds, stressed /ɜ˞/ and unstressed /ɚ/. Jackie emits two approximations of initial, prevocalic blends, /tr/ and /kr/, but all other productions are totally incorrect. The clinician then decides to see if these close approximations might be improved and generalized to other phonetic contexts. A further decision is to try to teach stressed /ɜ˞/ in isolation if necessary.

The techniques for using the /tr/ and /kr/ phonetic contexts include presentation of a strongly produced /tr/ or /kr/ utterance followed by imitations by Jackie with the clinician reinforcing /r/ quality differences by saying "little better," "not so good," "that's better," "much better," "perfect." Once /tr/ or /kr/ or both reach ninety percent correct imitation with FR–1, on three sets of five stimuli presented by the clinician, the phonetic contexts are changed to include an added vowel, for example, "trō, trī, krō." To improve the likelihood of success for these stimuli, the clinician instructs Jackie to "hold" the first part or prolong the /r/ before producing the vowel, that is, "tr → ō." Both /tr/ and /kr/ are trained this way, and after reaching criterion levels of ninety percent across four sets of ten stimuli each, using modeling and approximations, the clinician fades out the /t/ and /k/ in the syllables and has Jackie imitate a stressed /ɜ˞/ and the vowels; thus: r–ō, r–ē, etc. Each of the long vowels is imitated ten times following /r/, the criterion level is set at eighty percent, with FR–1. It appears that stressed /ɜ˞/ is in production at a minimal level. From this point forward, it is practiced in a variety of phonetic contexts using nonsense syllables that Jackie would imitate for some time.

Step Four

To increase the demands on Jackie's error-detection system, the clinician prepares a tape of sentences containing errors of /tʃ/, /θ/, and /l/. These errors occur randomly in words embedded in sentences of various length and complexity. Jackie is instructed that he would win a point in a game against the clinician for every "bad word" spoken, but he has to correct it to do so. To reach criterion he has to do this thirty times, since ninety percent has been set and thirty-six words are on the tape. The sentences were earlier recorded by the clinician at a slow rate. A second tape containing errors on /r/ (of all types) and errors on the sounds above is also used for this purpose. Following this, Jackie is told a fairy story by the clinician, who also presents portions of it in picture form. Leaving the pictures before Jackie, the clinician asks him to tell her/him the story as "best as you can." His speech is tape recorded, and he is told that he has made ten errors on various sounds and words, and if he can find eight or more of them and correct them, he will earn a reward (a balloon). To do this he is allowed to listen to the tape completely twice. All corrected words are also reinforced with verbal praise.

At the end of the sixteen weeks of therapy, the primary, spontaneous, connected-speech probe is readministered. A few errors persist on the w/l substitution, but it is basically gone. The /s/ and /z/ errors no longer can be found, nor can the t/ʃ and t/tʃ errors; and the d/ʤ is considerably improved. Errors on all types of /r/ persist, although the sound is in production in some of its forms, echoically, at least. Some words show changes to a demise in the d/ð substitution as well. The three defective phonological patterns have literally been eliminated.[2]

Step Five

A set of special instructions is provided to Jackie's mother who has participated in almost every step in therapy to reinforce his learning in the clinic by home practice. In particular she is instructed and given practice materials on /r/ in syllables which Jackie is to imitate. No word practice on /r/ is to be attempted for some time. Additional practice on the discrimination of /r/ and vowels (which the mother had done in home practice earlier), is also recommended. Finally, she is cautioned not to correct articulation errors on other sounds except in a fun way, for example, playing the game of snapping her fingers occasionally when Jackie makes an error that she knows he can correct, then smiling at him when he corrects it without anything being said.

In summary, the Wedge Approach is a set of special measurements, the generation of some working hypotheses, and an effort to destroy patterns of speech defectiveness that many of the younger, articulatory-defective children manifest. Its therapy techniques, *per se*, are not uniquely different from the traditional ideas. The concept of clear, precise distinction among speech sounds is hardly new, but it maintains a great significance in many approaches to articulatory correction. The fun of articulation therapy (for the author at least) rests in the challenge of taking a multisound problem and using a multisound, continuously probing, decision-making approach to its solution. The operant paradigm used with the Wedge Approach

---

[2] The author's clinical example is actually based on the changes made in two preschool children of Jackie's age when very similar therapy was provided over a span of about the same number of weeks in a university speech clinic.

allows for the experimental analysis of the behaviors. That's where the fun is: Using the responses given by the child to make new decisions that can be tested one by one.

SUMMARY

In this chapter I have attempted to describe and illustrate some of the approaches to the correction of defective phonology in young children. Many of the distinctive feature recommendations implied in the phonological process analysis approach are basically promising but inadequately tested. In particular, the usual lack of comparative, experimental studies characterizes the literature in this respect. With innovation and creativity, perhaps these more phonological approaches will prove highly effective with certain young phonologically defective children. It is obvious, however, that unless the young child's speech is rather severely defective, these approaches may not be warranted or even possible.

The extent to which response generalization occurs to enhance the efficacy of therapy as a result of distinctive feature or phonological process training seems not yet to have been determined. That sound generalization occurs in therapy seems more convincingly established, but even this phenomenon lacks adequate and comprehensive verification across its many phonemic possibilities. The practitioner awaits the outcome of many more experiments and investigations to come to a stronger set of conclusions concerning both the efficacy and efficiency of intervention based on the concepts and recommended procedures for these phonological approaches.

We also lack adequate verification of the notion that directing phonological improvements can be achieved both effectively and efficiently by targeting not on phonological errors but on some other aspect of defective language that accompanies the disorder, and this is most often syntax. Confirmation of this belief does not appear to be present to any convincing degree in our literature. Again, the question may be "for whom is such an approach more effective than a nonlinguistic or traditional articulation therapy approach?" Perhaps a subtype of phonological defective that shows certain patterns of accompanying linguistic defectiveness is the benefactor of an approach teaching syntax for example, while others may improve as well under an approach that strikes directly at correction of the defective phonemes.

The impact of the operant paradigm to the treatment of phonological errors of children is obvious in most of the published literature. In the Wedge Approach for the more severely defective young child, which may be effective in some instances, the essence is multi-dimensional: possible distinctive feature and/or sound generalization phenomenon operational, measures of speech applied to assist in making therapy choices, parents trained and participating in the correction process, and use of operant technology to foster documented speech improvement. This is not a panacea and is not for everyone—but what approach do we enjoy that is?

The operant paradigm applied to articulation remediation

○ OPERANT TECHNOLOGY AND NOMENCLATURE

Some of the principles of operant conditioning and examples of how to apply them in speech/language therapy have been excellently presented by members of this profession (Brookshire, 1967; Holland, 1967; McReynolds, 1970), and the reader is urged to check these sources. A review of the basic elements of the operant paradigm will be presented at this point, since by its very nature the operant one is a highly disciplined, rigorous, and explicit system of analyzing and modifying behavior, and a speech/language clinician working within this system should be conversant with the precise definitions and descriptions of its elements. Furthermore, most applications to articulation therapy and other speech and language disorders have frequently not taken advantage of all the power and opportunities that are possible using operant technology.

Among the elements and their precise definitions and the principles that they embody, we have the following:

> *Operant conditioning:* A process in which the frequency of occurrence of a behavior is modified by the consequences of the behavior.
>
> *Probability:* Likelihood that a bit of behavior will occur. In the operant sense it is the absolute rate of occurrence of the behavior, and it will occur more now than formerly if the behavior occurs more than it did formerly.
>
> *Operants:* Responses that become more probable when they are followed by reinforcers. For example, in articulation therapy a clinician uses the technique called "approximations" (or shaping in the operant sense) to modify a child's production of /ɜ'/. Improvements toward improved production are reinforced with "good." The bit of behavior that is emitted in an improved form by the child increases its probability of occurrence and can be considered as an operant.
>
> *Consequences:* These involve either the effects of behavior seen in the appearance of an additional aspect of the environment or the disappearance of an aspect of it. Consequences can be seen to function in either regard. A *positive reinforcer* affects the appearance of a stimulus as a consequence of a response, thus increasing the probability that the response will reoccur. A *negative reinforcer* involves the disappearance of a stimulus as a consequence of a response resulting in an increased probability that the response will reoccur. In articulation therapy an example might be reinforcing a correct imitated /s/ response by removing

90 dB of white noise from a child's ear when correct /s/ responding occurs. In this example the white noise is called an *adversive stimulus*. The therapy is *punishment*. This involves the reduction of the rate of responding for error responses using adversive stimuli. For example, in an article of some vintage the author told of using a mild fardic shock to extinguish the error responding of a young adult lisper—a procedure not widely recommended in the profession.

Schedules of reinforcement: Rules that dictate the conditions under which responses will be reinforced. These rules have significant and orderly effects on the organism's rate of responding. Commonly used schedules of reinforcement in speech/language training include fixed-ratio schedules such as FR–1 in which each correct response is reinforced. Variable-interval (VI) schedules in which the amount of time that must elapse before a response is reinforced are rarely used for speech/language training programs. In a VR–10 schedule, for example, the ten indicates the average value of the ratios and the schedule might consist of reinforcing responses in an irregular but repeating way, for example, 5, 25, 15, 10.

Extinction: This process involves the nonreinforcement of a response previously reinforced which ultimately reduces the frequency of responding to a very low level or eliminates it completely.

Discriminative stimulus (SD): These are stimuli that influence the probability of the occurrence of the operant. When present in the environment, the probability for occurrence is great; when absent the probability is low. Operants are brought under *stimulus control* by SDs because the operants have been reinforced in their presence. Based upon the responding rate, the influence of an SD can be determined; and by finding the powerful ones, the organism can be brought under tighter stimulus control. An example of a potentially powerful SD is the mother of an articulatory-defective child. The child has been responding with high rates of correct /s/ production using picture stimuli and reinforced in the mother's presence by the clinician. Next the mother does this same training and reinforces the child for correct responding. The mother may have assumed some power as an SD for correct responding at this point and may continue as such.

Conditioned reinforcers (CRs): These are acquired reinforcers of behavior that may operate throughout a lifetime. They occur when a new stimulus is repeatedly presented to the organism either simultaneously or right before another stimulus which has the power to reinforce behavior. The new stimulus may also develop the power to reinforce the behavior that precedes it, and the behavior becomes more probable in the future. For example, we have seen in articulation therapy how a poker chip can be used as a conditioned reinforcer. A child's correct modeling of a clinician's /s/ productions is reinforced with "good" each time. When the child produces twenty correct /s/ responses, he receives a poker chip which now becomes a reinforcer. When ten poker chips are earned, the child exchanges them for a toy, also a reinforcer. Because the poker chips have been exchanged for a toy, they become conditioned reinforcers.

Chains: Orderly sequences of stimuli and responses comprise chains. The most efficient and complex learning seems directly related to the establishment of chains. In the operant sense chaining involves literally "changing hats" so that discriminative stimuli and conditioned reinforcers play dual roles. In the example of a child in articulation therapy the functions may occur as follows: The child is reinforced with "good" for each correct /s/ response. After twenty consecutive correct /s/ responses, he receives on poker chip. After getting three poker chips, he gets a red piece of paper, 8½" by 11". After getting three pieces of red paper, he earns the right to collect a toy of his choice from the "toy store." The response of making twenty consecutive /s/ responses is made in the presence of the discriminative stimuli afforded by the clinician and is reinforced by the appearance of the poker chip, a conditioned reinforcer. The poker chip is also now a discriminative stimulus (the second in the chain) in whose presence the response of exchanging three of them for a piece of red paper makes the red paper a conditioned reinforcer (the second one in the chain). The red paper now becomes the third discriminative stimulus in whose presence the response of exchanging the paper for a toy becomes the final reinforcer in the chain.

○INTRODUCTION TO OPERANT THERAPY

Previously, we saw an operant method to articulation therapy for a young child having multiple misarticulations based upon the Wedge Approach. The purpose now is to detail an operant approach to group articulation therapy for older articulatory-defective children who only misarticulate /s/. These types of children are commonly placed in group therapy in school settings, and many of them are in grades three to six and enrolled in regular not special classes. The description of the operant approach used will not deviate a great deal from what one might consider to be a "traditional operant articulation approach."

The program will use both positive reinforcement for correct responding and punishment for incorrect responding. The first contingency used will be positive reinforcement. Punishment will be used later after the correct form of /s/ for all four children will have advanced nearly to the end of the transfer stage of therapy, but it will be accompanied by positive reinforcement also when some activities are in process. Verbal praise consisting of the usual "good," "right," "yes," and "fine" will be used as will nonverbal praise consisting of nodding or smiling. Later, when punishment is used, each of the four children and the clinician will be armed with a toy clicker to be used when an individual emits an incorrect response under a specific stimulus condition.

Basic to the operant approach, of course, is the counting and charting of behavior. Here we will count and chart both correct responses for each child in the group and incorrect ones. To facilitate this process we devise a talley sheet (Figure 5–1) that, hopefully, will be attractive to the children and serve also as a strong positive reinforcer as they develop greater skill at sound production. The clinician has introduced "Mr Goodspeech" as a jolly, happy, willing-to-try-and-listen person and his counterpart, "Mr.

FIGURE 5-1 Tally Sheet

Mumbles," as lonely, sad, and unwilling to try and listen. The children learn quickly that a positively reinforced response is tallied on Mr. Goodspeech's half of the tally sheet while a negatively reinforced one is tallied on Mr. Mumbles' half of the sheet. Depending upon which comes first, the number of points that each child receives are counted at the conclusion of each therapy task or at the end of each session. After this, the percent of correct responses are computed. A second recording device, a wall chart, is then used to record the percent of correct responses for each session or stage of therapy.

Preprogram stage During the speech assessment of each of the four children grouped together for /s/ therapy, the *McDonald Deep Test,* the *Carter–Buck Prognostic Speech Test,* and a measure of connected, spontaneous speech showed that all subjects were consistently misarticulating /s/, but two of the four had very favorable stimulability scores while the other two had near-zero scores. Of the low-scoring children one had a one-sided lateralization of /s/ and the other a pronounced lingual–dental distortion of this sound. The clinician decided to provide individual production therapy to each of these children until the correct /s/ had stabilized in its isolated form. Therefore, each received two twenty-minute periods of therapy and phonetic placement techniques were used successfully to get correct production. Then they were placed in group therapy for periods of forty-five minutes twice weekly. Thus, all four children began group articulation therapy at approximately the same production skill level.

147

Stage one In this stage echoic production of /s/ in isolation was undertaken with each child modeling the clinician's productions over ten presentations one at a time. A criterion level of ninety percent was used with an FR−1 schedule using verbal praise for reinforcement. As each child responded individually, members of the group were urged to "watch and listen." The clinician randomized the order of children's recitation over three trials of ten echoic stimuli each and gave the first child to reach the ninety percent criterion (nineteen of twenty consecutive correct /s/ productions) a red chip (4 points), the next child a blue chip (3 points), the next a green chip (2 points), and the last a white chip (1 point). Using the tally sheet, each child wrote the number of points denoted by the chip on the Mr. Goodspeech side of the sheet.

The next step involved the same criterion and schedule of reinforcement, verbal praise, but the task involved production of correct /s/ in isolation evoked by the stimulus presented by the clinician individually to each child of "What is your sound?". Chips were again used as reinforcers when criterion levels were met, and each child tallied his points on the Mr. Goodspeech side of the sheet as before.

In the last step the clinician presented the grapheme S printed on a card and flashed it once to each child in the group one at a time. The first child to produce ten correct responses received the red chip, etc., and points were tallied as before.

Stage two This is syllable-drill stage, which is preceeded by a probe. The probe is designed to assist the clinician in choices for stimulus material to be used for each child (by its definition an operant approach must look at the level of responding of each organism for each stimulus presented). The clinician prepares ten CV (sx, si, soʊ, sʌ, su), ten VC (æs, is, oʊs, ʌs, us), and ten VCV combinations (æsæ, isi, oʊsoʊ, ʌsʌ, usu). While three of the members of the group repeated the last step of stage one, each one taking turns as "teacher," the clinician presented the echoic probe to the fourth child in a corner of the room. Each stimulus was presented individually in a random order, for example, first /sæ/, then /ʌsʌ/, then /is/. The correct ones in each category were counted, and in each child's case the easiest syllable type was identified to be used initially in this stage of therapy. The results showed that three children found the CV form to be easiest and one the VC form. Thus, the syllable drills proceeded using the same material for three children and different syllables for the fourth.

Two skills trained in this step included echoic and spontaneous responding. In the first the clinician modeled the syllable appropriate to the child simultaneously presenting a syllable drill chart (see Figure 5–2). As the clinician presented the spoken syllable, she pointed to its written form and moved her/his finger from the S to the vowel spoken or from the vowel to the S (for the one child working on VC syllables). In the spontaneous stimulus condition the clinician discontinued the verbal stimulus, and the syllable chart was used by itself to generate responses. With FR–1 at the beginning of both the echoic and spontaneous presentations, the criterion was set at ninety percent for three sets of ten syllables each (27/30). After the first set, FR–3 was used. Data from the syllable probe were then reviewed in each child's case to determine whether CVC, VC, or CV syllables should be trained next. Identical procedures for echoic and spontaneous responding were followed until all three types of syllables under both responding conditions reached criterion levels to advance to the next major step involving word production.

A probe for word production involved testing out /s/ in the initial, medial, and final positions. Each child was tested individually (no reinforcement) using three lists of nouns that were presented randomly across lists. Individual words were presented echoically by the clinician. Since the probe's results indicated that the initial position was easiest for all four subjects, this step was introduced. (High levels of correct responding by all subjects on the initial word probe caused the clinician to set FR–3.) In the echoic presentation the clinician showed each child in turn a picture of the common noun containing /s/ in the initial position and simultaneously spoke the word. A record was kept of each child's pass/fail on each presentation, and the first one to reach the criterion level of one hundred percent over three sets of ten stimuli earned the blue chip, the next child the red chip, etc. Points were entered on each child's tally sheet as before at the end of this phase, and the next one involving spontaneous respond-

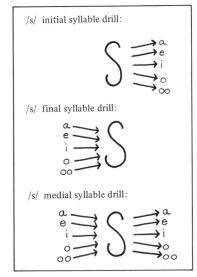

FIGURE 5–2 Syllable Drills

ing from picture stimuli was completed. The same procedures, criterion, and requirements were maintained.

The next step required each child to use a carrier phrase consisting of "I want. . . ." The clinician showed each child in turn a pictured noun; the child said its name using /s/ correctly and then, for example, said, "I want *soap*" (or other /s/ words such as "sandals," "sandwich," etc.). Again, the first child to reach the criterion of ten correct responses out of eleven presentations with FR–1 set received the red chip, etc.

In the last step in stage two the children were requested to generate an original statement about each picture using the /s/ correctly in the stimulus word. The clinician presented a stimulus card, the child named it (using the /s/ correctly, of course) and generated a short, meaningful sentence, such as, "I like hamburger *s*andwiches." The picture stimuli were randomized across subjects who took turns doing the task. The criterion of ten correct /s/ productions in original, spontaneous sentences was used, and the first child to reach the criterion got the red chip, etc. The schedule of reinforcement was FR–1, since four children took turns and the task was more complex.

Following the successful completion by all four children of the sentence-creation task, work proceeded to the production of /s/ in the medial and final positions in words, which the child first must produce from the isolated picture, followed by correct production in a word embedded in an original sentence. Probe data relative to the position of /s/ in words served to guide the clinician's choice of pictorial stimuli for individual children within the group setting. The criterion level, schedule of reinforcement, and techniques were the same in these steps as they were in the first one involving the /s/ in the initial position in words and the use of the word in an original sentence.[1]

Children within the group who suffer from difficulties in the correct use of /s/ in various word positions in spontaneous sentences may require additional training, while others who can accomplish these steps may be given appropriate words containing /s/ in various positions to practice in reading materials. As the clinician works individually within the group with the child requiring more assistance at this level, the three remaining children practice reading aloud the /s/ words in sentences that they read.

---

[1] It is not the author's intent here to illustrate an idealized therapy program. Rather, the intention is to show a typical application of operant technique in articulation therapy and in addition provide the reader with some ideas about how operant group therapy may be effectively applied. Many persons seems to believe that such approaches are limited to individual applications, possibly because little or nothing has been written about their use in group therapy. Morover, the use of parents trained to assist, while very desirable, is typically limited with older articulatory-defective children, and a problem in many operant approaches (carryover stages) is rarely stressed, thus weakening the program (Gerber, 1973). Therefore, our example here will not seek to be exemplary—merely representative.

As other members of the group detect errors of /s/ production in target words, they use the clickers to "punish" the error. The child reading is then trained to stop and make a correction of the /s/ production error. His audience then reinforces the correction by saying "good" in unison.

For those members of the group who show reluctance to forgo /s/ in the classroom and at home or elsewhere, additional devices can be used to condition responses, a suitable one, perhaps, being the use of a wrist strap (functioning as a discriminative stimulus) or perhaps a wrist counter to allow for a count of speech errors outside the therapy room. Counting and charting errors at home with assistance from family members is also recommended to help gain automaticity.

To assist the reader to conceptualize the application of the basic program described two examples will be provided:

Example one   This child, aged eight, was enrolled in a regular third grade class. His Carter–Buck stimulability score for /s/ was 33.3 percent, and deep testing revealed almost totally consistent error performances as did observations of his spontaneous speech. The wall graph for George (Figure 5–3) shows his progress over time and various stages of therapy. George attained the fifty percent-correct level of responding on imitating the clinician's production of /s/ in isolation during the first session on October 26th. On October 28th he reached the ninety-percent criterion level for this task. On November 3rd he attained the ninety-percent

FIGURE 5–3 Wall Chart Showing George's Progress in Articulation Therapy

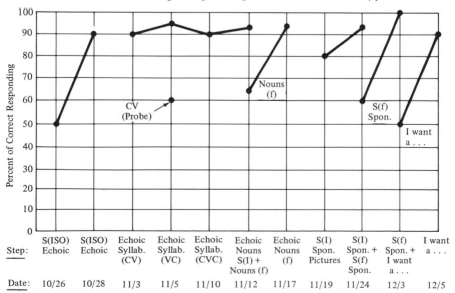

criterion for the imitation of /s/ CV syllables, and he reached this level on November 5th for VC syllables echoically presented. A probe for VCV showed sixty percent echoic responding. On November 10th he achieved the ninety percent criterion for CVC syllables. Echoic nouns with /s/ in the initial position reached the criterion level on November 12th and echoic nouns in the final position a sixty-five percent level of correct responding. On November 17th George reached the criterion level for echoic nouns with /s/ in final position. On November 19th he attained the eighty percent level of success producing /s/ from pictures with the sound in the initial position, and he reached the ninety percent level for doing this during the next session on November 24th. He also was trained to produce /s/ in the final position via picture stimuli on this date, and he reached the criterion level on this task on December 3rd. He also responded successfully to the "I want a. . . ." task fifty percent of the time, and at the last session he reached the ninety percent criterion on this task. The *McDonald Deep Test of Articulation* was readministered on December 10th, and George achieved a score of eighty-nine percent correct.

Example two   Charles was a fifth grade student. In fourth grade he enrolled in articulation therapy for severe lateral distortions of /s/, /z/, /ʃ/, /tʃ/. His progress was not satisfactory, possibly owing to a poor attitude about therapy and poor attendance. In fifth grade his attitude and attendance improved, and the operant approach to therapy began. The wall chart (Figure 5–4) shows his progress on the program. In ten sessions Charles advanced from a base rate of zero, as determined by the *Deep Test of Articulation* to being able to produce the ten initial-/s/ nouns in spontaneous speech and the ten final-/s/ nouns in connected speech.

In summary, although the author's personal bias is to apply an experimental approach to speech therapy, such as the use of the operant paradigm in articulation therapy, we have no overpowering evidence to support the use of such approaches to the exclusion of others at this time. It is conceivable that traditional articulation methods, usually accomplished using classical S–R conditioning, can be equally effective in the elimination of many young children's articulation errors. We can examine some experimental evidence which has addressed the question of whether behavioral modification approaches (largely based on the use of the operant paradigm) are more effective than traditional ones in the improvement children can make in sound discrimination and articulatory production.

Although debate on the efficacy issue seemed to abound some years ago (particularly in the latter part of the 1960 decade when teaching machines programmed using operant techniques were being tested), no real resolution of it appears to characterize the literature. Many variables probably relate to the determination that one treatment approach is superior to another, and this contributes to the difficulties and complexities of arriving at clearly valid conclusions.

Data were presented by Holland and Matthews (1963) to support the assertion that behavioral modification programs presented via teaching machines were more effective than traditional ways of teaching sound discrimination to /s/ defective children. Training of the discrimination of /s/ was conducted in isolation, in words, and again in words in which the sound was correctly or incorrectly produced. An operant-type program was presented on tape using a teaching machine which automatically advanced to the next item to be discriminated if the subject made the correct choice by pushing one of three buttons. An incorrect choice resulted in a tape review followed by another presentation of the item.

A four-phase program was devised by Holland and Matthews (1963) to train second- and third-grade children. In the first phase the presence or absense of /s/ in isolation was trained using sixty-two items. In phase two the position of the subject of a sentence was taught as well as training to accomplish placing it in the medial and final position of other paired words. The number of /s/ sounds contained in thirty other words was also part of this phase's discrimination training. In phase three the subject discriminated and signaled the position of /s/ in ninety-five words, and in phase four of the program subjects had to discriminate /s/ misarticulations from correct /s/ productions in 168 items. Basically, the children easily operated the teaching machine after as little as ten minutes of instruction,

FIGURE 5–4 Wall Chart Showing Charles's Progress in Articulation Therapy.

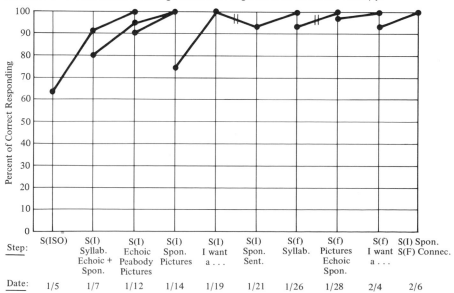

Step:	S(ISO)	S(I) Syllab. Echoic + Spon.	S(I) Echoic Peabody Pictures	S(I) Spon. Pictures	S(I) I want a . . .	S(I) Spon. Sent.	S(f) Syllab.	S(f) Pictures Echoic Spon.	S(f) I want a . . .	S(I) Spon. S(F) Connec.
Date:	1/5	1/7	1/12	1/14	1/19	1/21	1/26	1/28	2/4	2/6

and Holland and Matthews concluded that many children could advance in their discrimination-skill development almost independently.

In a related study Holland (1967) conducted a project over a span of two years to determine the effectiveness of a programmed instructional series in improving children's sound-discrimination performances. She concluded that there was generally sufficient evidence to show that the programmed instructional approach was superior to a traditional one in improving sound discrimination for numbers of different consonants.

The research activity of Garrett (1969) for some time dealt with the efficacy issue as he tested his Automated Speech Correction Program (ASCP) against traditional approaches to the correction of articulation. Using one hundred elementary school-aged children who had a variety of misarticulations as subjects, Garrett reported that his automated program was successful in making significant improvements in both speech/sound discrimination and articulatory production. However, when comparisons were made with the outcome of traditional therapy approaches, his automated program was not more effective in improving sound discrimination or sound production.

The most comprehensive study of the effectiveness issue was undertaken by Mumm (1973). Using 204 children and thirty speech/language clinicians, she conducted a experiment in which articulation changes of six groups were studied over a span of twenty-four weeks. The six groups of subjects were the following:

GROUP	DESCRIPTION
I: Experimental	Comprised of fifty children ranging in age from eighty-two to 124 months, selected to receive "traditional" therapy for their /r/ defects
II: Experimental	Comprised of fifty children ranging in age from seventy-eight to 124 months, selected to receive "behavior-modification" /r/ therapy
III: Control	Consisted of twenty-six /r/ defectives aged seventy-eight to 144 months, who functioned as untreated controls and did not receive therapy
IV: Experimental	A total of twenty-four /s,z/ defectives ranging in age from seventy-eight to 112 months, selected to receive "traditional" therapy
V: Experimental	A total of thirty-seven subjects defective in /s,z/ , ranging in age from seventy-three to 126 months, and chosen to receive "behavior-modification" therapy
VI: Control	Seventeen /s,z/ defectives aged seventy-nine to 126 months left untreated for their defects

Thirty speech/language clinicians in school settings were allowed to choose traditional or behavior-modification therapy for each child in the study. Apparently, many of the clinicians chose the approach that they were most confortable in using with /r/ or /s,z/ problems. The majority of the subjects who received behavior-modification approaches were seen individually while those selected for traditional therapy were seen in groups. To equate this in terms of direct therapy time per subject Mumm reasoned that if a child in a group was provided with traditional therapy along with three others for a thirty-minute period, the proportionate "direct-therapy time" for the subject in her experiment was one fourth of thirty minutes or seven and a half minutes. Records of therapy time for all subjects were made, and when the data were analyzed any differences between subjects in the traditional or behavior-modification groups were taken into account statistically using analysis of covariance.

Unfortunately, Mumm's written description of this project does not provide samples of the specific nature of the traditional and behavior-modification therapy approaches used by the thirty clinicians. No one "model" program for either approach was spelled out by the investigator, and, presumably, each clinician used some form of each type. The sophistication of the behavior-modification approaches is thus unknown, but it does seem likely that most consisted of some basic elements of the operant paradigm.

To test her hypotheses, which were basically in the null form, of no significant differences in children's articulation improvements when traditional was opposed to behavior-modification Mumm used pre- and post-scores or /r/ and /s,z/ Sound Production Tasks (Diedrich, 1971).

Judges listened to words imitated by each subject at the beginning and end of the experiment and rated them on a one to nine scale of defectiveness. Statistical evaluation of these data revealed nonsignificant mean differences between the /r/ subjects who received traditional and behavior-modification approaches, and this same finding merged from the data related to the performances of the /s,z/ subjects as well. Compared to the untreated controls, both /r/ groups showed significant improvements. While the trend for the /s,z/ subjects was to improve more than the untreated /s,z/ controls, differences failed to reach statistical significance (a finding Mumm thought related to more difficulty judging these misarticulations from taped sample of the type used).

In summary, the comprehensive effort to tease out some relevant factors related to the improvements of some articulatory defectives yielded few findings. Age, for example, was not found related to the effects of one type of therapy versus the other or which type of articulation error was treated. Both approaches seemed equally effective; however, Mumm reported that in the early sound-acquisition stages the behavior-modification approach generally resulted in more rapid sound production skill than the traditional approach. Later in therapy early rapid growth often slowed and the traditional approach seemed to become more effective. One has to ponder the issue of whether the approach *per se* was the dominant independent variable in this study, since we have seen some evidence that group articulation therapy is as effective in gaining improvements as individual therapy when traditional approaches are used (Sommers et al., 1966).

○ OPERANT APPROACHES TO ARTICULATION THERAPY FOR THE RETARDED

The use of operant technology to correct defective articulation has been stimulated by applying it to the challenge of correcting the speech of retarded persons. In particular, a series of systematic efforts have been undertaken and researched by McLean and his colleagues at the Parsons State School and Hospital in Parsons, Kansas. Basic approaches to articulatory correction were devised and tested by McLean (1965) and others, and many of these seem to have served as models for other later efforts to apply operant principles and procedures to articulatory-defective children of normal mental ability, stuttering children and adults, and persons with voice disorders or language impairments.

Almost by definition, mental retardation is a primary restrictor of generalization in learning. Thus, efforts to develop cognitive, linguistic, or motor skills frequently require that the instructor provide for a wide range of appropriate stimuli which are systematically and intensively presented. There is no good reason to believe that generalization of any type, whether stimulus generalization or response generalization, will occur after some learning has taken place; and, if mental retardation is severe enough, any that does can be considered "a gift from the gods." These major restrictions provide a fertile field for the use of the operant paradigm because of its systematic and accountable nature, and there is good evidence that its application can allow for some degree of success even with more severely mentally retarded persons.

One of the very basic early questions related to the application of operant technique to the articulation impairments of retarded children centered around the use of stimulus materials. What types of stimulus materials would be productive in evoking correct responses? What steps in the presentation of stimulus materials would be effective? How many trials of presentation of such material would be required to stabilize a step in learning? Would any stimulus generalization be found? These and other questions were researched, and the resultant information applied again and again to seek new evidence and chart new steps that might improve learning efficiency and effectiveness. Underlying the original work was the question of whether it was possible to shift stimulus control effectively with severely retarded persons.

As mentioned earlier, many of the steps in teaching the correct form of a speech sound emanated from this early work to help the retarded. As expected, early efforts stressed the development and testing of early stages in the process, namely, moving the individual from mastery of the new sound from one step of complexity to another and evoking the correct response using stimuli of varying degrees of abstractness. Because of its completeness and careful evaluation, an early investigation reported by McLean (1965) will be used to demonstrate how stimulus shift was used with mentally retarded children in articulation therapy.

Four male retarded children aged eleven to nineteen years and having moderate to severe articulation impairments served as subjects in an investigation designed to determine if an operant conditioning method would be effective in gaining correct responding from an auditory-visual stimuli which in turn is shifted to the control of picture, printed word, and intraverbal stimuli. Four related areas, probed for an understanding of the impact of learning on generalization, were stimulus types not trained, position generalization, across-position generalization, and over-generalization. After articulation testing which included a stimulability assessment, a phoneme was selected for each subject which was capable of being imitated correctly in its isolated form. This resulted in the fact that /s/ phoneme was selected for one subject, the /l/ for one, the /r/ for another, and two others the /tʃ/.

In the next phase ten different words were selected to be evoked using stimulus materials consisting of ten stimulus pictures and ten cards with the words written on them in manuscript. Also used were ten short phrases to evoke these same ten words but in an intraverbal context. Testing using each of these stimuli showed that none of the subjects would produce his target sound correctly on any word under any stimulus condition. The subjects could, however, be stimulated to correct production in the initial position some portion of the time by imitation.

In McLean's training program each child received individual instruction to bring his correct articulation response under the control of each type of stimuli using positive reinforcement as the consequent event. The positive reinforcer consisted of a penny dropped into a shallow box by a coin dispenser operated by the experimenter. For each five pennies found in the box at the end of the session a subject was allowed to keep one.

The basic operant program called for evoking correct target sound responses from each subject under the echoic-stimulus condition, followed by a shift of the response to the control of each of the three remaining proposed stimulus conditions. Training consisted of four conditions, after which posttreatment testing was undertaken.

In the first condition training was intended to bring correct responding to high rates using the echoic stimulus type. Subjects watched the examiner's face and were told to listen to the word spoken and then say it. Positive reinforcement using FR–1 was used. Stimuli were presented in blocks of ten words until the subject's responses were correct on his phoneme on at least fifty percent of the words occurring in each of four successive blocks of ten words each.

In the second condition McLean shifted the subjects to a modified first-condition stimulus so that each was instructed to watch the experimenter's face, listen, and say the word spoken; but, in addition, a picture depicting the word was held next to the experimenter's mouth as he presented each word for imitation. Again, FR–1 was used with positive reinforcement (penny in the box). These paired stimuli were presented in blocks of ten words until each subject achieved a criterion of twenty correct resposes in twenty attempts, after which the auditory-visual stimulus (S^1) was terminated. From this point on, the stimulus was the picture alone. Training continued using the picture stimulus (S^2) until each subject could attain a criterion level of at least thirty-eight correct responses in forty tries.

The shift in the third condition was from the picture stimulus to the printed word. Placing a stack of pictures and a stack of printed words matching them face down on a table, the experimenter proceeded to present each pair simultaneously by showing them together. After each subject demonstrated the ability to emit twenty correct phonemic responses in twenty attempts, the picture-stimulus stage was terminated and training continued using the printed-word stimulus (S^3). Correct responses in forty trials were achieved by each subject, effectively ending the third training condition.

In the final condition training proceeded to shift the printed-word stimulus to the intraverbal one (S^4). All the procedures and the criterion for success were identical to conditions two and three. Each subject was told that he would hear a sentence in which a word was "left out" and that his job was to say the omitted word. As the experimenter presented each intraverbal phrase, he exposed the printed-word card at the moment that the subject needed it to complete the task. After each subject had emitted twenty consecutive correct responses to the paired stimuli, the printed word one was discontinued. Training continued without it until the criterion of thirty-eight emitted correct phoneme responses in the intraverbal condition in forty trials terminated it. After this, the posttesting and assessment procedures were used to investigate the outcome and study the generalization questions.

The effectiveness of training was evaluated by comparing each subject's pre- and posttraining production of ten training words in all four stimulus conditions. As a test for generalization within the training sequence, probes were used by McLean to determine if the successful completion of one training condition allowed for generalization of elements in the successive one. (For example, at the end of S^2 a probe investigated a subject's responding to S^3.)

Subsequently, other tests for generalization effects were made by McLean. These were: (a) a new item generalization, (b) overgeneralization, and (c) across-position generalization. To test for new item generalization, he presented pictures of five new word items in which a subject's trained phoneme occured in the initial position. Each subject was told to name the picture; and if the target phoneme was articulated correctly, new item generalization was thought to have taken place. Overgeneralization, a phenomenon that occurs occasionally in articulation therapy, was tested using five new words in picture form in which a phoneme previously used as a substitute for the target phoneme was in the initial position. If the subject produced the phoneme on which he had been trained rather than the correct phoneme, overgeneralization was deemed to have taken place. The across-position generalization testing also used five new pictures, in which each subject's target phoneme occurred in the medial position. Across-position generalization was thought to have taken place if a subject correctly articulated the phoneme in the untrained, medial position in each word.

Training curves were developed by McLean to show the individual responding to the operant method. It was clear that responding rates varied considerably from subject to subject; however, some general conclusions were reached concerning the effectiveness of the stimulus-shift experiment. The general conclusions of this pioneer experiment can be stated as follows: Four of five retarded children trained by operant techniques were successful in shifting their responding from simpler to more complex stimuli. Using the evoking of correct responses under one stimulus condition, reinforcing such responses with pennies, and pairing them with new stimuli resulted in a continuum of learning. Experience with four of the five subjects showed that once stimulus control was stable, the shift to a new and different stimulus was possible. The generalization studies tended to reflect that once a phoneme was trained and emitted correctly under all of the stimulus types, generalization of the responses to new items occured along with some overgeneralization to their old substitution phonemes. Position generalization failed to occur in these retarded subjects, and one subject failed to show any form of generalization. A week after the termination of the program, all four subjects could articulate correctly their ten training words, and their original generalization patterns were maintained.

McLean experimented to determine the conditions under which the operant paradigm can be successful in training severely retarded children to articulate defective phonemes which they imitate in isolation. His experiments reflect the dedication required of early researchers in uncovering the learning skills and the rates of acquisition of severely handicapped children. The usefulness of the operant model is the driving force behind training skills in other types of communicatively impaired persons.

○ ACCOUNTABILITY AND PROGRAMMING IN ARTICULATION THERAPY

The major emphasis of the 1970 decade in many areas of education and the behavioral sciences was to "become accountable" for our expenditures of time, money, and energy. Industrial cost accounting at last had stricken speech and language therapy; effectiveness and efficiency issues were vogue and urgently pursued. All of this stirred the ladle in the pot called speech/language therapy. The result was a professional outcry for the "prove it," "show me," and "document" orientation toward professional work not so dramatically seen before in the speech/language professions. The behavior-modification approaches were a natural reply to such questions and challenges, since they were naturally attuned to the documentation and accountability issues because of their quantification and systematic analysis.

While the success of behavior-modification approaches to answering questions of cost effectiveness and efficiency was not to be denied, some astute observers of the professional scene slowly began to tabulate the costs of such approaches in terms of long-range professional goals. Not all behavior-modification approaches, although published and available commercially, were accepted by members of the profession. Serious questions, not fully answered at this time, were raised concerning many of the "canned" behavior-modification approaches. A common concern arose from B.F. Skinner's original conceptualization that the use of the operant paradigm had a basic, unifying concept: The experimental analysis of behavior was only related to an individual organism's rate of responding and this was unique to each experiment (or individual under study). Thus, behavioral approaches using operant techniques, by definition, could not cope with the wide range of individual variation that must be accounted for using the operant approach. Programs for groups of persons seemed inappropriate and much less defensible under the guise of the original doctrine, because if one went from the specific to the general the power of the operant paradigm might be diminished appreciably. Finally, it should be pointed out that some of the commercial operant programs for articulation remediation were heavily promoted by state departments of education for use by school clinicians in some states as part of inservice training. The outcome of many of these expensive, commercial endeavors to use operant principles in speech/language therapy remains unknown, but it is clear that many of these professional persons were exposed.

○ LIMITATIONS OF THE COMMERCIAL ARTICULATION PROGRAMS

Whereas a pigeon is trained to peck his own audiometric profile using strict operant technology (chaining being particuarly important), the human organism is basically much more complex; hence, it is subject to influences by many environmental and historical determinants of behavior. Those hoping to use the operant strategy to modify behavior may be unfamiliar with the historical determinants; therefore, predicted response from subjects fails to occur or responses occur that were not forseen. If the environmental determinants of behavior are not evaluated and anticipated in their influences upon a person's emitting a behavioral response, a great deal of variability of responding may be found. Therefore, this hypothesis is basically that the human represents the most difficult of all animals to predict in terms of the effect of events on responding. This is to deny the ability of "standardized" programs to emit the desired responses in many persons for whom the operant paradigm is the chosen learning/training tool. There are serious limitations to preconstructed articulation programs that find resolution of such problems *en masse.*

Few have written about the limitations of preconstructed operant programs for articulation remediation. The most cogent and comprehensive series of arguments was raised by Gerber (1977). She reviewed nine preconstructed articulation programs and compared their content and scope in light of a number of factors that concern speech/language clinicians. Many of her criticisms may apply to similar behavioral modification "programs" that have been commercially distributed since her report.

Among the salient inadequancies in many of the nine programs that Gerber reviewed were the following:

> Developers of many commercial programs fail to agree on the terminal behavior that is intended. This is a serious problem, because knowledgeable persons in programming have stressed that the program is developed from the terminal behavior forward to the initial behavior in small, sequential steps. Many of the programs that she reviewed showed limitations in their specification of the terminal behavior; and there was a wide variety of choices, some only within the clinic setting, a possible deficiency in terms of the completeness of the articulation-therapy process.

> Entrance Level. This was found by Gerber to vary considerably, and and in her review the beginning of articulation therapy was often not carefully specified in terms of how the clinician was able to get correct responding to defective phonemes. While some had provisions for phonetic placement activities, other programs ignored the importance for teaching a child the correct isolated or syllable form of the defective phoneme. Thus, some programs made vast assumptions that children can learn how to produce defective phonemes easily and quickly without intensive instruction—a questionable assumption at best.

> Quality Control. Her evaluation of the nine programs pointed out the lack of variability of response patterns in articulation therapy. As she stated, "A prewritten script, aiming at efficiency and economy, may actually prove less efficient by virtue of decreased effectiveness." She suggested that standard and continued phraseology such as "Say____" in the echoic mode or "What is this?" in the picture mode may be stifling and act to reduce responding, whereas the use of novel verbal statements may continue the likelihood of a high rate of responding. Therefore, mundane procedures may not prove productive in the long run.

> Provision of Prompts and Cues. Gerber cited the need for flexibility in appropriate cues and prompts during the process of shaping a person's articulatory productions. Some of the commercial programs that she ana-

lyzed failed to provide adequate prompts and cues to facilitate the type of learning needed to modify articulation toward the correct form. In particular, she emphasized the *individual* verbal prompts that are often accompanied by specific visual or touch-and-pressure cues to increase the probability of target acquisition as rapidly as possible. For example, elicitation and reinforcement of actions such as tongue elevation, tongue tensing, or lip retraction illustrate the acquiring of preliminary subgoals which advance the individual systematically toward the target goal. Deficiencies of this type abound in many "canned" programs.

Systematic Reinforcement. A single and dictated method of reinforcement may be tedious and lose effectiveness with some individuals receiving articulation therapy, because human responses tire of what is presented and vary considerably in their responses to the consequence of a behavior. Thus, a general recommendation concerning the nature and timing of reinforcement is contraindicated for some persons.

Quantification and Scoring of Responses. While almost all operant programs reviewed stressed the systematic and detailed counting and charting of behavior, Gerber reflected some concern that this practice, which has a discrete, fragmentary nature, may represent an oversimplification of the whole speaking process and not relate well to the characteristics of spontaneous, communicative speech. This potential loss may be overshadowed, however, by the values obtained from careful data analysis; and, while the operant method may be stilted to some extent, decisions about the course of action cannot be made without the counting and charting of behaviors. (This is the present author's opinion.)

Criticism of some operant programs that she reviewed was also advanced by Gerber to what she called "issues of methodology." Citing studies of traditional articulation-therapy approaches, which emphasized the values of using intrapersonal feedback mechansim to gain correction of defective sounds (Van Riper and Irwin, 1958; Mysak, 1959; Carrell, 1968, and her own study, Gerber, 1966), she observed that operant programs usually fail to stress the development of the subject to analyze accurately his/her own speech production. Since she considered this type of training to be of significant value for many articulatory-defective persons and most operant programs did not (and do not) train this skill, Gerber deemed it a serious shortcoming.

A second serious shortcoming of the operant programs reviewed related to "deliberate vs. automatic production." She concluded that many of the operant programs were deficient in inclusion of provisions for determining whether a subject was capable of producing his target sound(s) correctly without deliberately trying—an automatically produced correct response. The goal of carryover was often left to the individual with the problem and his associates. The typical operant preconstructed program failed to detail steps for the training of the target sound into the automaticity required (by some at least) for one-hundred percent correct responding under all stimulus conditions. In effect, she claimed that many such programs stopped too short. Some operant preconstructed programs, she reported, even purported to train for automatic production but were actually practicing responding to deliberate acts to emit correct sound productions.

Finally, Gerber concluded that

> The greatest weakness of some preconstructed programs is the practice of writing mandated prescriptions for target sound acquisition. This practice is regarded as insidious, because undue reliance on single prewritten approach restricts the flexibility, limits the resourcefulness, and lowers the level of function of the clinician, thereby performing a disservice to the client and the profession.

The clinician, sensitive, skilled, and knowledgeable, was deemed by Gerber as the backbone of the articulation-modification process.

Operant approaches to articulation therapy, she suggested, required modification themselves. The present author has perceived a decline in the promotion and use of "preconstructed programs" during the past five years, although many such programs probably continue to be used today.

SUMMARY

The use of operant technology to improve or correct children's misarticulations is now of relatively long-standing acceptance. Most of the evidence to show efficacy have come from studies of speech changes in retarded children's articulation. Indeed much of the detailed pioneering of procedures for fostering stimulus and, to a lesser degree, response generalization we owe to a small group of dedicated professionals who spent many years experimenting with retarded children. On the other hand, good evidence to support the assertion that the articulatory defects of children having intelligence within a normal range benefit more by strict operant approaches than more traditional stimulus-response methods is largely nonexistent with the exception of a few studies cited in this chapter.

The operant paradigm has served to draw the attention of many to the issue of accountability in speech-language therapy. Can we count and chart meaningful units of change? Are data emanating from the child reliably telling us what to teach next? Are speech-language pathologists providing the most effective stimuli in sufficient numbers and types to get rapid and consistent responses from the child or do we talk too much in therapy? While not primary, these may be valuable benefits of using a systematic and controlled technology in articulation therapy.

Of concern is the all-too-frequent use of "canned" therapy programs. In this chapter we saw strong criticisms raised about the acceptance of commercial therapy approaches—their limitations and restrictions. The author's experience has taught him that graduate students in training in speech-language pathology and audiology can learn to write very acceptable and highly specific operant therapy programs for their clients. Thus, many can master this powerful tool and learn to shape it to the individual characteristics of their clients—and wasn't this what B.F. Skinner intended in his timeless *The Behavior of Organisms* (1938).

Articulation-therapy aspects of orofacial abnormalities and neurological disorders

○ INTRODUCTION

Owing to an expanding population of older adults, greater availability of speech/language pathologists to serve their needs, and third-party payments to support services, professional interest in therapy approaches for older persons has grown. Graduate-level preprofessional training is increasing in these areas, and more inservice training of various types is being conducted across the country. The author's intention in this brief chapter is to outline some of the basic elements related to the diagnosis and remediation of various types of dysarthrias found frequently related to serious illnesses, neuropathologies, cerebral vascular accidents, physical injuries, and other conditions. Some attention will then be directed at the nature of dysarthric conditions in children, looking most directly at the cerebral palsied child. Finally, the articulatory component of cleft-palate speech will be briefly discussed, and an approach to the reduction of hypernasality as it occurs in various phonetic contexts will be described. Much more comprehensive accounts of neurogenic speech disorders and cerebral palsy can be found in other books in this Prentice–Hall series and in references cited.

○ DYSARTHRIC SPEECH IN ADULTS

As aptly expressed by Hardy (1968), the intense interest in aphasia and other related communication disorders overpowered interest in the speech dysfunctions of the neuromotor systems for many years. Although earlier writings by Froeschels (1943), Peacher (1950), Grewel (1957) and Canter (1967) did discuss elements of the nature of neuromotor-system speech disorders and some principles of therapy, the literature concerning neuromotor speech disorders was sparse. Vast experience with adult persons having forms of dysarthric speech led Darley, Aronson, and Brown to publish a comprehensive account of the nature and basic remedial strategies for dysarthric speech of various types. In their work, *Motor Speech Disorders*, published in 1975, they presented detailed new information about dysarthrias. Earlier, in 1969, they defined dysarthria very precisely as

... a collective name for a group of speech disorders resulting from disturbances in muscular control over the speech mechanism due to damage of the central or peripheral nervous system. It designates problems in oral communication due to paralysis, weakness, or incoordination of the speech musculature. It differentiates such problems from disorders of higher centers related to the faulty programming of movements and sequences of movements (apraxia of speech) and to the inefficient processing of linguistic units (aphasia).*

While earlier discussions of dysarthria treated it as a single entity (Preacher, 1950; Froeschels, 1953), later ones (Darley, Aronson, and Brown, 1969) specified seven different neurologic groups of dysarthria. Preacher (1950) had described dysarthric patients as having motor-control disorders related to weaknesses due to paralysis, incoordination of the muscles needed for speech, abnormal muscle tone, and motor impairments affecting respiration, phonation, resonance, and articulation. To this classical list Darley, Aronson, and Brown (1969) added impairments in the prosodic aspects of speech. Additionally, they described some of the motor impairments as single-process disorders of the type seen in a singular problem, such as defective articulation due to impairment of the hypoglossal nerve, a problem in achieving velopharyngeal closure adequate for speech due to neurogenic impairment, or an isolated dysphonia related to unilateral vocal-fold paralysis.

The importance of the movements and synchrony in speech production was stressed by Rosenbek (1978) as basic to a loss of control that some dysarthric persons have with direction, range of motion, endurance, timing, and force. Not only can all of these basic rudiments for normal speech be impaired; but, in some instances, there is extraneous and inappropriate activity, thus showing the range of possibilities for a lack of normal motor control.

Dysarthria is thought to reflect a wide range of congenital and acquired neuropathologies that complicate the normal activity of speaking. These etiologies range from CNS damage to the cortical areas, the cerebellum, and the brain stem or from damage to the peripheral nervous system, which consists of the cranial and spinal nerves along with their associated ganglia (LaPointe, 1975). Among the acquired conditions are infections, demyelinating diseases, space-occupying neoplasms. The most common type of congenital cause for dysarthria in its severe form is cerebral palsy.

The complex constellation of behaviors and events that relate to the overall diagnosis of dysarthria was clarified by Darley, Aronson, and Brown (1969) based upon their clinical studies of 212 persons at the Mayo Clinic. Subjects fell into seven distinct neurogenic groups consisting of pseudobulbar palsy, bulbar palsy, cerebellar lesions, Parkinsonism, amy-

* F.L. Darley et al., *Motor Speech Disorders* (Philadelphia: W.B. Sanders Company, 1975), pp. 272–276. Reprinted by permission.

otrophic lateral sclerosis, dystonia, and chorea. By rating samples of their spontaneous speech on a seven-point severity scale across thirty-eight dimensions of speech and voice, these investigators were successful in locating five types of dysarthrias. Based upon the natural clustering of their thirty-eight measures, the types they constituted are

flaccid dysarthria, found in bulbar palsy
spastic dysarthria, found in pseudobulbar palsy
ataxic dysarthria, found in cerebellar disorders
hypokinetic dysarthria, found in Parkinsonism
hyperkinetic dysarthria, found in dystonia and chorea

Dysarthric conditions were also found to be of the mixed type usually associated with multiple motor-system impairments of the type seen in some forms of amyotrophic lateral sclerosis, multiple sclerosis, and Wilson's disease.

A basic description of each of their five types follows, but the reader is urged to study the comprehensive material presented by Darley, Aronson, and Brown (1969; 1975). In *flaccid dysarthria*, in which bulbar palsy is present, a primary speech symptom is hypernasality resulting from velopharyngeal port musculature, followed by the tongue, lips, mandible, and larynx. When weakness of the larynx is developed, imprecise consonants are apparent; and a breathy voice may be heard, related to poor adduction of the vocal folds. Weakness in flaccid-dysarthric persons results from impaired cranial nerve innervation affecting the lower motor neurons.

In *spastic dysarthria*, found in pseudobulbar palsy, damage to the pyramidal tract and extrapyramidal tracts cause signs of a negative and positive nature. Persons having multiple sclerosis may develop these behaviors, which involve consonant distortions due to inadequate articulatory valving; slurred articulation due to poor tongue movements; and abnormal pitch and inflectional patterns (Farmakides and Boone, 1960). A slow rate of speaking, or the converse, a fast rate of speaking, plus occasional problems in initiating speech may also characterize their difficulties (Darley, Aronson, and Brown, 1975). Hypertonicity is also thought to cause the harsh and strained vocal quality found in some persons having spastic dysarthria, since this condition causes abnormal constrictions of the laryngeal musculature.

In *ataxic dysarthria*, seen in cerebellar disorders in which acute lesions may be present but also in some persons having multiple sclerosis, the presenting symptoms include tremulous voice quality possibly related to tremors of the respiratory and/or phonatory musculature. According to Kent, Netsell, and Bauer (1975) ataxic dysarthric persons often have slow speaking rates, vowel prolongations, imprecise consonants, equal and excessive stress patterns, and occasional "telescoping" of syllables. In spite of the fact that affected muscles are hypotonic and feel flabby due to a jerkiness resulting from irregularities of the speed and force of articulatory systems, such persons may perform articulatory contacts abnormally tightly resulting in occasional sound prolongations and complete blockage of speech may result at times.

In *hypokinetic dysarthria*, which can be observed in Parkinsonism, severe monopitch and monoloudness problems are prominent distinctions (Darley, Aronson, and Brown, 1969). Canter (1963) thought this condition was related to restrictions in Parkinson patients' range of fundamental frequencies. Many hypokinetic dysarthrics display a cluster of speech deviations which may represent a type of prosodic insufficiency. This condition manifests itself in short rushes of speech, variable rates of speaking, and inaccurate consonant production. It is related to a reduction in the range of motion in muscles needed to articulate, according to Darley, Aronson, and Brown (1975), who reported the common finding that lack of flexibility of function reduced control of the mechanism needed for phonation and could be seen in measures of pitch range and ability to shift pitch and vocal intensity.

In *hyperkinetic dysarthria*, seen in dystonia and chorea patients, the presenting speech symptoms consist of quick, unsustained, involuntary movements and slowness of movements. Apparently, the course of intended movements is impeded by abrupt muscular contractions which occur when the speech musculature is in repose. Muscle contractions also result in disturbances affecting required movements for proper respiration, phonation, resonance, and articulation (Darley, Aronson, and Brown, 1975) Contractions of an irregular nature can be found in the diaphragm, thoracic muscles, laryngeal structures, and muscles of the tongue and lips. Imprecise articulation, variable rate of speech production, vowel distortions, variations in loudness, and irregular articulatory breakdowns characterize hyperkinetic dysarthrias. The excessive, irrelevant movements that are imposed on musculature which is in the process of functioning to produce speech is a characteristic of this type of dyspraxia. These characteristics particularly relate to those having hyperkinetic dysarthria from chorea. Those resulting from dystonia are similar, and inefficiencies of phonation show themselves in prolonged vocal harshness and intervals between syllables. As with chorea, dystonia may cause the insertion of inappropriate silence in communication.

Although the articulatory component of dysarthric speech is most relevant to the present discussion, it is obvious in the conditions described that such a component is always associated with other difficulties in speech production such as disturbances in the prosodic aspects of speech and phonatory production. It therefore becomes somewhat difficult to specify how the complex set of skills required for correct articulation can be treated without some overlap to other aspects of speech. We may be able to see some general principles of therapy for dysarthrias of various types in adults and improvement of basic aspects of the articulatory process. Since normal speech production requires highly precise coordination of all its components, namely, respiration, phonation, resonance, and articulation and many dysarthric conditions have loss of control over some of these components, treatment may stress one over the other (and this is frequently the articulatory one), but all need attention. For example, not only the articulatory component affects speech intelligibility; the prosodic and supersegmental components and the phonatory ones can impair overall intelligibility as well.

Moderately high relationships between intelligibility of speech in dysarthria and reduced stress have been reported as have similar relationships between variable speaking rates and monoloudness and intelligibility (Darley, Aronson, and Brown, 1975). In the treatment process, therefore, we may find that efforts to improve the articulatory component must be coupled with efforts to adjust the defective overall speaking system of the dysarthric person to facilitate the development of compensatory motor control movements. If, indeed, the essence in speech therapy for dysarthric persons is to teach compensatory ways of going about the process, then the superior clinician working with such persons probably has excellent insights into how the various components of speech interface and is highly adroit at finding ways for individuals to adjust these components to improve speech intelligibility. As experienced clinicians know and authorities in this disorder acknowledge freely, there is no cure for dysarthric speech: only improvements are possible and only in some persons. Some approaches to the improvement of speech intelligibility in adult dysarthric persons follows, with stress on the articulatory component but including dicussion of the relationship between articulation training and the training of other defective components.

○ARTICULATION DIAGNOSIS AND THERAPY FOR DYSARTHRIC SPEECH

The choice of how to improve speech intelligibility in dysarthric persons includes consideration of the following:

which of the five types of dysarthria is present
diagnostic studies of all aspects or components of speech production
sensory, perceptual, and motor integrity of the individual
attitudinal and motivational variables related to the individual's participation
specific training, orientation, and biases of the clinician

Earlier, we saw evidence that five types of dysarthria identified by Darley, Aronson, and Brown (1969) have some common and unique characteristics of speech production. Since spasticity is seen in some, weakness in others, slow rates in some, variable rates in others, prosodic and surpersegmental disorders in many, and various types of respiratory and phonatory defectiveness in many but not all types, no overall prescription is possible (Rosenbek and LaPointe, 1978). Clearly, the exact extent to which each of the various components of speech are affected and contribute to overall loss of speech intelligibility is the primary goal of the diagnostic process for such persons, since these variables need to be manipulated by the clinician to "fine-tune" the patient.

Specific assessment of the articulatory component usually involves tape-recorded samples of sufficient length of both spontaneous, conversational speech and speech based upon reading phonetically balanced material. Standard articulation tests, such as the *Deep Test of Articulation* (sentence form) (McDonald, 1964), may also be used for a controlled evaluation of the possible presence of inconsistent misarticulation related to certain phonetic contexts. Tests of diachokinetic rates using /puh/, /tuh/, /kuh/ are also often made, and, in some instances, tests of oral–sensory discrimination may be used to evaluate aspects of the perceptual/motor speech mechanisms. As in other disorders, some clinicians may investigate the extent to which the dysarthric person can detect aspects of defectiveness in his own speech production by replaying portions of taped material to them and asking them to identify "poorly produced words," followed, if successful, by "poorly produced sounds within words." Such information may encourage the careful monitoring required by the clinician if he/she is to help dysarthric individuals gain better control over the speaking process.

Although Tikofsky (1970) completed an item analysis of fifty single words that represented nine difficulty levels of speech production and determined that they were highly clinically useful for estimating single-word intelligibility, results from an investigation by Yorkston and Beukelman (1978) suggested that no one measure was capable of making precise and reliable intelligibility measures across the range of speech sound in dysarthric individuals. Again, choices by clinicians of how to make useful and reliable assessments of intelligibility may have to depend upon which type of dysarthria one is evaluating.

Efforts to understand how some of the neuromuscular aspects of various types of dysarthrias impede speech using instrumentation have been made by Darley, Aronson, and Brown (1975) and others. One approach, palatatography, has the advantage of allowing the speech pathologist to see the contact of the tongue with the alevolar ridge and palate as single sounds or syllables are produced by the subject. A powerful technique used to study movements of the articulators in connected speech samples is cineradiography. Its use for routine checks for sufficient and precise movement has been drastically curtailed due to the potential risk involved in using radiographic techniques.

A technique that appears to yield a good deal of information about aspects of the speech production of dysarthric persons was reported by Netsell (1969) who studied simultaneous recordings of intraoral airpressure, rate of nasal air flow, and the speech signal to assess the competency of velopharyngeal valving. A study of intraoral air pressure and velopharyngeal valving, in particular, would probably be very helpful in those dysarthrics who often have muscle weaknesses of the articulators (flaccid dysarthria). For example, if a gradient of hypernasality and intraoral breath pressure could be located and found related to the adequacy of speech sound production, this gradient might be used to establish a hierarchy of training in a systematic and potentially effective way. Many of the fine points in speech therapy for the dysarthric patients may depend upon the specific identification and use of this and related types of information. This may also be the case for other organic speech disorders, such as cleft-palate speech.

Some of the commonly recommended areas for training in speech of many dysarthric persons include:

Slowing rate of speech The precise articulatory movements and contacts required for some speech sounds cannot be accomplished if dysarthric persons continue to use their premorbid speaking rates. Thus, the clinician should strive to test the efficiency of various rates and their effectiveness in gaining improved articulation. A particular rate may be best for accurate articulation in any individual's case.

Manipulation of supersegmental and prosodic factors In some dysarthrias the clinician may want to experiment with various forms of speech sounds in various, controlled phonetic contexts and systematically vary pitch, loudness, and the duration of the target sounds and occasionally those contiguous to it. In some instances, rather dramatically improved articulation of the target sounds and adjacent ones may be identified and used to advance articulatory performances.

Overarticulation This is probably a form of putting the word and/or phonemes within it into unusual supersegmental conditions in an effort to generate some type of integration of function within the overall speech production system. It is potentially useful and should be tried in many cases.

Phonetic placement Basic description of articulatory movements and patterns may be required. The mirror is essential in many instances of severe, consistent articulation errors. Aspects of the motokinesthetic approach may be needed to get better control over tongue movements. Compensatory training for cranial nerve damage affecting the ability of the dysarthric to elevate his tongue tip may be required. Touch, movement patterns, keen observation, and imitation of the clinician's sound production may be required for severe cases.

Syllable by syllable production It is often recommended that the clinician

train the dysarthric to approach syllable production with premotor planning. This is taught using polysyllabic words which the dysarthric learns
to separate into the syllables contained in it, followed by a deliberate effort
to produce each syllable accurately. This basic step is efficacious for
many such persons.

Biofeedback approaches Teaching tongue control and the feeling of contact when consonants are produced may be enhanced if various forms of
bio-feedback systems are used. Various forms of visual displays of individual speech sounds are available using oscilloscopic devices, modified
television sets, videotape playback units, and others. Automatic tape records can be used for auditory monitoring of speech production. Tactile
biofeedback devices of various types also exist and have been used with
dysarthric persons in many clinical settings.

Since many dysarthric adults are basically free from disorders involving
language comprehension and use (including reading and writing), therapy
is largely aimed at the defective speech production and the systems that
are affected. Therapy is basically not remarkably different for dysarthric
persons from what might be considered appropriate for more severely
involved persons having neuromotor disorders. The gradient is from the
best production of speech sounds in linguistic units, which may be from
sound in isolation to syllables, to words, to phrases, and then to sentences
(as usual). The work is tedious and requires highly structured therapy
characterized by drill. Therapy is almost always provided individually.
Unlike therapy for aphasia, controlled studies to show that therapy for
dysarthria is effective are nonexistent at this time. Most of those engaged
in it appear to believe that significant improvements can be made in some
individuals.

○DYSARTHRIA IN CHILDREN

The most common cause for dysarthria in children is cerebral
palsy. However, head traumas due to accidents of various types, diseases
acquired postnatally, and other conditions can result in dysarthric speech.
Since cerebral palsy almost always is present at birth, the child has never
acquired the process of normal speech production. (A large number of
the more severely cerebral palsied have defective speech.) While many
similarities exist in the nature of dysarthrias in children and adults, there
are also many differences. In terms of treatment for speech impairments
a common denominator is the frequent disruption in many or all of the
component parts needed for normal speaking. Each child's disorder needs
careful study to determine the extent to which modifications in one system
or more than one can influence the precision of speech production—a
principle clearly espoused for treating the speech disorders of adult
dysarthrics. However, a basic difference is that the motor-control systems
of cerebral palsied or other dysarthric children are developing but with

restrictions. There is a developmental aspect or potential that the adult dysarthric does not have which implies that some natural maturation process may come into play and should be considered when therapy for dysarthric speech is contemplated.

Since almost all children who are victims of cerebral palsy begin life with vital elements of their CNS impaired, the disorder in its more severe forms is far more pervasive than many forms of acquired dysarthrias in adults. It affects reflexes of many types, respiratory activities such as yawning and coughing, and other basic human functions such as biting, chewing, swallowing, and sucking. Programs of management for many young cerebral palsied children often stress the training of these basic functions prior to any consideration that might involve a direct attack upon defective tongue-movement patterns, for example, to gain the correct articulation of a speech sound. Indeed, until some improvement is made in this basic human function, the likelihood for successful indirect speech training is dismal.

To put the articulatory component in cerebral palsy speech into perspective requires the realization that the disorders occur in different forms depending on the specific site of the CNS impairment; for example, in a common form, spasticity, the component impaired is the pyramidal tract; in another common form, athetosis, the component impaired is the basal ganglia. Ataxic cerebral palsy involves impairment of the cerebellum. Many cerebral-palsied persons show a mixed form of the disorder. The result is that patterns of reflexes, movement, and physical posturing are frequently different, and approaches such as the neurodevelopmental one (Bobath and Bobath, 1972) take these basic differences into account as they strive to release primitive postures and movements which tend to be inhibited in many different ways. Improvement in posturing includes improvement in posturing for speech, and it is believed that the release of primitive reflexes enhances the possibility that volitional control over many muscle systems may be improved including those involving the vital functions of the speech, such as respiration and motor control of the articulators. Included in comprehensive programs of management for many young cerebral palsied children is training to develop volitional motor-control patterns, development of basic normal vegative functions (particularly training in eating and swallowing), stabilization training, perceptual stimulation, and training to use special devices, such as braces, wheel chairs, and others. A team of professionals consisting of physical therapists, occupational therapists, physicians, and speech/language pathologists most often coordinates the training activities, setting priorities and establishing short-term and long-term goals. Eventually, the speech/language pathologist and team members determine when the cerebral-palsied child has a basic readiness for direct speech training.

Recommendations for direct speech intervention in the more severe forms of cerebral palsy frequently vary to some extent depending upon which type of cerebral palsy is involved. Since it has been estimated that about eighty percent of the cases are spastic or athetoid forms (Phelps, 1949) and studies have shown (Hopkins, Bice, and Colton, 1954; Hoberman and Hoberman, 1960) that the majority of the severe speech disorders were found in the more severely impaired quadriplegic types with many milder hemiplegic and diplegic types having essentially normal speech, we can direct much of this brief overview towards the specific problems presented by these two types in their severe form.

Aggravated muscle tone is characteristic of spasticity. Muscle movements are often mass produced and abnormal postural arrays can be seen. If a spastic muscle is stretched deliberately by an examiner or by the muscle's antagonist, the result will be the rapid presence of the "stretch reflex," and the muscle will become rigid. Both extension and flexon activities can be impaired in such a way that if a spastic tries to extend one part of his body (an arm, perhaps, or his tongue), the effort will cause his whole body to extend. Conversely, if the person attempts to flex his leg, for example, failure will result, and the whole body will flex instead.

In the athetoid type of cerebral palsy we characteristically find "overflow," which is a condition in which voluntary movements are impaired. In some instances the disorder can be violent, and the individual may show sudden and powerful involuntary movements resembling jerking and pushing. Athetosis can be hypertonic or hypotonic, going from extreme muscle tonus in the former condition and extreme flaccidity of muscle tonus in the other. When the tense form of the condition is present, an examination of the tongue may show it oscillating continuously; and similar movements have been seen in the vocal cords and epiglottis. In this condition there are also abnormal postural patterns of the type seen in spasticity.

Due to the excessive muscle tension and presence of stretch reflexes, the spastic individual's pattern of articulating is bombastic and seems to occur as a series of muscle spasms that are released in a jerky fashion. At times the speaking process seems blocked, and long pauses may result before the spastic is able to speak again. The athetoid's speech is more variable in form. Some athetoids cannot speak at all. Generally, the speech problems of athetoids are more severe than those of spastic individuals; and it has been found that significantly smaller numbers of athetoids than spastics have intelligible speech, a condition perhaps related to the additional finding that athetosis appears to have a greater affinity to impair many of the muscles of the articulators, larynx, and respiratory systems (Wolfe, 1950).

As stated earlier, cerebral palsy speech is dysarthric, and this condition is more than simply related to impaired articulation. It involves prosodic, supersegmental, phonatory, respiratory, and resonance characteristics. Although isolated in therapy, each articulatory component relates to every other one to give the dysarthric speech its characteristic acoustic nature and efforts to fragment the process may be artificial and simplistic. The speech/language pathologist would have to consider all aspects of the disorder and establish priorities for remediation. For example, certain commonly defective speech sounds in cerebral palsy are fricatives and affricatives, and some sounds within each class have high requirements for intraoral breath pressure if they are to be produced adequately. The impaired respiration of some persons will not allow for sufficient amounts of pressure (particularly coordinated with speech) to allow for the adequate production of some of these speech sounds. Therefore, either the clinician sets out to improve the adequacy of respiration for speech prior to training production of some of these sounds or works on respiration and their articulation concurrently.

○ EVALUATION OF THE ARTICULATORS

A speech/language pathologist interested in improving the articulatory component in cerebral-palsy speech would need to know the extent to which each articulator, and its set of muscles is functional. In particular all movements of the jaw, lips, and the tongue need to be explored, both in nonspeech and speaking tasks. The soft palate may be impaired in some of the more pervasive types of the disorder, and one would need to know if adequate velopharyngeal closure can be achieved under speaking and reflexive conditions. If the soft palate appears nonfunctional under any speaking condition attempted, it may continue to show a normal reflexive action which can be demonstrated by touching of either the membrane covering the musculus palatogollus muscle or the pharyngeal wall and noting the rise of the soft palate. Testing of other reflexes, such as the masseter one, is also recommended to see if any form of possible basic innervation and movement can be accomplished even at the very primitive reflex level of function. Both the range of motion of the articulators and the strength of their performance need to be studied. Dentition, alignment of teeth and jaw, swallowing behaviors, sucking abilities, and other basic functions need to be evaluated in light of their bearing upon the acquisition of new speech sounds or the modifications of existing ones to more acceptable forms. In severe instances the goal is largely to provide the best possible set of performance variables which will allow compensation for defective structures and result in improved speech intelligibility. The clinician must patiently evaluate the individual's potential for change and devise a set of strategies to accomplish this act.

○ ARTICULATION THERAPY

Therapy approaches for cerebral-palsy speech are not uniform across the disorder due to the wide range of variables that can exist. For example, articulation of low front vowel sounds, such as /æ/, can be attempted with a child sitting in a wheel chair and the clinician holding his head up so that he looks directly at the clinician. This stabilization of the head posture and firm positioning in the wheel chair may result in a better movement of the jaw, thus allowing for better oral resonance and vocal-tract shaping resulting in an improved approximation of the vowel. If the child is spastic and has numerous stretch reflexes, better speech under some specific instances may be achieved if the attempt is made while he is relaxed by the clinician having been placed in a supine position on a plinth. In the neurodevelopmental approach the speech/language pathologist works directly with physical therapists and others and attempts speech production with the individual in a variety of postural patterns that may reduce or eliminate athetoid overflow or spastic stretch reflexes. Often by repeated trials involving the production of individual speech sounds, syllables of various types, words, phrases, or even short sentences, a better "match" of speech unit and physical positioning may be found that facilitates the accuracy of speech production.

Much of the motokinesthetic approach to speech therapy has been aimed at the improvement of cerebral-palsy speech (Stinchfield–Hawk and Young, 1938). The clinician uses tongue depressors, her fingers, brushes, and related tactile and kinesthetic tools and techniques to teach the motor movement pattern for a speech sound or unit of speech such as a syllable or word. The movements for the jaw and tongue may be stimulated by the clinician using her hands and fingers to take the individual through the movement pattern until voluntary skills are acquired. The clinician, for example, might place her fingers against the individual's top front teeth and then ask him to try and produce an /s/ sound or hold his lips together, provide verbal instruction for impounding air, and then, on signal, release his lips for production of /p/. These very old ideas are not necessarily antiquated in helping some cerebral-palsied persons to learn new articulatory skills; in fact, they remain very basic to techniques to improve the speech of such persons.

A well known approach to many of the motor-movement problems that accompany cerebral palsy was devised and promulgated by Rood (1954; 1962). Based upon the assumption that stimulation of muscles using chemical, tactile, and thermal stimuli would facilitate the development of functional mobility because the reflexes would be discriminated and brought into play as active motor engrams, Rood detailed a series of training activities for such persons. To develop functional mobility rapid tactile stimuli and cold stimuli, tapping of the tendon, or resistance during movement might be effective techniques.

The widespread use of phonetic-placement techniques along with the related motokinesthetic ones shows the need for intensive, special tactics in the improvement of articulation. Many cerebral-palsied children, for example, can benefit from imitation of articulatory positions by sitting beside the clinician and monitoring their performances in a mirror that is large enough to show both the clinician and themselves. Auditory discrimination and perceptual training is needed by many of them to teach the parameters of the newly acquired speech sounds. The use of tape recorders and automatic tape playback devices is often very valuable in teaching self-monitoring of speech and in showing the child in a repeated form that progress is being made under a special set of conditions.

Many of the approaches advocated for so-called "functional articulation disorders" will not be effective with a vast number of the more severely impaired cerebral-palsied persons. Since many of them are very consistently defective in the production of speech sounds, little hope for use of techniques that rely upon some correct production in some type of linguistic unit, such as key word, specific phonetic contexts, seems possible. For many clinicians, improvement of the articulation of many such children is tedious and painstaking and requires a special type of dedication. However, it is the present author's opnion based on his own clinical experience with such cases that many of even the most involved cerebral-palsied persons can improve their speech to some degree and the vast majority of them will develop some degree of functional speech. For those who cannot after a thorough effort has been made to teach them, nonverbal communciation systems may be valuable as a facilitator for speech development and, if necessary, can become the sole system for communication.

○ BIOFEEDBACK AS A TOOL FOR MOTOR CONTROL IN DYSARTHRIA

Some preliminary data suggest that biofeedback, a condition in which an individual receives information concerning the state of his body, is a valuable adjunct in motor training of dysarthric children and adults (Andrews, 1957; Marinacci and Horande, 1960; Shankweiler, Harris, and Taylor, 1968; Leanderson, Pierson, and Ohman, 1970; Netsell and Cleeland, 1973; Finley, Niman, Standley, and Ender, 1976; Finley, Niman, Standley, and Wansley, 1977). One of the more common forms of biofeedback consists of the use of electrodes placed on the surface of the skin or inserted in it to detect the electrical discharge of a muscle. This is electromyography (EMG), and selected studies of its use to improve speech motor movements in children and adults indicate its potential therapeutic usefulness. Normally, electrical information is detected by the electrode, amplified, rectified, smoothed, and displayed in some form, often on a voltage meter. The subject is then provided with information about the transaction, which is either in a visual display, an auditory mode, or a kinesthetic mode. This information guides the manipulation of the subject toward the desired behavior, for example, specific motor movement desired by the clinician.

Earlier attempts to show that EMG feedback can be beneficial by Andrews (1957) and Marinacci and Horande (1960) indicated that success could be gained with adults having hemiplegia and those having upper and lower motor-neuron paralysis. Studies of the effects of biofeedback training in children, such as the one by Simard (1969), indicated that children as young as seven can learn to control fine-motor movements under its purview. Subsequently, two investigations of the usefulness and effectiveness of cerebral-palsied children were reported by Finley and his associates. In the first Finley, Niman, Standley, and Ender (1976) found that four of six athetoid cerebral-palsy persons, some children and some adults, showed significant improvement in the reduction of EMG activity of their frontalis muscles. This resulted in significant improvements in speech, as seen in abilities to sustain consonant and vowels in isolation and in syllable production based upon the time it took the subjects to initiate requested syllables. These preliminary results, therefore, suggested that speech efforts might be enhanced if subjects could control their specific muscle activity in the defective frontalis muscle.

In a related effort, Finley, Niman, Standley, and Wansley (1977) also reported that four spastic cerebral-palsied children, aged seven to twelve years, could be trained to decrease frontal EMG activity with a resultant improvement in speech and motor skills after six weeks of training, thus suggesting again that EMG feedback might be very useful in controlling the aberrant muscle-movement activities associated with spastic cerebral palsy.

Hanagan (1977) applied EMG feedback training to a seven-year old, male child who had been medically diagnosed as having pseudobulbar palsy subsequent to rubella at age one. His speech disorder consisted of spastic dysarthria. Most of his motor impairment was limited to his oral musculature. Lip movements were particularly impaired, and he drooled a great deal under most circumstances. Tongue movements were rather grossly impaired for lingualveolar or linguadental placements in both speech and nonspeech acts; but he could make linguapalatal contact for production of linguapalatal speech sounds, and he had hyperactive gag reflex.

Biofeedback training using EMG was attempted for four hours weekly with his mother (a physical therapist) assisting in it, and training was directed at a variety of muscles required for oral-motor control. After assessing early findings, the emphasis shifted to control of lip movement during speech stressing the control over the superior orbicularis oris, the inferior orbicularis oris, and the angle of the mouth where the levator anguli oris and the depressor anguli oris cross.

To accomplish her simultaneous articulation and EMG training, Hanagan set the electrodes in place and urged her subject to move his lips and mouth in any way possible, which tended to increase the occurrence of auditory clicks which he heard. He was then instructed to imitate speech consisting of the following items:

VOWELS:

/i, o, a, ʋ, u, æ, ʌ, and ɝ/

CONSONANT–VOWEL SYLLABLES:

/m/ + above vowels
/b/ + above vowels
/w/ + above vowels

VOWEL–CONSONANT SYLLABLES:

above vowels + /m/
above vowels + /b/

WORDS:

bike, bee, boo, book, bye, bird, and boat
mild, me, moo, my, man, mom, mine, and mop
way, why, win, won, wheel, and woo

As he produced the target sound, he was asked to increase the rate of auditory clicks. The subject earned poker chips during each session or points toward a toy or a specific privilege for improved articulation of target sounds. The increase in auditory clicks simultaneous with the production of the target sound was reinforced on a continuous schedule which was changed to an intermittent one in later sessions. When auditory clicks increased but the target sound or any noticeable approximation of the movement required for its production occured, the clinician did not provide reinforcement. Oral-movement training was also accomplished without speech as part of the single-subject research investigation.

To assess effectiveness video tapes were made following the first training period on several speech and oral-motor tasks consisting of vowels, CV and VC syllable imitation, and the eliciting of words using the *Goldman–Fristoe Test of Articulation* (1969). The subject also imitated lip movements of various forms and was tested for diadochokinesis. Thirty hours of simultaneous speech therapy and intensive EMG feedback training were provided, three sessions weekly of twenty to thirty minutes duration. Repeated video tapes were completed at the end of approximately fifteen hours of instruction and again at the end of thirty sessions using the same measures used at the end of the initial training session. The results indicated that significant improvements occurred on some speaking tasks (particularly the easiest ones), but evidence to show that some oral motor movements were improved was not found by judges who viewed the three video tapes. Flanagan's findings seemed encouraging concerning the use of EMG feedback with a spastic dysarthric child in terms of improvements in some of the basic aspects of speech production. Controlled research studies of the effectiveness of such approaches using untreated and treated groups and groups in which other (nonfeedback) techniques are used are obviously required before we can formulate more conclusive opinions.

○ THE ARTICULATORY COMPONENT IN CLEFT-PALATE SPEECH

As we have seen in the earlier discussion of cerebral-palsied speech, the types of conditions associated with the disorder are myriad, and this appears to be the case in cleft-palate speech also. Understanding cleft-palate speech disorders is not easily accomplished because the variables that need to be appraised revolve around the extent of the physical limitations imposed by the size and extent of the cleft condition, age of the child, type of restoration attempted, individual motivational and training factors, the type of compensation used by the individual in order to speak more intelligibly, and the impact of all this on the normal speech development process in young children. One thing that has become clear in the past years is that the defective articulatory aspect of this condition is the major obstacle to normal speech.

The hypernasality condition, which relates to specific phonetic contexts in many cleft-palate speakers, obviously changes resonance, limits the intraoral breath pressure that many speakers can muster, and, in some cases, may influence the nature of voicing. There is evidence, as well, that tongue-movement speed and accuracy may be impaired in some cleft-palate persons (Mathews and Bynne, 1953; Fletcher, 1978). Both the place and manner of the articulation of certain types of speech sounds are frequently affected, and when both are erroneous, the speech is badly impaired. Generally, speech/language pathologists consider that when place of articulation is affected the condition is less defective than when manner of articulation is affected. As we will see later, some propose to allow place-of-articulation changes if the manner feature of speech-sound production can be approximated when therapy attempts show the target sound cannot be developed in its true form. This form of compensation may be necessary under extreme conditions to allow for increased speech intelligibility.

The popular belief that some significant aspects of cleft-palate speech have been learned in childhood, reflected in views and data interpretation of numerous investigators (Koepp–Baker, 1957; Morley, 1958; Mysak, 1966; Morris, 1968) is probably an important concept for the speech/language pathologist to embrace. Some aspects of the defective articulation, for example, can be logically associated with the pathomorphology of the condition, while others present cannot and are perhaps "functional arti-facts" of the condition. This situation was adroitly explained by Morris (1968) when he discussed how the anatomical–physiological deficits in cleft-palate speech, when eliminated, failed to change functional mis-articulations:

> As an example, consider a child with velopharyngeal incompetence who demonstrates, among other errors, distorted /r/, /ɚ/ and /ɝ/ and a substitution of a glottal stop for the plosive /k/. Both types of articulation errors may have been learned. The use of the glottal stop for the /k/ may have come about because the child was not able to impound an adequate amount of intraoral pressure for an acceptable /k/, and because he rejected the faulty /k/ in favor of glottal stop for the reason that the glottal stop sounded better or more normal to him. The response then became generalized and in subsequent behavior the glottal stop was consistently substituted for the /k/. Clearly, the individual easily could have continued to use the /k/ which was characterized by nasal leak or oral breath pressure. The glottal stop error for /k/, then, is related both to the velopharyngeal incompetence and to inappropriate learning.

Morris went on to explain that the class of /r/ errors is not related to requirements for intraoral breath pressure but were related to tongue positioning, and he concluded in his example that they were learned.

types of speech-sound errors

For many years, it has been established that many cleft-palate speakers suffer most in their attempts to articulate from difficulties in producing certain classes of sounds, particularly fricative, plosive, and affricative sounds (Bzoch 1965; Spriesterbach et al., 1956; Moll, 1968). The usual explanation for this is that many of these sounds require greater amounts of intraoral breath pressure and air-flow rates for their produc-tion, and the "leaky" velopharyngeal seal of many such speakers bleed off a significant amount of this pressure and air flow thus making the sounds difficult to produce. Recently, however, Fletcher (1978) has reassessed the results of investigations on this point and added new data from a comprehensive study of seventy repaired cleft-palate speakers, and his findings show that older findings and his newer ones reflect a slightly altered and refined arrangement concerning the classes of speech sounds that may be most troublesome for cleft-palate speakers.

Comparing his newer data to those of Spriesterbach et al., 1956; Van Denmark, 1969; Byrne et al., 1961; and McWilliams, 1958, Fletcher found that fricatives, affricatives, and plosive sounds were almost always the most defective across a wide age range of from three to fifty-nine years, but the two most difficult sounds in all studies were /s/ and its voiced counterpart,

/z/. He reasoned that the older concept of classification was not realistic, and the data generally supported a reclassification in which /s/ and /z/, which had traditionally been classified with other fricatives such as /f/ and /v/, would be grouped with other more difficult sounds which are usually affricatives. These sounds, /tʃ/ and /dʒ/, would then be classified with other sibilant sounds, namely, /s/, /z/, and /ʃ/. The pattern of errors would then consist of sibilants, nonsibilant fricatives, plosives, glides, and nasals, ordered from most difficult to least. Fletcher's new data and findings from earlier studies appear to support his new classification system and offer a clearer conceptualization of the problems that cleft-palate speakers have in speech-sound production.

As students of speech science can attest, /s/ is a precise and demanding speech sound. Not only is the requirement for intraoral breath pressure high but requirements for velocity of air are vital to its production, and there is movement required to get its position accurately stabilized for each speaker as a function of tongue mobility, dentition–mandibular alignment, and coordination. Since many cleft-palate speakers who suffer from articulatory defects have some degree of difficulty in all these areas, it is no wonder that /s/ is the most frequently difficult sound for them to produce. For some cleft-palate speakers, /z/ is equally difficult or more so than /s/, while for others the added element of voicing, for some obscure reasons, masks a portion of the hypernasality that might be detected when /s/ is produced. There is a great deal of variation on /s/ and /z/ production across cleft-palate speakers, and this variation may relate to individual coupling of voicing, resonance, and resultant velopharyngeal closure when each of these two sounds is produced or possibly to specific phonetic contexts in which one is influenced more by adjacent speech sounds than the other resulting in improved or poorer articulation. Perhaps a favorable prognostic sign would be the existence of /s/ and /z/ production without nasality, substitutions, distortions, or omissions, since this condition of normal production might imply that other speech sounds in the sibilant family established by Fletcher (1978), such as /ʃ/, /tʃ/, and /dʒ/, might be amenable to correction if defective. Furthermore, the adequacy of velopharyngeal valving for correct /s/ and /z/ production might also suggest that nonsibilant fricatives, such as /f/ and /v/, might also have the potential for correct or nearly correct production. This might particularly be the case if /s/ and /z/ were articulated normally in spontaneous, connected speech, but even a rather optimistic view for their correction might be warranted if they were accurately produced. Rather interestingly, prognostic factors relating to cleft-palate speech have remained largely unexplored.

Understanding of some of the important underlying conditions that relate to defective articulation in cleft-palate speakers was enhanced by data obtained from seventy repaired cleft-palate speakers aged five to fifteen by Fletcher (1978). Using the Iowa Sound Pressure Test (Morris, 1966), he assessed their abilities to articulate forty-three items and added seven others to increase the sensitivity of the test for certain fricative sounds. He made a comprehensive series of related tests of tongue posture, velar height, length, thickness, retraction, pharyngeal depth, and velo-pharyngeal gap and other measures including a test for diadochokinesis. He used his data as predictors of their total errors on the modified Sound Pressure Test. This test is a form of regression analysis termed "the maximum R^2 improvement procedure" to identify the most powerful factors related to defective cleft-palate speech. He found three variables could account for fifty percent of the variance in the defective articulation presented by the speakers. In the order of greatest importance these three factors were reported to be as follows:

1. *Motor coordination* (polysyllable diadochokinesis)
   Velopharyngeal *valving*:
2. /s/ velar contact
3. /ɔ/ gap

Fletcher set the computer program in such a way as to request the best ten-variable model to explain cleft-palate speech. The first three most important variables were those presented above; the remaining important variables were

4. *Degree of original anomaly* (class of cleft, that is, palate and lip, etc.)
   Tongue position:
5. /s/ linguapharyngeal aperture
6. /ɔ/ tongue retraction
7. /i/ tongue fronting
   Jaw position:
8. /ɔ/ vertical interincisor aperture
9. /ɔ/ horizontal intercisor aperture
10. *Compensatory action* (velar retraction difference)

He found that his ten-variable model accounted for all but twenty percent of the total variance related to the articulation performances of his cleft-palate subjects. Fletcher's findings appear to be important, since they were based upon a reasonably large sample of repaired cleft-palate children and subjected to a powerful multivariate form of analysis. As in most prediction studies, however, replication is needed to confirm the strengths of the relationships determined.

Rather surprisingly Fletcher found that the most important variable related to the articulatory performances of his speakers was their accuracy and speed of production of the diadochokinetic task consisting of /p∧, t∧, k∧, f∧/. He was able to muster some evidence by recasting his data that scores for this task on the modified *Iowa Pressure Test* were not related to deficient velopharyngeal valving *per se* but to a lack of fine-motor coordination of the articulators. This conclusion is tentative of course, but it suggests that cleft-palate speech may have other elements of defectiveness existing concomitantly with the principal one of deficient velopharyngeal valving, at least for the types of surgically repaired cleft-palate children that Fletcher studied.

The second and third most important variables, /s/ velar contact and /ɔ/ gap, were evaluated using cephalometric observational techniques. These two items in particular were most importantly related to overall velopharyngeal valving. Fletcher concluded from his data that a vp gap of 2 mm. or less had an appreciable effect on the production of vowel sounds. General articulatory deficiencies were found to be linked to vp gaps of more than 2 mm., and consonants such as /s/ lack of contact closure were definitely related to poorer articulatory performances. His data also supported the fact that degree of velopharyngeal closure was different for vowels and consonants—a finding long recognized by many earlier investigators. Fletcher noted that differences in the degree of vp closure required before speech becomes nasal may relate the ages of the subjects studied and other variables.

Both tongue position and jaw position were linked to the accuracy of articulation in Fletcher's data. A range of tongue positions was found associated with superior speakers. Fletcher concluded that a defensible explanation was that a wide range of tongue positions for vowels characterized the inferior cleft-palate speaker. Additionally, he found that when vowels are produced using improper positioning of the tongue, consonant production may be negatively influenced, since speakers may not arrive at the ideal target positions for consonant production. The suggestion appears to be that combinations of syllables containing vowels and consonants may link together to impair articulation.

Previous information has rather consistently associated voice and voiceless environments and vowel articulation with the defectiveness of cleft-palate speech. Lintz and Sherman (1961) reported that perception of nasality was greater in syllables with voiceless environments than voiced environments and greater in front than back vowels. Earlier, Spriesterbach (1959b) produced evidence to show that high vowels were more nasal than low vowels, and Minifie et al. (1970) later confirmed that high vowels were more nasal than low vowels and went on to show that lateral pharyngeal wall movement during speech production was greatest on low vowels and least on high vowels. To add to this information Isshiki and Ringel (1964) reported that greater airflow rate was seen during the production of voiceless consonants than voiced ones, and airflow rate decreased from the highest for stops, followed by fricatives, to the lowest for vowel-like sounds (glides). Thus, airflow rate was linked to the most frequently defective consonants in cleft-palate speech. Further evidence for the impact of airflow requirements in speech production was provided by Lubker (1970) whose results attested to the fact that greater nasal airflow in prosthetically managed cleft-palate speakers occured on consonants than vowels with greater nasal airflow on high vowels than low vowels. He also reported that voiceless consonants had more nasal airflow than voiced consonants. Although voiced fricatives were found to have greater nasal airflow than voiced plosives, voiceless plosives had more nasal airflow than voiceless fricatives.

This literature and more not reported here stimulated the development of a hierarchy of perceived nasality in cleft-palate speakers devised by Moore and Sommers (1974) and investigation to determine its effects upon listeners' ratings of speech intelligibility in its different phonetic contexts. The combination of vowels and consonants resulted in a variety of phonetic contexts that were established from the least conceivable degree of nasality to the greatest using the factors found in the literature to guide decisions concerning the possible order. The order of perceived nasality was validated on the first study and the effects upon speech intelligibility in the second one. Finally, we shall see some preliminary

FIGURE 6–1 Mean scale scores of perceived nasality for consonants within vowel contexts. (From W.H. Moore and R.K. Sommers, "Phonetic Contexts: Their Effects on Perceived Nasality in Cleft-Palate Speakers," *The Cleft Palate Journal*, 10, 72–83 (1973). Reprinted by permission.)

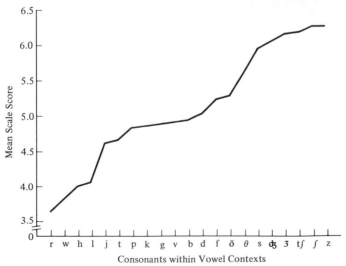

evidence to show that use of the hierarchy of perceived nasality across phonetic contexts is a valuable adjunct to guide articulation therapy in cleft-palate speech.

Sixteen repaired cleft-palate children, aged four years, eight months to thirteen years, five months, imitated CVC syllables in which the vowel was the same in the initial and final positions in the Moore and Sommers investigation. The following vowels were used with each of the consonants shown in Figure 6–1: /a/, /ɔ/, /u/, /æ/, /ɛ/, and /i/. The mean-scale score for nasality for all the vowels as a function of the consonant environments can be seen in Figure 6–1. These data constitute the hierarchy of perceived nasality across phonetic contexts for these speakers.

These results demonstrated that consonants were perceived to increase in nasality in the order of glides and glottal fricative /h/, plosives, and fricatives/affricates. Tests of linear trend revealed an almost perfect linear progression across vowel contexts. Nasality was perceived between vowel contexts from low- to high-vowel contexts, and vowel height was found to be a more significant variable in the perception of nasality than front- or back-vowel classification. Fricatives/affricates in /ɔ/ environments proved to be the best single predictor of perceived nasality in VCV syllables. A number of findings of earlier investigations were confirmed by these data, and a hierarchy of perceived nasality across phonetic contexts was determined comprehensively for the first time.

Therapy based upon the perceived hierarchy of nasality Findings from the Moore and Sommers investigation were systematically used by Lang (1974) to plan and conduct articulation therapy with cleft-palate children. A program to eliminate hypernasality in phonetic contexts having the least perceived nasality to those having more, in a monotonic, regular fashion, according to the Moore and Sommers data. The eleven subjects were repaired cleft-palate children, aged nine to thirteen years, who were attending an eight-week summer camp therapy program at Duke University. Six were males and five were females. All had some hypernasality in their spontaneous speech.

This program, presented on the following pages, stressed teaching each child to perceive hypernasality in phonetic contexts. Lang provided each child with individual and group therapy daily. She reported that pre- and postarticulation changes in a portion of the eleven children showed encouraging signs of progress. At the end of the eight weeks, she also noted that one child whose velopharyngeal valving was very poor, had successfully completed only step one of the program, three successfully completed step two, three step four, one step five, and two step nine. Lang considered the children's progress to be directly related to their degrees of velopharyngeal competency. In her opinion their overall progress following the hierarchy of perceived nasality as a guide in therapy was very valuable in gaining improvements in many children.

○PROGRAM FOR THE ELIMINATION OF HYPERNASALITY
IN PHONETIC CONTEXTS*

Rationale This program was developed and tested by Mary Lang (1974). It is based on the rationale that a hierarchy exists for degree of perceived nasality in both consonants and vowels. This hierarchy was first identified and described in an investigation performed by Moore and Sommers in 1973. Their findings revealed that judges perceived the phonemes listed below to fall into the following hierarchy from least to most nasal:

CONSONANTS

1. Glides and glottal fricatives /h/, /r/, /w/, /l/ and /j/
2. Plosives /t/, /p/, /k/, /g/, /b/, /d/
3. Fricatives /v/, /f/, /ð/, /e/, /s/
4. Affricatives /dʒ/, /ʒ/, /tʃ/, /ʃ/
5. /z/ was perceived as the most nasal consonant

VOWELS

1. /ɔ/
2. /a/
3. /ɛ/
4. /æ/
5. /u/
6. /i/

Terminal objective Normal resonance (no occurrence of hypernasality) on all phonemes produced with velopharyngeal closure in conversational speech.

STEPS (SUCCESSIVE APPROXIMATIONS):

1. Correct production of the following vowels. Practice in the order listed:
   /ɔ/, /a/, /ɛ/, /æ/, /u/, /i/
2. Correct production of VCV combinations utilizing each vowel (from least to most nasal) in combination with each consonant (from least to most nasal).

* M. Lang, "Program for the Elimination of Hypernasality," (Unpublished Manuscript, Kent State University, 1974). Reproduced by permission.

3. Correct production of CVC combinations utilizing each vowel (from least to most nasal) in combination with each consonant (from least to most nasal).

4. Correct production of the varied vowel and consonant combinations (from least to most nasal) in the initial and final positions of monosyllabic words.

5. Correct production of the varied vowel and consonant combinations (from least to most nasal) in bisyllabic words.

6. Correct production of the ten short phrases and sentences loaded with the following phonemes in combination with all of the vowels:

/r/, /w/, /h/, /l/, and /j/

7. Correct production of ten short phrases and sentences loaded with the following consonants in combination with all of the vowels:

/t/, /p/, /k/, /g/, /b/, /d/

8. Correct production of ten short phrases and sentences loaded with the following consonants in combination with all of the vowels:

/v/, /f/, /ð/, /θ/, /s/

9. Correct production of ten short phrases and sentences loaded with the following consonants in combination with all of the vowels:

/ʤ/, /ʒ/, /tʃ/, /ʃ/, /z/

10. Correct production of all consonant and vowel combinations in long sentences.

11. Correct production of all consonant and vowel combinations while reading a short paragraph. (If the child does not read, poems or nursery rhymes can be substituted at this step.)

12. Correct production of all consonant and vowel combinations in a structured conversational task.

13. Correct production of all vowel and consonant combinations in a spontaneous conversational task.

Stimuli Syllable lists were formulated containing all possible consonant and vowel combinations for steps two and three (see examples below). Word lists utilized for step four contained CVC, VC, and CV combinations listed from least to most nasal. On step five word lists containing CVCV, VCV, CVCVC combinations were utilized. Stimuli for steps six, seven, eight, and nine consisted of sentences which contained words taken from the word lists (see example below). Short paragraphs, poems, and nursery rhymes, utilized for step eleven, were randomly chosen based upon the clients level of linguistic functioning. Structured conversational tasks consisted of a question and answer period between the client and clinician. The client was encouraged to answer the clinician's question with a complete sentence.

EXAMPLES OF CONSONANT AND VOWEL COMBINATIONS

SYLLABLE LEVEL: STEPS 2 AND 3				WORD LEVEL: STEPS 4 AND 5	

VCV	VCV	MONOSYLLABIC		BISYLLABIC	
ɔhɔ	pɔp	wrought	/rɔt/	chopper	/+ʃapɚ/
aha	pap	rot	/rat/	checker	/+ʃɛkɚ/
ɛhɛ	pɛp	red	/rɛd/	channel	/+ʃenl/
æhæ	pæp	rat	/ræt/	chewy	/+ʃui/
uhu	pup	root	/rut/	cheaper	/+ʃipɚ/
ihi	pip	reel	/ril/		
ɔrɔ	sɔs	shock	/ʃɔk/	follow	/falo/
ara	sas	shot	/ʃat/	feather	/fɛðɚ/
ɛrɛ	sɛs	shed	/ʃɛd/	family	/fæmli/
æræ	sæs	shall	/ʃæl/	feeble	/fibl/
uru	sus	she	/ʃi/		
iri	sis				

SENTENCES FOR STEPS 6, 7, 8, AND 9

1. The red rat was wrong.
2. He hid the hat here.
3. The wet wagon went that way.
4. The lazy lion laughed.
5. Your yard is not yellow.
6. The root was rotted.
7. Harry hit his heel.
8. When will you win?
9. Larry lost lots of lollipops.
10. Yesterday he was eleven years old.

Criterion 1. A criterion of zero percent perceived nasality on the phonemes listed was met on one complete trial at each successive approximation before moving on to the next step. At the sentence and conversational levels, this criterion was applied only to those phonemes which were produced with velopharyngeal closure.

2. A criterion of one-hundred percent agreement with the clinician on the self-monitoring task was also met before movement was made from one step to the next (see procedure for description).

Procedure Each step (successive approximation) of the program was introduced at the imitative level. At this level, the clinician presented the verbal stimulus and the client imitated the syllable, word, or sentence after the clinician. When criterion was met on all stimulus items at one step, movement was made to the next step. Steps one to nine of the program were presented at the imitative level only. At step ten (sentence-production task) a spontaneous task was introduced after criterion was met at the imitative level. At the spontaneous level the client was shown a picture of an object and asked to make a sentence using the word in the sentence. Steps eleven, twelve, and thirteen were presented at the spontaneous level only. On these steps, the clinician would frequently remind the client to "use your good speech" throughout the course of the conversation. Verbal feedback was presented after each response regarding correct and incorrect production of the stimulus items. Client self-monitoring tabulations of correct and incorrect responses on each task were kept by every client on grocery counters. The client was taught to press the red button (dollar column) on the counter when they felt they had said the syllable, word, or sentence correctly. They were instructed to press the green button (cents column) on the counter when they felt they had made an error. Comparisons of correct and incorrect responses were made between the clinician and client at the end of each verbal task. If both tabulations were in agreement, criterion was met at the self-monitoring level. Movement was not made from one step to the next until criteria for both correct production and self-monitoring were met.

Phonetic contexts and speech intelligibility In a related investigation in which scaling of intelligibility, not hypernasality, was performed across the same vowels and consonant, a strong linear trend for a hierarchy of vowel intelligibility from low to high vowels was determined (see Figure

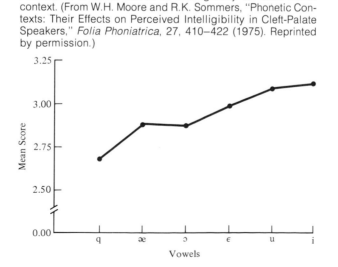

FIGURE 6–2 Mean scores of intelligibility for each vowel context. (From W.H. Moore and R.K. Sommers, "Phonetic Contexts: Their Effects on Perceived Intelligibility in Cleft-Palate Speakers," *Folia Phoniatrica*, 27, 410–422 (1975). Reprinted by permission.)

6–2); however, unlike the data based on scale values of hypernasality, the data which can be seen in Figure 6–3 show that no linear trend was found for intelligibility for consonant-manner-of-production subgroups. This suggests that listeners' perception of intelligibility across the CVC phonetic contexts and their judgments of perceived nasality, while found moderately correlated ($r = .56$), are most often not comparable across a wide range of phonetic contexts; and the line functions of hypernasality and intelligibility are highly dissimilar when tested with tests of trends.

These specifically different relationships may suggest that efforts to improve hypernasality do not necessarily result in improved intelligibility in many phonetic contexts. Furthermore, therapy planning for the improvement of intelligibility as a major goal may profit from relying upon a linear hierarchy across vowels but not across consonants. The vowel environments appear not to vary significantly in their influences on consonant manner of production when scale values of intelligibility are made by listeners. Since the interjudge reliability for scaling of both nasality and intelligibility for the trained listeners was very high, the large amount of curvilinear variance in the mean scores of intelligibility for consonants within vowel contexts, seen in Figure 6–3, cannot relate to poorer reliability for such measures.

The influence of other factors may affect the intelligibility scaling of phonetic contexts: for example, a wide range of events, such as whether glottal stops replaced /k/, changes in place of articulation causing distortions of consonants and vowels combined, and possible variations in other aspects of speech associated with articulation such as resonance and voicing. Listeners' judgments of nasality across phonetic contexts may be much more specifically related to the acoustic presence of the correlates

FIGURE 6–3 Mean scores of intelligibility for consonants within vowel contexts. (From Moore and Sommers, 1975. Reprinted by permission.)

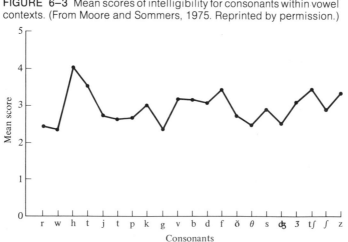

of nasality, thus reducing the impact of other distortions in the speech signal. Much more research is required to understand the complex nature of measurements of nasality and intelligibility in phonetic contexts. In the interim it appears reasonable to believe that speech/language pathologists can plan and conduct therapy using information of the type described to guide decisions and set overall goals and subgoals.

It is clear that the articulatory component of cleft-palate speech is a complex and basic deficiency as seen in the place, manner, voicing, and resonance aspects of the problem with most ties going directly to the specific articulatory function: the phonetic contexts of speech. Overall impressions of cleft-palate speech, gained from samples of connected, spontaneous speech, are valuable to obtain; but these data suggest strongly that the vital information for the clinician is at the level of the defective phonetic contexts.

In this broad and brief chapter I have attempted to present a small series of ideas and therapy implications for a number of the more frequently occurring orofacial and neurologic disorders that the speech-language pathologist diagnoses and treats. Literature for many of these conditions is abundant with many fine reference sources available to the serious student and practioner.

Perhaps due to political, social, and demographic factors, certain neurogenic disorders of both children and adults are becoming more prominent. Young, rather severely involved cerebral-palsied children, for example, seem to have surfaced in programs that saw their numbers many years ago but witnessed a rather slow decline over a decade. As a result of PL 94-142 with the "least restrictive environment" principle actively pursued, many of these individuals are appearing at local clinics, schools, and hospitals for treatment. The approaches for teaching speech and oral language to many of these children do not appear much different from those used twenty-five years ago with the exception of more technological aids such as biofeedback. Emphasis on nonverbal communication systems seems stronger at this time than was the case a quarter of a century ago.

The aging population of our country has been having and will continue to influence many of our decisions concerning treatment, types of treatment, extent of treatment, and others. More and more attention is being made toward therapy techniques for acquired apraxia of speech and language and dysarthria. Prominent in the research and development aspects of these adult disorders are speech-language pathologists from hospital settings, particularly a creative and dedicated group of individuals from Veterans Administration Hospitals.

Many of the orofacial and neurogenic disorders have components of articulatory defectiveness of significance. The result is that understanding of the entire set of conditions that appear to account for the speech disorder is requisite to effective therapy planning. The articulatory component is thus best seen in light of its interrelated ones, the diagnostic process becomes more intent, more challenging, and the clinician looks for the specific set of circumstances very covertly expressed in the word "specificity."

FINAL REMARKS

The impact of the old and the new approaches to articulation therapy have been touched upon with perhaps greater emphasis placed upon some of the more recent innovations in the process than the historical, time-tested ones. It is obvious that the major blueprints for the articulation-therapy process today reflect the insights and basic thinking of a rather small number of dedicated and creative pioneers in speech pathology. It was they who gave us the basic elements of the therapy process and detailed for us procedures for the correction of defective articulation. While some of their basic concepts concerning procedural matters have been abandoned by some modern workers, many fundamental ones remain with us for further development and use. These early, significant contributions were basically a set of assumptions concerning the nature of the corrective process; but they also contributed mightily to conclusions concerning the efficacy of articulation therapy generally, that is, that articulation therapy for children of many types has proved effective. This can be seen repetitively in controlled experiments, in operant case studies, and in the experiences of many speech clinicians who have seen significant changes in treated children and few if any changes in many nontreated ones. To our earlier ancestors we owe a hearty "thanks" for setting a course of action for all of us.

While we encourage speech pathologists and students in training to seek to master different approaches to articulation therapy, we have little information to guide us concerning the efficacy of different approaches under comparable conditions. Research to determine the many issues related to choices of approach is greatly needed; however, we are experiencing a decline in the number of reported studies on the efficacy of different approaches, and the number of studies in the past has been discouragingly low. Thus, while newer approaches may be more attractive at the moment than older ones, we remain with the responsibility of gathering our own clinical impressions of the value of them in light of the particular needs of the individual involved and, to some extent, the comfortableness of the approach as it fits our training, experiences, and personalities.

The historical concept of articulation, which was largely phonetics oriented, has given way to the phonological model. Fortunately, older concepts of motor phonetics and related ones have not entirely been defeated, and we can see some important basic areas of research concerning the normal process of articulation, such as studies of coarticulation, which are potentially very important in helping us to understand this complex process. Such understandings, hopefully, will provide us with clearer insights into the needs of the articulatory impaired. If we could understand all of this new information and translate it into direct implications for intervention, we might be able to increase therapy efficacy significantly. Our inability to use what is available to us in the past may suggest that training programs need to stimulate students to engage in creative thinking concerning the possible inclusion of basic speech-science knowledge into scenarios in which various types of impediments cause articulation to be defective, for example, motor-planning problems in adult apraxic speakers. Articulation-therapy approaches, not unlike other disorders that the speech/language clinician treats, suffer badly from a lack of creative thinking; yet we have a storehouse of basic information about the normal process, which we largely ignore.

The nature of the articulatory-defective person has also come in view. More and more evidence is being compiled to show that significant numbers of articulatory-defective persons have other deficiencies. While the term "functional articulation problems" has not been totally obliterated, we can locate an increasing body of literature to suggest that many such individuals are not equal to normal speakers in some perceptual, memory, and linguistic abilities. To our offspring we give the challenge of developing more sensitive and generally superior tests and measures to apply to such persons. New knowledge will strengthen our understanding of many of these problems, and we may see some relevance it is for therapy decisions.

Finally, the fresh, new stimulation given to us by linguistics and psycholinguistics should be productive in improving the quality of service that we provide to some articulatory-defective children. The intricate and largely unknown relationships between the phonological elements and other elements of language may be better understood in the future. Implications for studying and treating phonological disorders may be exciting and revealing even for matters as seemingly mundane as knowing the importance of choices of linguistic units in which to imbed a target sound. Information of many types may result in modifications of therapy procedures for many types of articulatory-defective children and adults, particularly aphasics who suffer from apraxia.

The pervasive nature of articulatory defectiveness in many speech and language disorders signifies the importance of teaching and training clinicians and students in its treatment. Although other types of related disorders, such as language weaknesses in children, gain more attention from some professional workers, the reality remains that defective articulation is the most prevalent aspect of many speech and language problems. The need is to understand it better.

ANDERSLAND, P.B., Maternal and environmental factors related to success in speech improvement training. *Journal of Speech Hearing Research,* 4, 79–90 (1961).

ANDERSON, P.W., The relationship of normal and defective articulation of the consonant /s/ in various phonetic contexts to auditory discrimination between normal and defective /s/ productions among children from kindergarten through fourth grade. Unpublished masters thesis, State University of Iowa (1949).

ANDREWS, J., Electromyography. *Journal of the American Osteopathic Association,* 56, 354–355 (1957).

ANGLIN, J.M., *Word, Object, and Conceptual Development.* New York: Norton (1977).

ARKEBAUER, H., HIXON, T., and **HARDY, J.,** Peak intraoral air pressures during speech. *Journal of Speech Hearing Research,* 10, 196–206 (1967).

ARNDT,W.B., SHELTON, R.L., JOHNSON, A.F., and **FURR, M.L.,** Identification and description of homogeneous subgroups within a sample of misarticulating children. *Journal of Speech and Hearing Research,* 20, 263–292 (1977).

AUNGST, L.F., The relationship between oral otereognosis and articulation proficiency. Unpublished doctoral dissertation, Pennsylvania State University (1965).

AUNGST, L.F. and **FRICK, J.V.,** Auditory discrimination ability and consistency of articulation of /r/. *Journal of Speech Hearing Disorders,* 28, 76–85 (1964).

BACKUS, O. and **BEASLEY, J.,** *Speech Therapy with Children.* Boston: Houghton Mifflin Company (1951).

BARNES, I.J. and **MORRIS, H.L.,** Interrelationships among oral breath pressure ratios and articulation skills for individuals with cleft palate. *Journal of Speech Hearing Research,* 10, 506–514 (1967).

BARR, D.F., Letter: Comment on auditory processing factors in language disorders. *Journal of Speech Hearing Disorders,* 39, 227–228 (1974).

BARRETT, K.H., KEITH, R.W., AGNELLO, J.G., and **WEILER, E.M.,** Central auditory processing of stutterers and nonstutterers. Paper presented at the annual convention of the American Speech–Language–Hearing Association, Atlanta, Georgia (1979).

BECKEY, R.E., A study of certain factors related to retardation of speech. *Journal of Speech Hearing Disorders,* 7, 223–249 (1942).

BENTON, A.L., Developmental aphasia and brain damage. *Cortex,* 1, 40–52 (1964).

BINGHAM, D.S., VAN HATTUM, R.J., FAULK, M.E., and **TAUSSIG, E.,** Program organization and management. In research committee of the American Speech and Hearing Association, public school speech and hearing services. *Journal of Speech Hearing Disorders Monograph Supplement,* 8, 33–49 (1961).

BLANK, M., Cognitive processes in auditory discrimination in normal and retarded readers. *Child Development,* 39, 1091–1101 (1968).

BLOCH, E.L. and **GOLDSTEIN, L.D.,** Functional speech disorders and personality: A decade of research. *Journal of Speech Hearing Disorders,* 36 (3), 295–314 (1971).

BLOOM, L. and **LAHEY, M.,** *Language Development and Language Disorders.* New York: John Wiley and Sons, Inc. (1978).

BOBATH, K. and **BOBATH, B.,** Cerebral palsy, part II: The neurodevelopmental approach to treatment. In P.H. Pearson and C.E. Williams (Eds.), *Physical Therapy Services in the Developmental Disabilities.* Springfield: Charles C Thomas (1972).

BOUNTRESS, N., Use of distinctive features in articulation training. In C.W. Bennett, N.G. Bountress, and G. Bulls (Eds.), *Contemporary Readings in Articulation Disorders.* Broadway, Va.: Teaching Texts (1979).

BROOKS, A.R., SKELTON, R.L., and **YOUNGSTROM, K.A.,** Compensatory tongue–palate–posterior pharyngeal wall relationships in cleft palate. *Journal Speech Hearing Disorders,* 30, 166–173 (1965).

BROOKSHIRE, R.H., Speech pathology and the experimental analysis of behavior. *Journal Speech Hearing Disorders,* 32, 215–227 (1967).

BRYDEN, M.P., Ear preference in auditory perception. *Journal of Experimental Psychology,* 65, 103–105 (1965).

BRYDEN, M.C., SKELTON, R.L., JR., and **DIEDRICK, W.M.,** Articulatory skills, physical management and classification of children with cleft palates. *Journal Speech Hearing Disorders,* 26, 326–333 (1961).

BYRNE, M.C., SHELTON, R.L., DIEDRICH, W.M., Articulatory skill, physical management, and classification of children with cleft palates. *Journal of Speech Hearing Disorders* 26, 326–333 (1961).

BZOCH, R.R., Articulation proficiency and error patterns of preschool cleft palate and normal children. *Cleft Palate Journal,* 2, 340–349 (1965).

CANTER, G.J., Speech characteristics of patients with Parkinson's disease: I, Intensity, pitch, and duration. *Journal of Speech Hearing Disorders,* 28, 221–229 (1963).

CANTER, G.J., Speech characteristics of patients with Parkinson's disease: II, Physiological support for speech. *Journal of Speech Hearing Disorders,* 30, 44–49 (1965).

CANTER, G.J., Neuromotor pathologies of speech. *American Journal of Physical Medicine,* 46, 659 (1967).

CARRELL, J., *Disorders of Articulation.* Englewood Cliffs: Prentice–Hall, Inc. (1968).

CARROW, E., *Test for Auditory Comprehension of Language* (5th Ed.). Austin: Learning Concepts (1973).

CARTER, E.P. and **BUCK, W. McK.,** Prognostic testing for functional articulation disorders among children in the first grade. *Journal of Speech Hearing Disorders,* 23, 124–133 (1958).

CHOMSKY, N., *Aspects of the Theory of Syntax.* Cambridge: The M.I.T. Press (1969).

CHOMSKY, N. and **HALLE, M.,** *The Sound Pattern of English.* New York: Harper & Row (1968).

CLARK, B.J., Using a short-term lisp correction program for more effective distribution of clinicians' time. *Language, Speech, Hearing Services for the Schools*, 5, 152–155 (1974).

CLARK, E.V., What's in a word? On the child's acquisition of semantics in his first language. In T.E. Moore (Ed.) *Cognitive Development and the Acquisition of Language*. New York: Academic Press (1973).

COMPTON, A.J., A generative analysis of articulatory deviations. Paper presented at the annual convention of the American Speech and Hearing Association, Denver, Colorado (1968).

COMPTON, A.J., Generative studies of children's phonological disorders. *Journal of Speech Hearing Disorders*, 35, 315–39 (1970).

COOPER, F.S., Research techniques and instrumentation: EMG. *American Speech Hearing Association Reports*, 1, 153–168 (1965).

COOPER, R., The method of meaningful minimal contrasts in functional articulation problems. *Journal Speech Hearing Association.* 10, 17–22 (1968).

COSTELLO, J., Articulation instruction based on distinctive features theory. *Language Speech and Hearing Services in Schools.* 6(2), 61–72 (1975).

COSTELLO, J. and ONSTINE, J., The modification of multiple articulation errors based on distinctive feature theory. *Journal of Speech Hearing Disorders.* 41(2), 199–216 (1976).

COUNIHAN, D.T., Articulation skills of adolescents and adults with cleft palate. *Journal of Speech Hearing Disorders* 25, 181–187 (1960).

COX, M., Evidence for sound generalization in young children. Unpublished research report, Kent State University (1974).

CRICKMAY, M.C., *Speech Therapy and the Bobath Approach to Cerebral Palsy*. Springfield: Charles C Thomas (1977).

CROCKER, J., A phonological model of children's articulation competence. *Journal of Speech Hearing Disorders* 34, 203–213 (1969).

CURRY, R. and GREGORY, H., The performance of stutterers on dichotic listening tasks thought to reflect cerebral dominance. *Journal Speech Hearing Disorders*, 12, 73–82 (1969).

DARLEY, F.L., ARONSON, A.E., and BROWN, J.R., Clusters of deviant speech dimensions in the dysarthrias. *Journal of Speech Hearing Research*, 12, 462–496 (1969).

DARLEY, F.L., ARONSON, A.E., and BROWN, J.B., *Motor Speech Disorders*. Philadelphia: W.B. Saunders (1975).

DAVENPORT, R.W., Dichotic listening in four severity levels of stuttering. Paper presented at the annual convention of the American Speech–Language–Hearing Association, Atlanta, Georgia (1979).

DAVIS, K.V., Linguistic correlates of dichotic speech processing in language and speech defective young children. Unpublished master's thesis, Kent State University (1978).

DeRENZE, E., PIECZURO, A., and VIGNOLO, L., Oral apraxia and aphasia. *Cortex* 12, 50–73 (1966).

DeVILLIERS, J.G. and DeVILLIERS, P.A., *Language Acquisition*. Cambridge: Harvard University Press (1978).

DICKSON, S., Differences between children who spontaneously outgrow and children who retain functional articulation errors. *Journal Speech Hearing Research*, 5, 263–271 (1962).

Diedrich, W.M., Procedures for counting and charting a target phoneme. *Language Speech, Hearing Services in Schools,* 5, 18–32 (1971).

Diedrich, W. and **Bangert, J.,** *Articulation Learning.* Houston: College–Hill Press (1980).

DuBois, E. and **Bernthal, J.,** A comparison of three methods of obtaining articulatory responses. *Journal of Speech Hearing Disorders,* 43(3), 295–305 (1978).

Dukes, P. and **Pangos, J.M.,** Reception of comprehensible sentences by children with deviant speech. *British Journal of Disorders of Communication,* 8, 139 (1973).

Durkin, D., *Teaching Young Children to Read.* Boston: Allyn and Bacon (1972).

Edwards, M., The use of favorite sounds by children with phonological disorders. Paper presented at the annual convention of the American Speech and Hearing Association, Detroit, Michigan (1980).

Eisenson, J., *Aphasia in Children.* New York: Harper and Row (1972).

Eisenson, J. and **Ogilvie, M.,** *Speech Correction in the Schools.* New York: The MacMillan Company, 83–96 (1971).

Epstein, A.G., Auditory memory span for language. *Folia Phoniatrica,* 16, 271–289 (1964).

Fairbanks, G., Systematic research in experimental phonetics: a theory of the speech mechanism as a servosystem. *Journal of Speech Hearing Disorders,* 19, 133–139 (1954).

Faircloth, M.A. and **Faircloth, S.R.,** An analysis of the articulatory behavior of a speech-defective child in connected speech and in isolated-word responses. *Journal of Speech Hearing Disorders,* 35, 51–61 (1970).

Farmakides, M.N. and **Boone, D.R.,** Speech problems in patients with multiple sclerosis. *Journal of Speech Hearing Disorders,* 25, 385–390 (1960).

Fay, W.H. and **Butler, B.V.,** Echolalia, I.Q., and the developmental dichotomy of speech and language systems. *Journal of Speech Hearing Research,* 11, 365–371 (1968).

Finley, W.W., Niman, C.A., Standley, J., and **Ender, P.,** Frontal EMG biofeedback training of athetoid cerebral palsy patients. *Biofeedback and Self-Regulation,* 1, 169–182 (1976).

Finley, W.W., Niman, C.A., Standley, J., and **Wansley, R.,** Electrophysiologic behavior modification of frontal EMR in cerebral palsied children. *Biofeedback and Self-Regulation,* 2, 59–79 (1977).

Flanagan, J., *Speech Analysis, Synthesis and Perception.* New York: Academic Press (1965).

Fletcher, S.G., *Diagnosing Speech Disorders from Cleft Palate.* New York: Grune and Stratton, 1978.

Freeman, G.G. and **Sonnega, J.A.,** Peer evaluation of children in speech correctness class. *Journal of Speech Hearing Disorders,* 21, 179–182 (1956).

Frisch, F. and **Handler, L.,** A neuropsychological investigation of functional disorders of speech articulation. *Journal of Speech Hearing Research,* 17, 432–445 (1974).

Fritzell, B., The velopharyngeal muscles in speech. *Acta Oto–Laryngologica Supplementum,* 250 (1969).

Froeschels, E., *Dysarthric Speech.* Magnolia: Expression Company (1952).

FROESCHELS, E., Hygiene of the voice. *Archives of Otolaryngology*, 38, 122–130 (1943).

FUCCI, D.J. and ROBERTSON, J.H., Functional defective articulation: An oral sensory disturbance. *Perceptual and Motor Skills*, 33, 711–714 (1971).

FUDALA, J.B., ENGLAND, G. and GANOUNG, L., Utilization of parents in a speech correction program. *Exceptional Children*, 1972, *38* 407–412.

GALATHRIS, C., Sociological factors related to defects of inner city children. Unpublished nonthesis master's paper, Kent State University, 1977.

GARRETT, E.R., An automated speech correction: A pilot study. *American Speech Hearing Association*, 5, 796 (1963).

GERBER, A., The achievement of /r/ carryover through intensification of simultaneous auditory feedback. *Pennsylvania Speech Hearing Association Newsletter*, 7, 7–11 (1966).

GERBER, A., *Goal: Carryover*. Philadelphia: Temple University Press (1973).

GERBER, A. Programming for articulation modification. *Journal of Speech Hearing Disorders*, 42(1), 29–43 (1977).

GILLILAND, A., *A Practical Guide to Remedial Reading*. Columbus: Charles E. Merrill (1974).

GOLDMAN, R. and FRISTOE, M., *Goldman–Fristoe Test of Articulation*. Circle Pines: American Guidance Service (1969).

GORDON, L.V., *Gordon Personal Profile, Manual*. New York: Harcourt Brace Jovanovich (1963).

GOWMAN, M., and SOMMERS, R.K., Distinctive feature acquisition and children's articulatory behavior. Unpublished research paper, Kent State University (1979).

GREENBERG, K.R., A study of the relationship between articulatory disorders and personality in the intermediate grades. Unpublished master's thesis, Ohio State University (1952).

GREWEL, F., Classification of dysarthrias. *Acta Psychiatry Neurology*, 32, 325 (1957).

GREY, H.A. and STUNDEN, A.A., A preliminary study of the effect of meaning as a variable in the auditory discrimination ability of speech handicapped and normal grade school children. *American Speech Hearing Association*, 3, 187 (1961).

GROSSMAN, R.C., Sensory innervation of the oral mucosae: A review. *Journal of the Southern California Dental Association*, 38, 128–133 (1964).

GURALNIK, D.B., (Ed.)., *Webster's New World Dictionary*. New York: The World Publishing Company (1978).

HAAS, W., Phonological analysis of a case of Dyslalia. *Journal of Speech Hearing Disorders*, 28, 239–246 (1963).

HALLE, M., On the basis of phonology. In J.A. Fodar and J.J. Katz (Eds.), *The Structure of Language: Readings in the Philosophy of Language*. Englewood Cliffs: Prentice–Hall (1964).

HALLE, M. and STEVENS, K.N., Analysis by synthesis. In Wathen–Dunn and L.E. Woods (Eds.), *Proceedings of the Seminar on Speech Compression and Processing*. 2 AFCRC–TR–5–198, Paper D7, U.S.A.F.: Cambridge Research Center (1959).

HANAGAN, M.K., The effects of electromyographic biofeedback training on the speech and oral motor abilities of a cerebral palsied child. Unpublished master's thesis, Kent State University (1977).

HARDY, T.C., Respiratory physiology: Implications of current research. *American Speech Hearing Association*, 10, 204–205 (1968).

HATHAWAY, S.R. and McKINLEY, T.C., *Minnesota Multiphasic Personality Inventory; Manual.* New York: Psychology Corporation (1951).

HESS, D.A. and McDONALD, E.T., Consonantal nasal pressure in cleft palate speakers. *Journal of Speech Hearing Research*, 3, 201–211 (1960).

HIER, C., LeMAY, C., ROSENBERGER, P., and PERLO, V., Developmental dyslexia *Archives Neurology*, 35, 90–92 (1978).

HILLARD, S.W. and GEOPFERT, S.W., Articulation training: A new perspective. *Language Speech Hearing Services in Schools*, 10, 139–144 (1979).

HIXON, T.J. and HARDY, J.C., Restricted mobility of the speech articulators in cerebral palsy. *Journal of Speech Hearing Disorders*, 29, 294–306 (1964).

HOBERMAN, S.L. and HOBERMAN, M., Speech habilitation in cerebral palsy. *Journal of Speech Hearing Disorders*, 25, 111 (1960).

HOLLAND, A.L., Some applications of behavioral principles to clinical speech problems. *Journal of Speech Hearing Disorders*, 32, 11–18 (1967).

HOLLAND, A.K. and MATTHEWS, J., Application of teaching "matching" concepts to speech pathology and audiology. *American Speech Hearing Association*, 5, 473–482 (1963).

HOPKINS, T.W., BICE, A.V., and COLTON, K.C., *Evaluation and Education of the Cerebral Palsied Child: New Jersey Study.* Washington, D.C.: I.C.E.C. (1954).

HUFFMAN, L. and McREYNOLDS, L., Auditory sequence learning in children. *Journal of Speech Hearing Research*, 11, 179–188 (1968).

INGRAM, R., *Phonological Disorders in Children.* New York: Edward Arnold Publishers (1976).

IRWIN, O.C., Infant speech: Consonant sounds according to manner of articulation. *Journal of Speech Hearing Disorders*, 13, 320–326 (1948).

IRWIN, R.B., Speech therapy and children's linguistic skills. *Journal of Speech Hearing Research*, 5, 377–381 (1962).

ISSKIKI, N. and RINGEL, R., Air flow during the production of selected consonants. *Journal of Speech Hearing Research*, 7, 233–244 (1964).

JACKSON, P. and SOMMERS, R.K., Performances of articulatory-defective and minimal cerebral-dysfunctioning children on selected language and speech tasks. Paper presented at the American Speech and Hearing Association convention Chicago, Illinois (1971).

JAKOBSON, R., FANT, G., and HALLE, M., *Preliminaries to Speech Analysis: The Distinctive Features and Their Correlates.* Cambridge: M.I.T. Press (1951).

JENKINS, E. and LOHR, F.E., Severe articulation disorders and motor ability. *Journal of Speech Hearing Disorders*, 29, 286–292 (1964).

JORDON, E.P., Articulation test measures and listener ratings of articulation defectiveness. *Journal of Speech Hearing Research*, 17, 122–123 (1960).

KENNEDY, G.M., The relationship among articulatory speech defects, personality maladjustments, educational and retardation and physical deviations. Unpublished master's thesis, Emerson College (1951).

KENT, R.D., NETSELL, R., and BAUER, L.L., Cineradiographic assessment. *Journal of Speech Hearing Disorders*, 25, 355–390 (1960).

KENT, R.D., NETSELL, R., and BAUER, L.L., Cineradiographic assessment of articulation mobility in the dysarthrias. *Journal of Speech Hearing Disorders*, 40, 467 (1975).

KIM, R., The chronic residual respiratory disorder in past encephalitic Parkinsonism. *Journal of Neurologic Neurosurgery Psychiatry*, 31, 393–398 (1968).

KIMBLE, G.A., *Conditioning and Learning*. New York: Appleton Century Crofts, Inc. (1961).

KIMURA, D., Speech lateralization in young children as determined by an auditory test. *Journal of comparative physiology and psychology*, 56, 899–902 (1963).

KIRK, S., McCARTHY, J., and KIRK, W., *The Illinois Test of Psycholinguistic Abilities* (rev. ed.). Urbana: University of Illinois Press (1968).

KOEPP–BAKER, H., Speech problems of the person with a cleft palate and cleft lip. In L.E. Travis (Ed.), *Handbook of Speech Psychology*. New York: Appleton Century Crofts, Inc. (1957).

KRAMMERMEIER, M.A., A comparison of phonatory phenomena among groups of neurologically impaired speakers. Ph.D. dissertation: University of Minnesota, 1969. Cited in Darley, F.L., Aronson, A.E., and Brown, J.R., *Motor Speech Disorders*. Philadelphia: Saunders (1975).

KUCERA, A., Relationships among hemispheric speech processing linguistic abilities and fine motor skills in language and speech impaired children. Unpublished master's thesis, Kent State University (1980).

LADEFOGED, P., Sub-glottal activity during speech. In A. Sovijarvi and P. Aalto (Eds.), *Proceedings of the Fifth International Congress of Phonetic Sciences*. The Hague: Mouton and Company, 73–91 (1962).

LADEFOGED, P., Some physiological parameters in speech. *Language and Speech*, 6, 109–119 (1963).

LADEFOGED, P., DeCLERK, J., LINDAU, M., and PAPCUN, G., An auditory motor theory of speech production. *UCLA Phonetics Laboratory, Working Papers in Phonetics*, 22, 48–76 (1972).

LADEFOGED, P., DRAPER, M.H., and WHITTERIDGE, D., Syllables and stress. *Miscellanea Phonetica*, 3, 1–14 (1958).

LADEFOGED, P. and McKINNEY, N.P., Loudness, sound pressure and subglottal pressure in speech. *Proceedings of the Fourth International Congress of Phonetic Sciences*. The Hague: Mouton and Company (1963).

LANG, M., Program for the elimination of hypernasality. Unpublished manuscript, Kent State University (1974).

LaPOINTE, L.L., Neurogenic abnormalities affecting speech. In D.B. Tower (Ed.), *The Nervous System, Human Communication and its Disorders*. New York: Raven Press, vol. 3 (1975).

LEANDERSON, R., PIERSON, A., and OHMAN, S., Electromyagraphic studies of the function of the facial muscles in dysarthria. *Acta Otolaryngology*, 263, 89–94 (1970).

LEE, L., *The Northwestern Syntax Screening Test*. Evanston: Northwestern University Press (1969).

LEE, L. *Northwestern Syntax Screening Test*. Evanston: Northwestern University Press (1966).

LEE, L. and CANTER, S., Developmental sentence scoring: A clinical procedure for estimating syntax development in children's spontaneous speech. *Journal of Speech Hearing Disorders* 36:311–330 (1971).

LEITER, R.G., *The Leiter International Performance Scale*. Washington, D.C.: The Psychological Service Center Press (1951).

LEONARD, L., The nature of deviant articulation. *Journal of Speech Hearing Disorders*, 38–(2), 156–162 (1973).

LEREA, L. and WARD, B., The social schema of normal and speech defective children. *Journal of Social Psychology*, 69, 87–94 (1966).

LIBERMAN, A., HARRIS, K.S., EIMAS, P., LISKER, L., and BASTIAN, J., An effect of learning of speech perception: The discrimination of durations of silence with and without phonemic significance. *Language Speech*, 4, 175–195 (1961).

LIBERMAN, I.Y., LIBERMAN, A.M., MATTINGLY, D.G., and SHANKWEILER, D., Orthography and the beginning reading. Paper presented at cross-language conference on othography, reading, and dyslexia, sponsored by NICHD and Forgarty International Center of NIH, Bethesda, Maryland (1978).

LIEBERMAN, P., *Speech Physiology and Acoustic Phonetics: An Introduction*. New York: MacMillan Publishing Company (1977).

LINTZ, L.B. and SHERMAN, D., Phonetic elements and perception of nasality. *Journal of Speech Hearing Research*, 4, 381–398 (1961).

LISKER, L. and ABRAMSON, A., Distinctive features and laryngeal control *Language* 47(4), 767–783 (1971).

LOCKE, J.L., Oral perception and articulation learning. *Perceptual and Motor Skills*, 26, 1259–1264 (1968).

LOCKE, J.L., Short-term auditory memory, oral perception and experimental sound learning. *Journal of Speech Hearing Research*, 12, 185–192 (1969).

LOGEMEN, J.A., FISHER, H.B., BOSKES, J., and BLONSKY, R.E., Frequency and co-occurrence of vocal tract dysfunctions in speech of a large sample of Parkinson patients. *Journal of Speech Hearing Disorders*, 43, 47–57 (1978).

LOWE–BELL, S, BERLIN, C, and BERLIN, H, Dichotic speech perception: A developmental study. Unpublished paper presented to the convention of the American Speech and Hearing Association, San Francisco (1972).

LUBIT, E.C. and LARSEN, R.E., A speech aid for velopharyngeal incompetency. *Journal of Speech Hearing Disorders* 36, 61–70 (1971).

LUBKER, J.F., SCHWEIGER, J.W., and MORRIS, H.L., Nasal airflow characteristics during speech in prosthetically mangaged cleft palate speakers. *Journal of Speech Hearing Research* 13, 326–338 (1970).

MACALUSO–HAYNES, S., Developmental apraxia of speech systems and treatment. In D.F. Johns (Ed.), *Clinical Management of Neurogenic Communicative Disorders*. Boston: Little, Brown and Company (1978).

MacGINTIE, W.H., Auditory perception in reading. *Education* 87, 532–538 (1967).

MACHOWSKY, H. and MEYERS, J., Auditory discrimination, intelligence, and reading achievement at grade 1. *Perceptual Motor Skills*, 40, 363–368 (1975).

MARINACCI, A.A. and HORANDE, M., Electromyogram reeducation. *Bulletin of the Los Angeles Neurological Society*, 25, 57–71 (1960).

MARQUARDT, T.P. and SAXMAN, J.H., Language comprehension and auditory discrimination in articulation deficient kindergarten children. *Journal of Speech Hearing Research*, 15, 382–389 (1972).

MARTIN, J.A., Generalizing the use of descriptive adjectives through modeling. *Journal Applied Behavior Analysis*, 8, 203–209 (1975).

MATHEWS, J. and BYRNE, M., An experimental study of tongue flexibility in children with cleft palate. *Journal of Speech Hearing Disorders*, 18, 43–47 (1953).

MAYBERRY, R.I. and NISSEN, S.W., A comparison of distinctive feature and phoneme approaches to articulation therapy with the retarded. Paper presented at the annual convention of the American Speech and Hearing Association, Las Vegas, Nevada (1974).

McDONALD, E.T., *Articulation Testing and Treatment: A Sensory–Motor Approach*. Pittsburgh: Stanwix House (1964).

McDONALD, E.T., *A Deep Test of Articulation*. Pittsburgh: Stanwix House, Inc. (1964).

McGOVERN, J.E., Auditory perception: A review of the literature. *Academic Therapy*, 14, 445–460 (1979).

McLEAN, J., Shifting stimulus control of articulation responses by operant techniques. Unpublished doctoral dissertation, University of Kansas (1965).

McNUTT, J.C., Perceptual and motor performances of articulatory defective and normal speakers. Unpublished doctoral dissertation, Kent State University (1973).

McNUTT, J.C. and HAMAYAN, E., Subgroups of older children with articulation disorders. In R. Daniloff (Ed.) *Position Papers in Speech, Hearing, and Language*. Baltimore: College-Hill Press, 1982.

McREYNOLDS, L.V., Contingencies and consequences in speech therapy. *Journal of Speech Hearing Disorders*, 35, 12–24 (1970).

McREYNOLDS, L.V. and BENNETT, S., Distinctive feature generalization in articulations. *Journal of Speech Hearing Disorders*, 37, 462–470 (1972).

McREYNOLDS, L.V. and ENGEMANN, K.L., *Distinctive Feature Analysis of Misarticulations*. Baltimore: University Park Press (1975).

McREYNOLDS, L.V. and HUSTON, K., A distinctive feature analysis of children's misarticulation. *Journal of Speech Hearing Disorders*, 36(2), 155–166 (1971).

McWILLIAMS, B.J., Some factors in the intelligibility of cleft palate speech. *Journal of Speech Hearing Disorders*, 19, 524–527 (1954).

McWILLIAMS, B.J., Articulation problems of a group of cleft palate adults. *Journal of Speech Hearing Research*, 1, 68–74 (1958).

MENYUK, P., Comparison of grammar of children with functionally deviant and normal speech. *Journal of Speech Hearing Research*, 7, 109–121 (1964).

MENYUK, P., The role of distinctive features in children's acquisition of phonology. *Journal of Speech Hearing Research*, 11, 138–146 (1968).

MENYUK, P., *Sentences Children Use*. Cambridge: MIT Press (1969).

MILLER, S., Exploration and comparison of first grade children's performances on two predictive articulation tests. Unpublished master's thesis, Kent State University (1978).

MILLER, G.A. and JOHNSON–LAIRD, P.N., *Language and Perception*. Cambridge: Harvard University Press (1976).

MILLER, G. and NICELY, P.E., An analysis of perceptual confusions among English consonants. *Journal of the Acoustical Society of America* 27, 338–352 (1955).

MINIFIE, F., HIXON, T., KELSEY, C., and WOODHOUSE, B., Lateral pharyngeal wall movement during speech production. *Journal of Speech Hearing Research*, 13, 584–594 (1970).

MOLL, K.L., Speech characteristics of individuals with cleft lip and palate. In

Spriesterbach, D.C., and Sherman, D. (Eds.), *Cleft Palate and Communication*. New York: Academic Press (1968).

MOLL, K. and **DANILOFF, B.,** Investigation of the timing of velar movements during speech. *The Journal of the Acoustical Society of America,* 50(2), 678–684 (1971).

MOLL, K.L. and **DARLEY, F.L.,** Attitudes of mothers of articulatory-impaired and speech-retarded children. *Journal of Speech Hearing Disorders,* 25, 277–384 (1960).

MONROE, M., *Children Who Cannot Read.* Chicago: The University of Chicago Press (1932).

MONSEES, E.H., Temporal sequences and expressive language disorders. *Exceptional Children,* 35, 141–147 (1968).

MOORE, W.H., JR. and **SOMMERS, R.K.,** Phonetic contexts: their effects on perceived nasality in cleft-palate speakers. *The Cleft Palate Journal,* 10, 72–83 (1973).

MOORE, W.H., JR. and **SOMMERS, R. K.,** Phonetic contexts: their effects on perceived intelligibility in cleft-palate speakers. *Folia Phoniatricia,* 27, 410–422 (1975).

MORLEY, M., *Cleft Palate and Speech.* Edinburgh: E & S Livingstone (1958).

MORLEY, M., *Development and Disorders of Speech in Childhood.* Baltimore: Williams and Wilkins, 2nd ed. (1965).

MORRIS, H., SPRIESTERSBACH, D., and **DARLEY, F.,** An articulation test for assessing competence of velopharyngeal closure. *Journal of Speech Hearing Research,* 4, 48–55 (1961).

MORRIS, H.L., (Ed.), *Cleft Lip and Palate: Criteria for Physical Management.* Iowa City: University of Iowa Press (1965).

MORRIS, H.L., Etiological bases for speech problems. In Spriesterbach, D.C., and Sherman, D. (Eds.). *Cleft Palate and Communication.* New York: Academic Press, 1968, pp. 119–168.

MORRIS, H.L., The oral manometer as a diagnostic tool in clinical speech pathology. *Journal of Speech Hearing Disorders,* 31, 362–369 (1966).

MORSE, W.H., Intermittent reinforcement. In Honig, W.K. (Ed.), *Operant Behavior: Areas of Research and Application.* New York: Appleton Century Crofts (1966).

MUELLER, P.B., Parkinson's disease: motor speech behavior in a selected group of patients. *Folia Phoniatrica,* 23, 333–346 (1971).

MULLER, J., *The Physiology of the Senses, Voice, and Muscular Motion with the Mental Faculties.* W. Baly (trans.), London: Walton and Maberly (1848).

MUMM, M.N., A comparison of the results of "behavior-modification" versus "traditional approaches" in the treatment of misarticulations in a public school setting. Unpublished doctoral dissertation, Ohio State University (1973).

MURRAY, H., *Manual for the Thematic Apperception Test.* Cambridge: Harvard University Printing Office (1943).

MYSAK, E.D., A servomodel for speech therapy. *Journal of Speech Hearing Disorders,* 24, 144–149 (1959).

MYSAK, E.D., Phonatory and resonatory problems. In Rieber, R.W. and Brubaker, R.S. (Eds.), *Speech Pathology.* Amsterdam: North-Holland Publishing Company (1966).

NAGAFUCHI, M., Development of dichotic and monaural hearing abilities in young children. *Acta Otolaryngology*, 6, 409–414 (1970).

NELSON, O.W., An investigation of certain factors to the nature of children with functional defects of articulation. *Journal of Educational Research*, 47, 211–216 (1953).

NETSELL, R., Evaluation of velopharyngeal function in dysarthria. *Journal of Speech Hearing Disorders*, 34, 113 (1969).

NETSELL, R. and CLEELAND, C.S., Modification of lip hypertonia in dysarthria using EMG feedback. *Journal of Speech Hearing Disorders*, 38, 131–140 (1973).

ORTON, S.T., *Reading, Writing, and Speech Problems in Children*. New York: W.W. Norton and Company, Inc. (1937).

PANAGOS, J.M., QUINE, M.E., and KLICH, R.J., Syntactic and phonological influences on children's speech. *Journal of Speech Hearing Research*, 22, 841–848 (1979).

PARKER, F., Distinctive features in speech pathology: Phonology or phonemics. *Journal of Speech Hearing Disorders*, 41(1), 23–39 (1976).

PEACHER, W.G., The etiology and differential diagnosis of dysarthria. *Journal of Speech Hearing Disorders*, 15, 252 (1950).

PENDERGAST, K., DICKEY, S., SELMAR, J., and SODER, A., *Photo Articulation Test*. Danville, Ill.: Interstate Printers and Publishers (1969).

PERRIN, E.H., The social position of the speech defective child. *Journal of Speech Hearing Disorders*, 19, 250–252 (1954).

PERRIN, K.L. and EISENSON, J., An examination of ear preference for speech and non-speech stimuli in a stuttering population. Paper presented at the annual convention of the American Speech and Hearing Association, New York City, New York (1970).

PETTIT, J.M. and HELMS, S., Cerebral dominance of language and articulation disordered children as measured by dichotic listening tasks. Paper presented at the annual convention of the American Speech and Hearing Association, Las Vegas, Nevada (1974).

PHELPS, W.M., Description and differentiation of types of cerebral palsy. *Nervous Child*, 8, 107 (1949).

PINTER, R., LOFTUS, J., FORLANO, G., and ALSTER, B., *Manual of Directions: Aspects of Personality*. New York: World Book (1938).

PISKE, K.L., Children's short-term memory in relationship to articulatory competency. Unpublished master's thesis, Kent State University (1978).

PITZNER, J.C. and MORRIS, H.L., Articulation skills and adequacy of breath pressure ratios of children with cleft palate. *Journal of Speech Hearing Disorders*, 31, 26–40 (1966).

POLLACK, E. and REES, N.E., Disorders of articulation: Some clinical applications of distinctive feature theory. *Journal of Speech Hearing Disorders*, 37(4), 451–461 (1972).

PRATHER, E.M. and HEDRICK, D.L., Articulation development in children aged two to four years. *Journal of Speech Hearing Disorders*, 40, 179–161 (1975).

PRINS, T.D., Motor and auditory abilities in different groups of children with articulation deviations. *Journal of Speech Hearing Research*, 5, 161–168 (1962).

PUTNAM, A. and RINGEL, B., Some observations of articulation during labial sensory deprivation. *Journal of Speech Hearing Research*, 15, 529–542 (1976).

REES, N.S., Auditory processing factors in language disorders: The view from procustes' bed. *Journal of Speech Hearing Disorders*, 38, 304–315 (1973).

REID, C., The etiology and nature of functional articulatory defects in elementary school children. *Journal of Speech Hearing Disorders*, 12, 143–150 (1947).

RENFREW, C., Persistence of the open syllable in defective articulation, *Journal of Speech Hearing Disorders*, 31, 370–373 (1966).

REYNOLD, G.S., *A Primer of Operant Conditioning*. Chicago: Scott, Foresman, and Company (1968).

RINGEL, B., BURK, R., and SCOTT, C., Tactile perception: Form discrimination in the mouth. In J. Bosma (Ed.), *Second Symposium on Oral Sensation and Perception*. Springfield: Charles C Thomas (1970).

RINGEL, R.L., HOUSE, A.S., BURKE, K.W., DOLINSKY, J.P., and SCOTT, C.M., Some relationships between crossensory discrimination and articulatory aspects of speech. *Journal of Speech Hearing Disorders*, 35, 3–11 (1970).

RINGEL, R.L. and STEER, M.A., Some effects of tactile and auditory alterations on speech output. *Journal of Speech Hearing Research*, 6, 369–377 (1963).

ROOD, M.S., Neurophysiological reactions as a basis for physical therapy. *Physical Therapy Review*, 34, 444 (1954).

ROOD, M.S., The use of sensory receptors to activate, facilitate, and inhibit motor response, autonomic and somatic in developmental sequence. In Satterly, C. (Ed.), *Approaches to Treatment of Patients with Neuromuscular Dysfunction*. Dubuque, Iowa: William C. Brown Company (1962).

ROSENBEK, J.C. and LAPOINTE. L.L., The dysarthrias: description, diagnosis, and treatment. In Johns, D.F. (Ed.), *Clinical Management of Neurogenic Communicative Disorders*. Boston: Little, Brown, and Company (1978).

ROSENBEK, J.C. and WERTZ, R.T., A review of fifty cases of developmental apraxia of speech. *Language, Speech, and Hearing Services in Schools*, 3, 23–33 (1972).

ROSSETTI, L.M., The generalization of distinctive features. Paper presented at the annual convention of the American Speech and Hearing Association, Atlanta, Georgia (1979).

ROSSMAN, A., Identification of oral forms by articulatory defective speaker. Unpublished master's thesis, Purdue University (1970).

RUSSELL, G.O., *The Vowel*. Columbus: Ohio State University Press, 1928.

SAWASHIMA, M. and MIYAZAKI, S., Glottal opening for Japanese voiceless consonants. *Annual Bulletin, Research Institute Logopedics and Phoniatrics*, University of Tokyo (1973).

SAXMAN, J.H. and MILLER, J.F., Short-term memory and language skills in articulation deficient children. *Journal of Speech Hearing Research*, 16, 721–730 (1973).

SCHAEFFER, E.S. and BELL, R.Q., *Parental Attitude Research Instruments: Normative Data*. Bethesda: National Institute of Mental Health (undated mimeographed pamphlet).

SCOTT, C.M. and RINGEL, R.L., The effects of motor and sensory deprivation on speech: A description of articulation. *Journal of Speech Hearing Research*, 14, 819–828 (1971).

SCRIPTURE, M.K. and JACKSON, R.L., *A Manual of Exercises for the Correction of Speech Disorders*. Philadelphia: F.A. Davis Company (1927).

SHANKWEILER, D., HARRIS, K.S., and TAYLOR, M.L., Electromyographic studies of articulation in aphasia. *Archives of Physical Medicine and Rehabilitation*, 49, 1–8 (1968).

SHELTON, B.L., BROOKS, A.R., and YOUNGSTROM, K.A., Articulation and patterns of palatopharyngeal closure. *Journal of Speech Hearing Disorders*, 29, 390–408 (1964).

SHELTON, R.L., ELBERT, M., and ARNT, W., A task for evaluation of articulation change: A comparison of task scores during baseline and lesson series testing. *Journal of Speech Hearing Research*, 10, 578–585 (1967).

SHERMAN, D., SPRIESTERBACH, D.C., and NOLL, J.D., Glottal stops in the speech of children with cleft palate. *Journal of Speech Hearing Disorders*, 24, 37–42 (1959).

SHERRILL, D.D., Peer, teacher, and self-perceptions of children with severe functional articulation disorders. Doctoral dissertation, University of Nebraska (1967).

SHRIBERG, L., A response evocation program for /ɝ/. *Journal of Speech Hearing Disorders*, 40(1), 92–106 (1975).

SHRIBERG, L. and KWIATKOWSKI, J., *Procedure for Natural Process Analysis (NPA) of Continuous Speech Samples: NPA Application Manual*. New York: John Wiley and Sons, Incorporated (1980).

SHRINER, T.H., HOLLOWAY, M.S., and DANILOFF, R.G., The relationship between articulatory deficit and syntax in speech defective children. *Journal of Speech Hearing Research*, 12, 319–325 (1969).

SIMARD, T.G., Fine sensorimotor control in healthy children. *Pediatrics*, 43, 1035–1041 (1969).

SINGH, S., *Distinctive Features: Theory and Validation*. Baltimore: University Park Press (1976).

SINGH, S. and BLACK, J.M., Study of twenty-six intervocalic consonants as spoken and recognized by four language groups. *Journal of the Acoustical Society of America*, 39, 372–287 (1966).

SINGH, S. and FRANK, D., A distinctive feature analysis of the consonantal substitution pattern. *Language and Speech*, 15(3), 209–218 (1972).

SINGH, S. and POLEN, S., Use of a distinctive feature model in speech pathology. *ACTA Symbolica*, 3, 17–25 (1972).

SKINNER, B.F., *The Behavior of Organisms*. Englewood Cliffs, N.J.: Prentice-Hall, Inc. (1938).

SKINNER, B.F., *The Technology of Teaching*. Englewood Cliffs, N.J.: Prentice-Hall, Inc. (1968).

SMITH, C.B., Articulation problems and abilities to store and process stimuli. *Journal of Speech Hearing Research*, 10, 348–355 (1967).

SNYDER, D.B., MARQUARDT, T.P., and PETERSON, H.A., Syntactical aspects of developmental apraxia. A paper presented at the annual convention of the American Speech and Hearing Association, Houston, Texas (1976).

SOLOMON, A.L., Personality and behavior patterns of children with functional defects of articulation. *Child Development*, 32, 731–737 (1961).

SOLOMON, R.L., Punishment. *American Psychologist,* 19, 239–253 (1964).

SOLOMON, L.N., WEBSTER, J.C., and **CURTIS, J.F.,** A factorial study of speech perception. *Journal of Speech Hearing Research,* 3, 101–107 (1960).

SOMMERS, R.K., Factors in the effectiveness of mothers trained to aid in speech correction. *Journal of Speech and Hearing Disorders,* 1962, 27 (2), 178–186.

SOMMERS, R.K., Predicting children's speech and language using auditory–visual sequencing tasks. Paper presented at the annual convention of the American Speech and Hearing Association, Detroit, Michigan (1980).

SOMMERS, R.K., COCKERILLE, C.E., PAUL, C.D., BOWSER, D.C., FICHTER, G.R., FEN-TON, A.N., and **COPETAS, F.G.** Effects on speech therapy and speech improvement upon articulation and reading. *Journal of Speech and Hearing Disorders* 26, 27–38 (1961).

SOMMERS, R.K., BRADY, W.A., and **MOORE, W.H.,** Dichotic ear preferences of stuttering children and adults. *Perceptual and Motor Skills,* 40, 931–938 (1975).

SOMMERS, R.K., COX, S., and **WEST, C.,** Articulation effectiveness, stimulability, and children's performances on perceptual and memory tasks. *Journal of Speech Hearing Research,* 15, 579–589 (1972).

SOMMERS, R.K., ERDIGE, A., and **PETERSON, M.K.,** How valid are children's language tests? *The Journal of Special Education,* 12(4), 393–407 (1978).

SOMMERS, R.K., FURLONG, A.K., RHODES, F.E., FICHTER, G.R., BOWSER, D.C., CO-PETAS, F.G., and **SAUNDERS, Z.G.,** Effects of maternal attitudes upon improvement in articulation when mothers are trained to assist in speech correction. *Journal of Speech Hearing Disorders,* 29, 428–437 (1964).

SOMMERS, R.K. and **HATTON, M.E.,** School speech, language, and hearing programs: A survey of clinicians, programs, and services. *Ohio Journal of Speech and Hearing,* 14(2), 274–293 (1979).

SOMMERS, R.K. and **KANE, A.R.,** Nature and remediation of functional articulation disorders. In S. Dickson (Ed.), *Communication Disorders: Remedial Principles and Practices.* Glenview: Scott, Foresman (1974).

SOMMERS, R.K., LEISS, R.H., DELP, M.A., GERBER, A.J., FUNDRELLA, D., SMITH, R.M., REVUCKY, M.V., ELLIS, D., and **HALEY, V.,** Factors related to the effectiveness of articulation therapy for kindergarten, first, and second grade children. *Journal of Speech Hearing Research,* 10, 428–437 (1967).

SOMMERS, R.K., MILIKICH, M., and **SAVAGE, H.,** Distinctive feature analysis: A comparison of systems. Unpublished research report, Kent State University (1980).

SOMMERS, R.K., MOORE, W.H., BRADY, W., and **JACKSON, P.,** Performance of articulatory defective, minimal brain dysfunctioning and normal children on dichotic ear preference, laterality, and fine-motor skill tasks. *Journal of Special Education,* 10, 5–14 (1976).

SOMMERS, R.K., SCHAFFER, M.H., LEISS, R.H., GERBER, A.J., BRADY, M.A., FUN-DRELLA, D., OLSON, J.K., and **TOMKINS, E.R.,** The effectiveness of group and individual therapy, *Journal of Speech Hearing Research,* 9, 219–225 (1966).

SOMMERS, R.K. and **SITLER, S.,** Correlation between spontaneous and imitative speech tests in five and six-year-old children and their relationship to connected spontaneous speech. Unpublished research paper, Kent State University (1980).

SOMMERS, R.K. and TAYLOR, M., Cerebral speech dominance in language disordered and normal children. *Cortex*, 4, 3–16 (1972).

SPRIESTERBACH, D.C., Research in articulation disorders and personality. *Journal of Speech Hearing Disorders*, 21(3), 329–335 (1956).

SPRIESTERBACH, D.C., The effects of orofacial anomalies on the speech process. *ASHA Reports*, 1, 111–127 (1965).

SPRIESTERBACH, D.C., DARLEY, F.L., and MORRIS, H.L., Language skills in children with cleft palate. *Journal of Speech Hearing Research*, 1, 279–285 (1958).

SPRIESTERBACH, D.C., DARLEY, F.L., and ROUSE, M., Articulation of a group of children with cleft lips and palates. *Journal of Speech Hearing Disorders*, 21, 436–445 (1956).

SPRIESTERBACH, D.C., and POWERS, G.H., Nasality in isolated vowels and connected speech. *Journal of Speech Hearing Research*, 2, 40–45 (1959a).

SPRIESTERBACH, D.C. and POWERS, G.H., Articulation skills, velopharyngeal closure and oral breath pressure of children with cleft palates. *Journal of Speech Hearing Research*, 2, 318–325 (1959b).

SQUARE, P., Apraxia of speech in adults: Speech perception and production. Unpublished doctoral dissertation, Kent State University (1981).

STARKEY, K.L., The dichotic testing of young children: A new test for the speech and language impaired. Unpublished master's thesis, Kent State University (1974).

STINCHFIELD–HAWK, S.M. and YOUNG, E.H., *Children with Delayed or Defective Speech.* Stanford: Stanford University Press (1938).

STITT, C. and HUNTINGTON, D., Some relationships among articulation, auditory ability, and certain other variables. *Journal of Speech Hearing Research*, 12, 576–594 (1969).

SUBTELNY, J. and SUBTELNY, J., Intelligibility and associated physiological factors of cleft palate speakers. *Journal of Speech Hearing Research*, 2, 353–360 (1959).

SUBTELNY, J., KOEPP–BAKER, H., and SUBTELNY, J., Palatal function and cleft palate speech. *Journal of Speech Hearing Disorders*, 26, 213–224 (1961).

TEITELBAUM, P., The use of operant methods in the assessment and control of motivational states. In W.K. Honig (Ed.), *Operant Behavior: Areas of Research and Application.* New York: Appleton–Century–Crofts (1966).

TEMPLIN, M.C., *Certain Language Skills in Children.* Minneapolis: University of Minnesota Press (1957).

TEMPLIN, M.C., A study of aggressiveness in normal and defective speaking college students. *Journal of Speech Hearing Disorders*, 3, 43–49 (1938).

TEMPLIN, M.C., A study of the sound discrimination ability of elementary school pupils. *Journal of Speech Disorders*, 8, 127–132 (1943).

THORPE, L.P., CLARK, W.W., and TIEGS, E.W., *California Test of Personality.* New York: McGraw–Hill (1939).

TIKOFSKY, R.S., A revised list for the estimation of dysarthric single word intelligibility. *Journal of Speech Hearing Research*, 13, 59–65 (1970).

TRAPP, E.P. and EVANS, J., Functional articulatory defect and performance on a non-verbal task. *Journal of Speech Hearing Disorders*, 35, 176–180 (1960).

VAN DENMARK, D.R., Misarticulation and listener judgements of the speech of individuals with cleft palates. *Cerebral Palsy Journal,* 1, 232–245 (1964).

VAN DENMARK, A.A. and **MANN, M.B.,** Oral language skills of children with defective articulation. *Journal of Speech Hearing Research,* 8, 409–414 (1965).

VAN HATTUM, R.S., Articulation and nasality in cleft palate speakers. *Journal of Speech Hearing Research,* 1, 383–387 (1958).

VAN RIPER, C., *Speech Correction: Principles and Methods.* Englewood Cliffs: Prentice–Hall, Inc., 3rd ed. (1954).

VAN RIPER, C., *Speech Correction: Principles and Methods.* Englewood Cliffs: Prentice–Hall, Inc., 5th ed. (1972).

VAN RIPER, C., *Speech Correction: Principles and Methods.* Englewood Cliffs: Prentice–Hall, Inc., 6th ed. (1978).

VAN RIPER, C. and **IRWIN, J.V.,** *Voice and Articulation.* Englewood Cliffs: Prentice–Hall, Inc. (1958).

WALSH, H., On certain practical inadequacies of distinctive feature systems. *Journal of Speech and Hearing Disorders,* 39(1), 32–44 (1974).

WARREN, D.W. and **MACKLER, S.B.,** Duration of oral port constriction in normal and cleft palate speech. *Journal of Speech Hearing Research,* 11, 391–401 (1968).

WEATHERLAY–WHITE, R.A., STARK, R.D., DEHAAN, C.R., Acoustic analysis of speech: Validation studies. *Cerebral Palsy Journal,* 3, 291–300 (1966).

WEBER, J., Patterning of deviant articulation behavior. *Journal of Speech Hearing Disorders,* 35, 135–141 (1970).

WEBSTER, R.L., *Precision Fluency Shaping Program.* Roanoke: Communications Development Corporation (1975).

WECHSLER, D., *The Wechsler Intelligence Scale for Children.* New York: The Psychological Corporation (1955).

WEINBERG, B., LISS, G.M., and **HILLIS, J.A.,** A comparative study of visual, manual, and oral form identification in speech impaired and normal speaking children. In Bosma, J., *Second Symposium on Oral Sensation and Perception.* Springfield: Charles C Thomas (1970).

WEINER, P., Auditory discrimination and articulation. *Journal of Speech Hearing Research,* 32, 19–29 (1967).

WEISBERG, A., A distinctive feature approach to articulation therapy in a dysfluent child. Paper presented at the annual convention of the New York Speech and Hearing Association (1973).

WEPMAN, J.M., Relationship of auditory discrimination to speech and reading difficulties. *ASHA,* 1, 96 (1959).

WEST, C., Functional articulatory defects and reading defects, a correlational study. Unpublished research paper, Temple University (1969).

WESTLAKE, H. and **RUTHERFORD, D.,** *Cleft Palate.* Englewood Cliffs: Prentice–Hall, Inc. (1966).

WHITACRE, J.D., LUPER, H.L., and **POLLIO, H.R.,** General language deficits in children with articulation problems. *Language and Speech,* 12, 231–239 (1970).

WICKELGREN, W.A., Distinctive features and errors in short-term memory for English consonants. *Journal of the Acoustical Society of America,* 39, 388–398 (1966).

WILLIAMS, R., INGHAM, R., ROSENTHAL, J., A further analysis for developmental apraxia of speech in children with defective articulation. *Journal of Speech Hearing Research*, 24, 496–505 (1981).

WINITZ, H., *Articulatory Acquisition and Behavior*. Englewood Cliffs: Prentice–Hall, Inc. (1969).

WINITZ, H., *From Syllable to Conversation*. Baltimore: University Park Press (1975).

WINITZ, H. and BELLEROSE, B., Effects of pretraining on sound discrimination learning. *Journal of Speech Hearing Research*, 6, 171–180 (1963).

WINITZ, H. and BELLEROSE, B., Sound discrimination as a function of pretraining conditions. *Journal of Speech Hearing Research*, 5, 340–348 (1962).

WINITZ, H. and BELLEROSE, B., Phoneme cluster learning as a function of instructional method and age. *Journal of Verbal Learning, Verbal Behaviors*, 4, 93–102 (1965).

WINITZ, H., and LAWRENCE, M., Children's articulation and sound learning ability. *Journal of Speech Hearing Research*, 4, 259–268 (1961).

WINITZ, H., and PREISLER, L., Effects of distinctive features; Pretraining in phoneme discrimination learning. *Journal of Speech Hearing Research*, 10, 515–530 (1967).

WITKIN, B.R., Auditory perception: Implications for language development. *Language, Speech and Hearing Services in Schools*, 4, 31–52 (1971).

WOLFE, W.A., A comprehensive evaluation of fifty cases of cerebral palsy. *Journal of Speech Hearing Disorders*, 15, 234 (1950).

WOOD, K.S., Parental maladjustment and functional articulatory defects in children. *Journal of Speech Hearing Disorders*, 11, 255–275 (1946).

YORKSTON, K.M. and BEUKELMAN, D.R., A comparison of techniques for measuring intelligibility of dysarthric speech. *Journal of Communicative Disorders*, 11, 455 (1978).

YOSS, K.A. and DARLEY, F.L., Developmental apraxia of speech in children with defective articulation. *Journal of Speech Hearing Research*, 17, 399–416 (1974).